Migrant Daughter

Migrant Daughter

Coming of Age as a
Mexican American Woman

Frances Esquibel Tywoniak
and Mario T. García

UNIVERSITY OF CALIFORNIA PRESS

Berkeley   Los Angeles   London

University of California Press
Berkeley and Los Angeles, California

University of California Press, Ltd.
London, England

© 2000 by the Regents of the University of California

Library of Congress Cataloging-in-Publication Data

Tywoniak, Frances Esquibel, 1931–
   Migrant daughter : coming of age as a Mexican American woman /
Frances Esquibel Tywoniak and Mario T. García.
      p.   cm.
   ISBN 0-520-21914-7 (alk. paper). – ISBN 0-520-21915-5 (pbk. :
alk. paper)
   1. Tywoniak, Frances Esquibel, 1931–   .   2. Mexican American
women–California Biography.   3. Mexican American women–
New Mexico Biography.   4. Mexican American college students–
California–Berkeley Biography.   5. Mexican American migrant
agricultural laborers Biography.   6. Mexican American women–
Ethnic identity.   7. Central Valley (Calif. : Valley) Biography.
8. University of California, Berkeley Biography.   9. Artesia Region
(N.M.) Biography.   I. García, Mario T.   II. Title.
F870.M5T96   2000
979.4'0046872073–dc21   99-40594
                                                      CIP

Manufactured in the United States of America

08   07   06   05   04   03   02
10   9   8   7   6   5   4   3

To Ed
And to My Parents, Florinda and Teodoro
Frances Esquibel Tywoniak

To My Parents,
Alma Araiza García and Amado García Rodarte
Mario T. García

CONTENTS

ACKNOWLEDGMENTS

We want to first thank Marliese Esquivel for her inspiration in writing the initial oral history paper that led to the creation of this book.

For providing the facilities where we conducted our interviews, we are grateful to the Center for Chicano Studies at the University of California at Santa Barbara.

For transcribing the oral history tapes, we want to thank Carole MacKenzie.

Funding for this project came from the University of California at Santa Barbara.

At the University of California Press, we want to particularly thank Monica McCormick for her enthusiastic support of this project and for her patience in the long process of revising the manuscript. We are grateful to Marc Zimmerman of the University of Illinois at Chicago and to the two anonymous reviewers for their excellent assessments of the manuscript and for their thoughtful and valuable suggestions for improvements. We further appreciate the supportive editorial work of Sue Heinemann and Mimi Kusch at the Press.

Introduction

Mario T. García

For my mainstay Chicano history course at the University of California at Santa Barbara, I ask students to do an oral history project. They have to interview someone of Mexican American background or a Mexican immigrant who, through personal recollections, can shed light on different aspects of the Chicano experience in the United States. I encourage my students to seek out individuals who have lived long enough to have experienced various changes in their lives. Mexican American students, I suggest, may want to interview someone in their own families, perhaps a grandparent or parent.

These interviews, by both my Chicano and my non-Chicano students, usually turn out to be much better reads than the typical, often tedious college term paper. In the spring of 1990, one paper in particular caught my attention. Written by Marliese Esquivel, it presented the story of her aunt, Frances Esquibel Tywoniak, her father's sister. I was fascinated by this Mexican American woman's experiences and intrigued to know more.

With Marliese's assistance, I contacted Fran (the name she is known by). I told Fran about my own work in oral history, in particular about the narrative I was then completing of Bert Corona, the Mexican American labor and community leader.[1] Her story, I thought, was also worth telling, and I suggested doing some extensive interviewing with her. Fran, with the usual modesty and graciousness that I came to know so well, agreed to this plan.

FRAN'S STORY: HIGHLIGHTS

What fascinated me about Fran's life story? It is certainly very different from Bert Corona's very politicized story, since Fran was not enmeshed in the kinds of labor and political struggles that Corona was. Her story is far more personal—at least those aspects of her life that intrigued me the most. Her story traces a young Mexican American woman's coming of age during the thirties, forties, and early fifties.

Fran's story begins with her very early years in rural southeastern New Mexico and tells of the strong family network among the Hispanos of that area. Her story describes her family's move to California as part of the dust bowl migration during the Great Depression and their commencing a cycle of farm-labor sojourns in the central San Joaquin Valley. It details Fran's experiences growing up in various squalid farm-labor camps and working with her father in the fields at an early age—experiences right out of a John Steinbeck novel.[2]

Fran's story relates her experiences, good and bad, in the country schools that she attended. It tells of a young adolescent beginning to discover her gender, sexual, and ethnic identity in junior high school in Visalia, where the Esquibel family finally settled. And it relates how a young woman, excelling in high school, finds that she desires to make something more of her life than being a farm laborer, the future for most Mexican Americans in the valley.

Fran's story describes the exceptional circumstance of being the only one in her high school class to receive an academic scholarship to the University of California at Berkeley. It portrays her new life as one of the few Mexican Americans, and even fewer Mexican American women, to attend Berkeley in the post–World War II period. And it tells of Fran's adjustment to a seemingly new land, revealing how she crossed still another frontier when, in her junior year, she married Ed Tywoniak, a World War II veteran several years her senior, and a year later gave birth to her first child.

The story of Fran told here ends with her achieving her goal of graduating from Berkeley, in 1953. From there she pursued a successful career as a teacher and administrator in the San Francisco schools until her retirement in 1991.

BRIDGING CULTURES

As I listened to Fran tell her story, I was most fascinated by the years leading up to her graduation from Berkeley. They seemed to constitute a kind of Mexican American bildungsroman—a coming-of-age narrative. It was during those years that, like many other Mexican Americans and for that matter other ethnic Americans, Fran began the complicated and intricate process of bridging cultures.

However, this bridging process was not a simple binary process linking or negotiating solely between a Mexican-based culture on the one hand and a generic Anglo-American one on the other. Instead, it represents a more complicated dynamic in which the American ethnic experience and identity are as much a negotiation within the ethnic culture as with other subordinate ethnic cultures and with the hegemonic Anglo-American culture. Lisa Lowe has described this "cultural hybridity" in Asian American culture, and her remarks are equally valid for the Latino experience: "The boundaries and definitions of Asian American culture are continually shifting and being contested from pressures both 'inside' and 'outside' the Asian origin community."[3]

The "dialectics of difference" that literary scholar Ramón Saldívar stresses concerning the Chicano experience and its relationship to the hegemonic Anglo culture should be revised to include the "dialectics of difference" within Chicano culture.[4] As Juan Bruce-Novoa correctly observes, Chicano culture is certainly dialogical, but that dialogue is as much within the culture as it is with other ethnic cultures, including the Anglo one.[5]

Since most of the coming-of-age years are spent within the ethnic-based culture, the changes experienced by members of a particular ethnic community result as much from interactions within that community as from coming into contact with the dominant culture, which itself is highly differentiated and heterogeneous. The process of bridging cultures is thus more multifaceted than dual, as is too often suggested by ethnic studies scholarship, whether in the form of the African American/white or the Latino/Anglo paradigm. This contact of cultures—both within and outside the specific ethnic experience—represents what cultural critic George Lipsitz refers to as the "juxtaposition of multiple realities," or what Renato Rosaldo calls "cultural border zones."[6]

This bridging of cultures also involves more than the "border space" that writers such as Gloria Anzaldúa and others prioritize; it spans the "border spaces" within Chicano culture itself.[7] That is, the borderlands are not just the spaces where Mexican and Anglo cultures intersect, but also where the spaces within Mexican American culture reveal themselves. There are many borders and many cultures or subcultures involved just within Mexican American culture, to say nothing of its complicated relationship with other ethnic cultures. As José David Saldívar correctly notes: "Culture is by nature heterogeneous and necessarily works through a realm of borders."[8]

In Fran's particular case, this bridging of various cultural frontiers involved, first of all, her foundational experiences—what Albert Stone terms the "immediate community"—set in the rural and native Hispano culture of southeastern New Mexico and complicated by her father's Mexican immigrant background.[9] Fran's initial experiences were expanded and further complicated by later experiences: her family's deterritorialized migration to California in the 1930s, her exposure to a multiethnic farm-labor force in the San Joaquin Valley, her encounter with an English-language Anglo educational system, her own growing sense of difference with respect to other Mexican Americans, her experiences as one of the few Mexican Americans tracked into the more academic curriculum in her high school, her engagement at that school with a small circle of kindred spirits composed of Anglo girls, her winning a scholarship to the University of California at Berkeley in 1949 (where in four years she does not recall ever meeting another Mexican American student), her meeting and marrying a man of Polish American background, her giving birth to her first child during her senior year at Berkeley, and her successful completion of her degree in 1953.

Within these different experiences, Fran occupied multiple positions of identity, although many of them overlapped. As Anzaldúa writes of the "new mestiza," "she learns to juggle cultures. She has a plural personality."[10] Fran is never just one person: she is multiple persons or personalities. For example, while she was in junior and senior high school, Fran was a student, a daughter, a sister, a girlfriend, a movie theater cashier, a Catholic, a Spanish speaker at home, an English speaker at school, a Mexican American, an adolescent, a young woman, and so forth.

All these positions together—not any one alone—help explain Fran. Some, such as daughter and girlfriend, take place largely within a Mexican American context, while others, such as student, take place in the mixed world of Mexican Americans and Anglos. Hence, Fran's identity at any one time is never simply the result of a Mexican American/ Anglo binary of the kind that Fran herself subjectively intuits. It is never just made up of the kind of dual consciousness that W. E. B. Du Bois observed about African Americans.[11] Instead, Fran's identity is the result of multiple positions and relationships bridging subcultures within the Mexican American world and other marginalized cultures such as African American and, of course, Anglo. Rosaldo refers to these complex and hybrid cultural influences on identity as a "multiplex personal identity" in which "our everyday lives are crisscrossed by border zones, pockets and eruptions of all kinds."[12]

What I am stressing here is the importance of recognizing and acknowledging that the American ethnic experience, including the Mexican American and Latino one, is not a simple encounter between the ethnic or subaltern culture and the mainstream or dominant culture. It is never just "us" versus "them." Ethnic cultures and ethnic identity represent multiple encounters both within the ethnic culture and outside it. The result is a synthetic bridging—what Lipsitz refers to as a "fusion" of various subcultures, or in the Latino case a *mestizaje* of cultures and experiences.[13] Moreover, in this process not only does the ethnic "subject" change but so too does the dominant subject. Nothing in these relationships is static. There are no monolithic or essentialist or "authentic" cultures in this exchange, either from a subaltern or postcolonial perspective or from a colonial or neocolonial one. Individual as well as collective identity is always in a state of flux, constantly being reinvented and always open and fluid.

Although I do not want to reveal too much of the rich substance of Fran's story contained within the narrative, I do wish to call attention to some of Fran's specific experiences to further illustrate what I mean by the concept of bridging multiple cultures as opposed to viewing American ethnicity in strict binary terms. For example, Fran's learning English represented a response both to her "Americanized" school context and to her more "Hispanicized" home environment. Fran learned English mostly at school and at a certain point understood that her mastery of this language held the key to her future opportunities. As the artist Amalia Mesa-Bains notes, her own command of English as a child and young woman led to an empowering transformation, particularly in her relationships with non–Mexican Americans.[14]

Yet English also represented for Fran a reaction to her predominantly Spanish-language home culture, where her Mexican-born immigrant patriarchal father insisted that only Spanish be spoken. In this context, English became for Fran a subversive and oppositional cultural symbol of her growing rejection of Mexican American patriarchy and of her need for self-expression. English constituted her effort to negotiate her ethnic and cultural position both outside her Mexican American culture and also within it. Indeed, other Latina writers, because of their focus on issues of gender and sexuality within Latino culture, have been in the forefront of moving the discourse away from strictly Latino/Anglo binaries and toward one acknowledging differences, certainly gender and sexual differences, within the ethnic culture.

Another example of bridging multiple cultures in Fran's early life concerns her recognition of diversity within the Visalia barrio. Part of this diversity is gender based. For example, Fran rejected the model of womanhood portrayed by the *pachucas,* or Mexican American female gang members. She saw in the *pachuca* type everything she did not want to be: conformist, self-hating, anti-intellectual, and hopeless about the future. To Fran, the *pachucas* represented a hostile and threatening form of womanhood. There was no "sisterhood." The antagonism that Fran felt has nothing to do with Mexican American/Anglo relations and everything to do with intraethnic or Mexican American/Mexican American relations: that is, it was not Anglo girls whom Fran rejected or was afraid of but other Mexican American girls. Fran's discriminating attitude toward the *pachucas* reveals that she did not romanticize the barrio but rather possessed a more realistic understanding of the diverse and dialectical character of that space. Still, there is a fusion of cultural influences at work here in that Fran, despite her antagonism toward the *pachucas,* appropriated some of their style in how she dressed and wore her hair while she was in junior high school.

Fran's gender and sexual development provides another example of multiple and complex cultural crossings. In her first year in junior high school, she met Peter Nava, who, as Fran puts it, became the "love of her life." Peter was a few years older than she, but over a period of a few months, and hidden from the scrutiny of Fran's parents, Fran and Peter became very close. Under other circumstances, as Fran observes, she and Peter probably would have married and raised a family in Visalia. Yet already Fran desired a life beyond Visalia, beyond repeating her parents' lives, beyond what the future held for most other Mexican American young women in rural California. She did not want to become the wife of a farmworker or someone like Peter who, lacking education, would not achieve much outside the limited opportunities of the central valley of California. Fran wanted more, even if wanting more meant losing Peter.

In effect, Fran was developing certain class and cultural interests that went further than the predominantly working-class culture that her family and most Mexican Americans in Visalia and the surrounding country represented. Fran did not look down on her parents, Peter, or other Mexican Americans, but she did want to make more of her life. Although it pained her greatly and she would always measure other men in her life against Peter, Fran broke up with him. She did so because she understood that, given her desire for more education and eventual professional advancement, there was no future with him; Fran's desires transcended Peter's. The tragedy, if you will, of Fran and Peter's relationship was not based on ethnic differences but on developing class differences within the barrio itself.

A final example of Fran's multiple cultural bridge crossings is her interethnic marriage while she was a student at Berkeley. Although many of her early experiences were set in her particular Mexican American working-class culture, Fran was certainly influenced by her interactions with Anglo students and teachers of different ethnic backgrounds. The impact of these encounters with non–Mexican Americans was perhaps inevitable in Fran's case, given her wish to succeed beyond the barrio, in what was an Anglo world. Although not politically conscious of this process, Fran in effect pursued a strategy of ethnic integration. She accepted herself as Mexican American and retained what she believed to be positive from this background, but at the same time she understood, as did other Mexican Americans of her generation, that mobility and success would come only by integrating that experience with those of many other American ethnic groups.

It was at Berkeley that Fran became even more aware of this integrationist process, since it was there that she encountered an even greater diversity of ethnic groups and concomitantly an almost complete dearth of Mexican Americans or Latinos. Fran's Berkeley years provided her with a more significant appreciation of multiculturalism or, better, interculturalism and the bridging not of dual cultures—Mexican and Anglo—but of multiple ones within an American context.

In this regard, Fran's interethnic marriage in her junior year at Berkeley to Ed Tywoniak, an older man of Polish American background, makes sense. By the time Fran married Ed, she had already bridged many cultures or subcultures. Marrying Ed was not a rejection of her Mexican American background but an extension of that background into a new ethnic and cultural frontier— specifically, a Polish American one. Moreover, this marriage also involved a generational bridging, in that Ed was seventeen years older than Fran and so brought to their relationship the experiences and qualities of a more mature person. Of course, this interethnic relationship assumed even more profound dimensions with the birth of their three children, who represent another level of ethnic and cultural integration.

As Fran's story suggests, the Mexican American or Latino experience has never consisted of simple cultural maintenance, in which Mexican Americans retain and protect their "authentic" culture apart from other American ethnic influences. Yet it has also never been a complete assimilationist experience, with Mexican Americans undergoing the classic melting-pot transformation and emerging as generic Americans.

The Mexican American (and the broader Latino) saga, like that of other American ethnic groups, represents everything in between cultural maintenance and assimilation. And that "in between" is not just positioned in a binary Mexican/Anglo relationship. Rather, it takes place within different cultural positions and forms of identity first and foremost within a Mexican American sphere. Multiculturalism begins within the Mexican American experience itself. It calls attention to the "choir of voices" within that culture, or what Norma Alarcón refers to as "multiple-voiced subjects." As Alarcón further notes: "The need to assign multiple registers of existence is an effect of the belief that knowledge of one's subjectivity cannot be arrived at through a single 'theme.'"[15]

In Fran's case, her knowledge of her subjectivity involved particular family histories, specific and changing geographic settings, generational differences, class differences, the juxtaposition of native-born Mexican Americans and Mexican immigrants, language and cultural differences, particular religious influences, and specific gender and sexual experiences. This highly diverse and multi-intraethnic world at the same time encounters an equally complex and diverse Anglo world with its own set of multiple ethnic influences. The result is a nuanced, heterogeneous, and multiple bridging of cultures.

FRAN'S STORY AND CHICANO HISTORY

In historical terms, Fran's story speaks to at least three aspects of the Chicano or Mexican American experience. First, Fran's story concerns a period in Chicano history that is still not very well researched—the Great Depression, World War II, and the early cold war years in the United States. It is this era that I and others have referred to as the years of the Mexican American Generation, or the generation of Mexican Americans, many with immigrant parents, who, like Fran, came of age during this period and experienced the various pressures of growing up Mexican American in the United States. Members of that generation felt the effects not only of the Mexican/Anglo paradigm, or what Fran refers to as "parallelism," but also of the many other cultural frontiers that they encountered both within and outside the Mexican American context.[16]

The Mexican American Generation represented the first extensive bilingual, bicultural cohort of Mexican Americans in the United States since Mexicans were conquered after the U.S.-Mexico War (1846–48) and the appropriation from Mexico of what came to be called the American Southwest. Yet my previous work and that of a few other scholars primarily touch on the more political aspects of this generation and on the rise of new leadership in the Mexican American communities, including figures such as Bert Corona who struggled for the achievement of full civil rights for Mexican Americans.[17]

In Fran's case, although she is part of this new generation of Mexican Americans, her story reflects the more personal and grassroots changes experienced by this generation. Fran's story, like Mary Helen Ponce's coming-of-age autobiography, *Hoyt Street,* set in the 1940s, reveals the changes in identity, culture, and status within the Mexican American Generation at a very personal level. Ponce's narrative, like Fran's, portrays both generational continuity and change in a Mexican American family in Pacoima, California, as well as the intraethnic tensions and differences within the Mexican American community. The difference between Fran's story and Ponce's is that while Ponce reflects on these changes only through her elementary school years, Fran recalls her changes through early adulthood.[18]

A second historical aspect of Fran's story is that in commenting on her experiences, she indirectly questions certain assumptions about Chicano history that stem from the militant Chicano Movement of the late 1960s and early 1970s. Specifically, the Chicano Movement, including Chicano studies programs, focused on the "unified subject" or what Bruce-Novoa calls "monological unity."[19] The movement suggested that there was a holistic or monolithic character defining *the* Chicano. Rather than representing a diverse group and a dialogic culture, Chicanos, as a result of the politics of identity championed by the movement, came to represent an invented essentialist or homogeneous community.[20]

To the movement, being Chicano meant having had certain ethnic and cultural experiences, holding certain political beliefs, and being involved in certain militant actions. Yet this was hardly the reality of the Chicano experience. This ethnic community was far more diverse than the movement acknowledged. Within this culture were historical, regional, cultural, linguistic, generational, racial, and class differences—among others—as Fran's story reveals.

Indeed, Fran's story serves as a testimony to this diversity. For example, whereas the Chicano Movement stressed the urban immigrant experience, her narrative brings attention to those Chicanos whose deep roots lie in the Hispano rural tradition of New Mexico. Although Fran's farm-labor experiences in the San Joaquin Valley resonate, for example, with the later struggle by César Chávez and the farmworkers to achieve dignity and justice in the fields, her experiences are not completely in keeping with the Chicano Movement narrative. Unlike the movement's perspective, which denounced the process of acculturation or Americanization on the part of Mexican Americans and instead stressed cultural nationalism, celebrating those Chicanos who refused to give up their "culture," Fran's story is much more complicated.

Her tale speaks to the difficult process of being the product of multiple cultural positions and experiences. On the one hand, these experiences had less to do with choice and more to do with circumstances beyond her control and that of most other Mexican Americans of her generation. Acculturation was a fact of life, especially because of schooling and mass cultural influences. On the other hand, what is significant is that at a certain point Fran recognized that acculturation could be empowering for her status both as a Mexican American and as a woman. She came to understand what the movement refused to acknowledge and what some Chicano studies ideologues still refuse to recognize: that learning to speak English well and to function in American society means being able to have greater control over one's life and future. In this process—the bridging of cultures with all the subcultures involved—Fran's acculturation or transculturation represents historical agency. Fran makes history—at least her history—rather than simply being a victim of history.

For Fran to overcome the obstacles inherent in being Mexican American in a racialized American society and being a woman in a sexually repressive Mexican American culture meant that she had to succeed in learning English and mastering her school work and aspire to a professional status. In this sense, Fran faced challenges both outside and within her ethnic culture. For example, she had to break with or renegotiate certain Mexican American family and cultural traditions. Although she did not give up her Mexican identity, she did reconcile her background with becoming Americanized. For Fran bridging multiple cultures did not mean selling out her "authentic" culture but, as Ruth Behar notes in her study of gender in Mexico, translating that culture or cultures to her particular experiences and aspirations for the purpose of empowering herself and, indirectly, her community.[21]

Fran's story speaks to the hybrid and constantly changing experiences of Mexican Americans and other Latinos in the United States. Her experiences counter the stereotypes imposed by some Chicanos and perpetuated by those who fear the "Latinization" or "Hispanicization" of the United States. She does not conform to any image of a static, inward-looking Latina who purposefully remains on the margins of American society. Fran's story breaks with such stereotypes and instead reveals Mexican Americans with real complexities who refuse to be neatly packaged as a particular ethnic commodity. Her story points to Mexican Americans who constantly experience change, who do not remain in their hometowns, who have aspirations and desires, who are not immigrants, who are not "illegal," who speak English (and Spanish), who do not romanticize the barrio experience, who negotiate varied cultures, who are not gang members (*pachucos* or *cholos*), who are not politically correct, and who, as citizens of the United States, struggle to broaden the meaning of being Americans.

Finally, I should note the dearth of historical studies concerning the role of Mexican American women in U.S. history. Although some studies have appeared in the last few decades, Mexican American women's history is still very much in its initial phase. One of the obstacles to a greater production of such studies concerns the unavailability of sources. At least in the twentieth century, oral history and autobiographical texts are of major importance in providing a foundation for this history and in filling in gaps that archival documents alone cannot fill.[22]

This is particularly true for women's history in general, since women of all ethnic backgrounds in the United States until very recently have not played important roles in the public sphere—the sphere that generates most of the archival documents. For this reason, Fran's autobiographical narrative, especially of the years spanning the Great Depression to the beginning of the cold war, provides us with an important historical document. Her story addresses the role of Mexican American women in history with respect to migration, family, labor, education, issues of gender and sexuality in American history, and the role of leadership among Mexican American women. Because Fran's story in part concerns her childhood, her narrative also speaks to the role of children in American and Chicano history.

OPPOSITIONAL HISTORY

In my book on Bert Corona, I made much of the oppositional character of Corona's text. By "oppositional," I mean that his story represents a counternarrative to the mainstream depiction of American history, which for the most part, at least until fairly recently, has either totally excluded or at best marginalized ethnic/racial minority groups such as Mexican Americans. Chicanos and other Latinos simply have not been seen as key subjects in the American historical saga. Bert Corona's story, filled with the struggles of twentieth-century Mexican Americans to achieve social justice and full recognition as citizens of this country, opposes and challenges the more traditional approach to American history.[23]

By the same token, Fran's story also represents an oppositional or revisionist narrative. Although not as overtly political as the Corona story,

Fran's narrative observes the role of Mexican Americans in making history, especially in their family and personal struggles as well as in their economic contributions to this country in the form of labor. Fran's personal struggle to find meaning and a place for herself in American society gives substance to American feminists' assertion that the "personal is political." In this sense, Fran's story is not only a Mexican American or Chicano oppositional narrative but a feminist oppositional one as well. As Sonia Saldívar-Hull observes of nontraditional Chicana narratives: "In our search for a feminist critical discourse that adequately takes into account our position as women under multiple oppressions we must turn to our own 'organic intellectuals.'" [24] Although she is not a professional historian, Fran plays the role of historian by retelling her story.

DUAL AUTHORSHIP

It has become fashionable in some circles for a writer to explain why he or she chooses to write about a certain subject or, in this case, about a particular person. I am not sure what purpose this serves, since one can assume that in writing about a particular topic, the writer believes it to be important. I obviously believe that Fran's story is important, or I would not have spent several years working on it. But I will offer that choosing to work with Fran on her story is quite consistent with my past work in Chicano history, work that entailed incorporating, as much as possible, the roles played by women in this history.[25]

In my Bert Corona book, for example, even though Bert was the main subject, I strove to get him to talk about the role of women in the history that his *testimonio* addressed. Hence, not only did we include much about the role of Bert's mother and grandmother in shaping his life, but we also dealt with the key leadership roles that other Latina women, such as Luisa Moreno, Josefina Fierro, Dolores Huerta, and Chole Alatorre, played in the labor and community struggles in which

Bert participated. The story also includes the essential role performed by Blanche Corona, Bert's wife, in providing the support network critical for Bert's successes as an organizer.

The role of leadership in the making of history, specifically Chicano history, has been of major research interest for me, as is evident in my previous studies of the Mexican American Generation, including Bert Corona's story, as well as my work on Ruben Salazar, the foremost Latino journalist of his time.[26] I am interested in the process by which some individuals become leaders. Fran's story is also a story of leadership, of her determination to achieve a position of leadership—in this case, as a teacher—to help others achieve self-reliance and dignity.

Given this background, as well as the fact that my own life has been significantly shaped by the strong role models provided by my mother, grandmother, aunt, and sister, it was not difficult for me to collaborate in bringing Fran's story—the story of an independent-minded and determined young Mexican American woman—to fruition.[27]

There are undoubtedly many other themes and interpretations that can be attached to Fran's story, but we will leave them to other scholars and readers to provide. Before turning to the narrative, however, a word should be said about the collaborative authorship of Fran's story.

In the summer of 1990 Fran flew from her home in San Francisco to Santa Barbara, where we worked for five full days at the Center for Chicano Studies. We covered a great deal of ground but did not finish. That Christmas season, I interviewed Fran again in her home, and we concluded the interviews the following summer in Santa Barbara when Fran returned for another five days. The foundation of this narrative lies in these interviews, which provided approximately thirty-five hours of taped conversation. The tapes were then transcribed by Carole MacKenzie in Santa Barbara. These transcripts were reviewed by Fran, who then, as her memory was stimulated by her reading of the interviews, added considerably more recollections. Using these revised transcripts as a foundation, I wrote the initial drafts of each chapter. Fran reviewed each chapter and again either added new material or deleted some. As a good English teacher, she also corrected my sentence structure and spelling. Indeed, what I believe to be the sensitive and moving style of this narrative is without question the result of Fran's intervention.

Upon receiving her revisions, I made changes to the master disk. When the completed manuscript was finished, I sent it to Fran, who went over it entirely and made still more changes, which I incorporated into the final version. This collaboration or dual authorship between Fran and me was significantly different from my relationship with Bert Corona. Corona provided the "raw material" through the interviews but did not participate in the writing or the revisions to the extent that Fran did. Corona's authorship remained at the level of the spoken narrative, whereas Fran's extended to the written narrative.

Based on the comments of one of the reviewers of this manuscript, I believe that I should also address another aspect of the "politics" of my working relationship with Fran. Although a female interlocutor *might* have obtained a somewhat different narrative from Fran, as suggested by this reviewer, I see this assumption as reductionist and problematic, playing to the "politics of identity" that, as I have indicated in my critique of Chicano Movement writings, I am here rejecting. Throughout our working relationship, I believe that Fran was as open and frank with me as she could be about her life. Indeed, at various points I felt that the interviews became "confessional" on her part. She revealed to me certain personal and intimate experiences that I had not imagined would be forthcoming. Our relationship over the last several years, which has included not only the time spent doing the interviews but also the subsequent collaboration in going over the transcripts of those interviews as well as numerous drafts of the chapters of the manuscript, has been nothing short of confident and trusting. This has been a collaborative project in the best meaning of that term.

Like my experience with Bert Corona, my working relationship with Fran Esquibel Tywoniak has been memorable. I learned as much Chicano history from her as I did from Bert. I have lived with Fran's story for the last ten years, and now it is my pleasure to join her in sharing it with you.

NOTES

1. Mario T. García, *Memories of Chicano History: The Life and Narrative of Bert Corona* (Berkeley and Los Angeles: University of California Press, 1994).

2. See John Steinbeck, *The Grapes of Wrath* (New York: Viking Press, 1939).

3. Lisa Lowe, "Heterogeneity, Hybridity, Multiplicity: Making Asian American Difference," *Diaspora* 1, no.1 (Spring 1991): 28, 33.

4. Ramón Saldívar, *Chicano Narrative: The Dialectics of Difference* (Madison: University of Wisconsin Press, 1990).

5. See Juan Bruce-Novoa, "Dialogical Strategies, Monological Goals: Chicano Literature," in *Another Tongue: Nation and Ethnicity in the Linguistic Borderland,* ed. Alfredo Arteaga (Durham: Duke University Press, 1994).

6. See George Lipsitz, *Time Passages: Collective Memory and American Popular Culture* (Minneapolis: University of Minnesota Press, 1990), 152, and Renato Rosaldo, *Culture & Truth: The Remaking of Social Analysis* (Boston: Beacon Press, 1989), 217.

7. See Gloria Anzaldúa, *Borderlands/La Frontera: The New Mestiza* (San Francisco: Spinsters/Aunt Lute, 1987).

8. José David Saldívar, *Border Matters: Remapping American Cultural Studies* (Berkeley and Los Angeles: University of California Press, 1997), 9.

9. As quoted in Carolyn G. Heilbrun, "Non-Autobiographies of 'Privileged' Women: England and America," in *Life/Line: Theorizing Women's Autobiography,* ed. Bella Brodzki and Celeste Schenck (Ithaca: Cornell University Press, 1988), 62.

10. Anzaldúa, *Borderlands,* 79.

11. W. E. B. Du Bois, *The Souls of Black Folk* (Chicago: New American Library, 1969).

12. Rosaldo, *Culture & Truth,* 179, 207.

13. Lipsitz, *Time Passages,* 151.

14. See interview with Amalia Mesa-Bains in video documentary *Women of Hope: Latinas Abriendo Camino,* prod. Bread and Roses Cultural Project, Inc., 1996.

15. See Norma Alarcón, "The Theoretical Subject(s) of *This Bridge Called My Back* and Anglo-American Feminism," in *Criticism in the Borderlands: Studies in Chicano Literature, Culture, and Ideology,* ed. Héctor Calderón and José David Saldívar (Durham: Duke University Press, 1991), 37–38.

16. See Mario T. García, "Identity and Gender in the Mexican American Testimonio: The Life and Narrative of Frances Esquivel Tywoniak," in *Migration and Identity,* vol. 3 of *International Yearbook of Oral History and Life Stories,* ed. Rina Benmayor and Andor Skotnes (New York: Oxford University Press, 1994), 151–166.

17. Mario T. García, *Mexican Americans: Leadership, Ideology & Identity, 1930–1960* (New Haven: Yale University Press, 1989); Richard A. García, *Rise of the Mexican American Middle Class, San Antonio, 1929–1941* (College Station: Texas A&M Press, 1991); and Benjamín Márquez, *LULAC: The Evolution of a Mexican American Political Organization* (Austin: University of Texas Press, 1993).

18. See Mary Helen Ponce, *Hoyt Street: An Autobiography* (Albuquerque: University of New Mexico Press, 1993).

19. Bruce-Novoa, "Dialogical Strategies," 237.

20. See, for example, Carlos Muñoz, Jr., *Youth, Identity, Power: The Chicano Movement* (New York: Verso Press, 1989); Ignacio M. García, *United We Win: The Rise and Fall of La Raza Unida Party* (Tucson: University of Arizona Press); Ignacio M. García, *Chicanismo: The Forging of a Militant Ethos among Mexican Americans* (Tucson: University of Arizona Press, 1997); Juan Gómez-Quiñones, *Chicano Politics: Reality and Promise, 1940–1990* (Albuquerque: University of New Mexico Press, 1990); and Armando Navarro, *Mexican American Youth Organization: Avant-Garde of the Chicano Movement* (Austin: University of Texas Press, 1995).

21. See Ruth Behar, *Translated Woman: Crossing the Border with Esperanza's Story* (Boston: Beacon Press, 1993).

22. See, for example, Vicki L. Ruiz, *Cannery Women, Cannery Lives: Mexican Women, Unionization, and the California Food Processing Industry, 1930–1950* (Albuquerque: University of New Mexico Press, 1987); Sarah Deutsch, *No Separate Refuge: Culture, Class, and Gender on an Anglo-American Frontier in the American Southwest, 1880–1940* (New York: Oxford University Press, 1987); Patricia Preciado Martin, *Songs My Mother Sang to Me: An Oral History of Mexican American Women* (Tucson: University of Arizona Press, 1992); Cynthia E.

Orozco, "The Origins of the League of United Latin American Citizens (LULAC) and the Mexican American Civil Rights Movement in Texas with an Analysis of Women's Political Participation in a Gendered Context, 1910–1929" (Ph.D. diss., University of California, Los Angeles, 1993); Magdalena Mora and Adelaida R. Del Castillo, eds., *Mexican Women in the United States: Struggles Past and Present* (Los Angeles: Chicano Studies Research Center, University of California, Los Angeles, 1980); Deena González, "The Spanish-Mexican Women of Santa Fe: Patterns of Their Resistance and Americanization 1820–1880" (Ph.D. diss., University of California, Berkeley, 1985); Antonia I. Castañeda, "Presidarias y Pobladoras: Spanish-Mexican Women in Frontier Monterey, Alta California, 1770–1821" (Ph.D. diss., Stanford University, 1990); Adela de la Torre and Beatriz M. Pesquera, eds., *Building with Our Hands: New Directions in Chicana Studies* (Berkeley and Los Angeles: University of California Press, 1993); Alma M. García, ed., *Chicana Feminist Thought: The Basic Historical Writings* (New York: Routledge, 1997); and Vicki L. Ruíz, *From out of the Shadows: Mexican Women in Twentieth-Century America* (New York: Oxford University Press, 1998).

23. See Mario T. García, "Introduction: Redefining American History: Bert Corona and Oppositional Narrative," in García, *Memories of Chicano History*, 1–26.

24. Sonia Saldívar-Hull, "Feminism on the Border: From Gender Politics to Geopolitics," in *Criticism in the Borderlands,* ed. Calderón and Saldívar, 206.

25. See Mario T. García, *Desert Immigrants: The Mexicans of El Paso, 1880–1920* (New Haven: Yale University Press, 1981); García, *Mexican Americans;* García, *Memories of Chicano History;* and Mario T. García, "The Chicana in American History: The Mexican Women of El Paso, 1880–1920—A Case Study," *Pacific Historical Review* (May 1980): 315–337.

26. See Ruben Salazar, *Border Correspondent: Selected Writings, 1955–1970,* ed. Mario T. García (Berkeley and Los Angeles: University of California Press, 1995).

27. See Mario T. García, "The Double Autobiography of Testimonio: Writing the Bert Corona Story," in *Confrontations et métissages: Cultures d'Amérique Latine aux États-Unis,* ed. Elyette Benjamin-Labarthe et al. (Bordeaux, France: Maison des Pays Ibériques, 1995), 25–33.

ONE

My Roots in New Mexico

My most vivid memory of my early childhood in New Mexico is of the surrounding environment. This is the visceral part of my memory. I remember the sky, the earth, the wind, the trees, the animals, the smell of rain before a storm, the horses prancing and sensing the rain coming, the wind blowing the buckets across the yard, the lightning—nature's elements as a display of power, inspiring awe.

I was so little and everything seemed so big. I remember the flat land and a very flat and immense horizon. I recall images of the trees being very tall, memories of the wind and of the trees responding to the wind. I can still visualize the cotton fields, the expanses of dry land. I remember the hot sun—lots of hot sun. I remember also the cold—intensities of heat and cold that were palpable but never oppressive or restrictive. They simply defined the vastness of the land.

I was born on April 2, 1931, in Atoka, just outside Artesia in southeastern New Mexico. I was the second child; actually, I was the third, but the first had died in infancy. My parents had named her Epifania because she was born on January 6, the day of the Epiphany in the Catholic calendar. She was a little princess, a beautiful fair-haired girl. The rest of us never knew her, but she remained a princess in our memories— part of the family mythology.

The real number-one child was my sister Antonia, or Toni, as she later came to be called. We were all named after saints. I was named Francisca after Saint Francis of Paola. I had been scheduled to be delivered by a doctor, but he was busy performing another delivery, so a midwife was called in at the last minute.

The birth was difficult for my mother, because the midwife was not all that proficient. She literally wrested me from the womb without giving my mother any anesthesia. For some time after my birth, my mother suffered a partial paralysis in her lower extremities. She attributed this paralysis to the difficulties of this birth.

I remember my mother's family well. She was the fifth of fourteen children, and I remember many of my aunts and uncles with warmth. Some of the positive things in life you just kind of take for granted and don't particularly appreciate. Family support has always been there for me, even when I didn't nurture it.

When I returned to New Mexico for a visit for the first time in almost forty years, my aunts greeted me as if I had never been away. "She is our own daughter," they affirmed. "She is *una de las nuestras*" (one of ours).

My grandfather was Vicente Flores and my grandmother was Genoveva Pineda de Flores. He was born in Socorro and she in Picacho, both towns northwest of Atoka. I think that my grandfather's family history originates in the Santa Fe area and my grandmother's in Las Cruces. Certainly, my mother's family has lived in New Mexico for many generations. I'm at least fifth-generation New Mexican on my mother's side.

My grandfather owned land, where he raised sheep and some cattle and grew cotton. He had inherited land from his family, and he added to it through lease-purchases and homesteading. We referred to this land as *los terrenos,* for Spanish was our language at home.

My grandfather sold sheep and wool in New Mexico and also transacted some business in Kansas. He conducted his sales in Roswell, which was the nearest "large" town. The sheep were driven to Roswell along rock-strewn gravel roads. In his final years, just before his death, he began negotiating the shipment of some cattle to Mexico by rail.

But my grandfather lost most of his land in the 1920s. I learned about this from listening to my aunts and uncles. The family talked about it all the time; to this day they still talk about it. The family's financial problems were evidently the result of both a family dispute and fraud and embezzlement by a mortgage company and a bank. The family dispute involved a brother-in-law's claim that part of my grandfather's land belonged to him. I don't think my grandfather ever gave up title to any of this land to the brother-in-law or his family.

Mineral and water rights as well as land titles were contested. There were even threats of violence. None of it was clear to me, but I could see that my uncle Vincent was regarded as the voice of authority on the subject after my grandfather died. Grandmother remained noncommittal. She believed the issues should be handled by the oldest surviving male, but she cautioned against family feuding. She was the peacemaker.

That my uncle Vincent had a wife whose loyalties were questionable complicated matters and heightened my sense of drama. It didn't occur to me until years later that I had never met or even seen the other participants in the dispute. They were all family members by marriage but consigned to the role of "the others."

What was really the immediate cause of my grandfather losing his land was the bank's claim that he had outstanding debts on a number of mortgages, a claim that my grandfather knew was false. Discussions always returned to the familiar theme—accounts of alleged legal chicanery. Still, the bank foreclosed and my grandfather lost most of his property. He did retain some land and tried to make a go of it, but by then, as the result of the onset of the Great Depression, there was no market for sheep.

My grandfather died of a heart attack with complications in 1932, one year after I was born. Yet because my grandmother remained on the ranch, my memory of New Mexico is that of "our land."

Since my grandfather died when I was still a baby, I don't remember him except through the stories I heard about him. I'm told, for example, that I was his favorite granddaughter. He would hold me on his lap and share his food with me. It wasn't the kind of thing he did for his own children, but he did it for me. He also enjoyed taking me for rides in his buggy.

I do remember my grandmother. She was a tiny lady—probably less than five feet in height—with very dark wavy hair and light green eyes. She was soft-spoken but somehow the center of our world. Everyone called her "mamá."

I've always wondered how she could have had all those children beginning at age fifteen, when she married my grandfather, while at the same time finding energy to help my grandfather on the ranch. At that early age, she was also a primary caregiver to four brothers and a sister, because her own mother had died. I have an image of her as a partner to her husband.

This image and what I was told about her have influenced my thinking. As I see the concern today over the role of working women, I recall that in my grandmother's time women also worked, perhaps not for a salary, but as working partners with their husbands in the home and, as in my grandmother's case, on the ranch.

I remember my grandmother being very much like the other women on the ranch, like my mother and my aunts. She was very open, accepting, nonjudgmental, nonauthoritarian, and noncritical of others. I remember her quiet love. She did not engage in overt or loud demonstrations of affection.

However, I also remember that she always had migraine headaches.

She had an interesting cure for them. She would lie down and put a cold compress of vinegar and raw potato on her head. This ritual was particularly intriguing, because it was observed only by her. I remember peeking into the bedroom to look at her knowing that she was to be left alone.

I also knew that she was a very religious person. Religious, but not obsessive about it. Being Roman Catholic was simply what defined us, at least in part.

My mother, Florinda, was born in Picacho right off the Hondo River. For the most part, throughout her life my mother retained pleasant memories of her childhood. Her memories, like mine, began with the land: memories of the ranch and of the sheep and of her mother helping to shear the sheep and feeding the men who worked on the ranch. She remembered my grandmother as being a good companion to my grandfather.

My grandparents had lots of children, and there was always a lot of work to be done. The work on the ranch involved everyone. In addition, the workload increased whenever there were problems with the sheep, such as when they were infested with lice and had to be bathed in a sulfur solution. At such times, caring for the sheep also entailed additional expenses.

My mother remembered her father as a good businessman and as a good provider. As a young girl, she often accompanied him as he made his rounds. He taught her at an early age how to saddle a horse and how to tend the sheep. She learned to milk cows. And he taught her to pick cotton when that crop became part of the family economy.

My mother never experienced any physical want or hunger. Ranch life was a self-sufficient existence. It's not that my mother grew up pampered or privileged but rather that there was a sense of purposefulness, an overall spirit of cooperation.

My mother obtained some formal education, but not much. During her childhood in New Mexico, schooling was not readily available and not always an option. What few schools existed were far away and limited in grade levels. My mother walked several miles to get to her school, which was a segregated public school. The Anglo kids in the area were bused to a separate school.

Her early experiences at school left her with both positive and negative impressions. She recalls liking school and that the teachers liked her. Arithmetic was her favorite subject, and she was an adept and eager learner. "*La maestra estaba impuesta a que yo aprendía a la nada,*" she would say. (The teacher was used to having me learn my lessons easily.)

But she also remembered racial and ethnic divisions. Perhaps the worst thing I remember hearing was my mother's recollection that a teacher of hers once told the class in Spanish: "*Si supiera donde tengo la sangre mexicana, me l'arrancaría.*" (If I could, I would eradicate any trace of Mexican blood in me.)

When I was still very young, I began picking up from my mother a generalized consciousness of ethnic differences. "*Nosotros somos de allá, al lado de Santa Fe,*" my mother would say. "*La gente es muy españolada.*" (We are from up in that area, near Santa Fe, where the people are very Hispanicized.) (The verb *somos* might be rendered in its characteristic regional form, *semos.*) We had a family history originating in the Santa Fe area, and people from around there were oriented toward a Spanish rather than a Mexican heritage.

I was also vaguely aware that there were language differences. Individuals were identified as Mexican (as opposed to New Mexican) by the way they spoke Spanish—with what I identified as a singsong quality. "*¿Qui 'uvo manito?*" (What's happenin' bro'?) I remember hearing words such as *chicanito* or *manito,* for example, which were used to distinguish people born in Mexico (*chicanito*) from native New Mexicans (*manito*), but I must have heard them in the fields. That type of language was not used in our home.

My mother went as far as the third grade, which was all that was available to her. After suffering major financial losses, her father had been unable to pay for needed school supplies, a requirement in public schools at that time. Furthermore, as one of the older children, my mother was expected to help supplement the family income. Doing housework for townspeople was one way in which she helped. Throughout her life, Mother recalled her lack of further schooling with regret and a sense of loss.

Her parents had obtained even less schooling, but her father was literate in both Spanish and English. Limited schooling was the norm for all my mother's siblings as well. Back then there were no compulsory attendance laws.

My mother remembers a well-meaning Anglo teacher who was moving away and offered to adopt my mother to enable her to continue her education. My grandparents actually considered this offer, but in the end they loved their daughter too much to give her up.

Despite her meager formal education, my mother was an intelligent and resourceful woman. She could read and write in both Spanish and English. I remember her ordering clothes for us out of what was either a Sears Roebuck or a Montgomery Ward catalog. I would watch her compute the prices, weights, and shipping costs.

"I think we can send for this one," she would declare, thinking aloud, as she consulted various tables and order forms in the back of the catalog. Her use of English in this context seemed natural to me, even though there were traces of what I always considered a southern-influenced elongating of vowel sounds and a Spanish-language influence in the stress she placed on certain syllables.

She would read to us the color options for clothes and fabrics. "Look, Frances," she would say, "I think this is real pretty." All the colors bore unusual qualifiers and were not expressed, for example, as simply red or blue. The descriptions meant nothing to me, but I loved hearing the sound of the words. My favorite was teal blue. These words had a liquid sound that fascinated me.

These moments with my mother linger as memories of an auditory, visual, and emotional experience—moments of joyful anticipation shared through the medium of a catalog, the wish book.

꿍웧

Life on the ranch in Atoka also meant an extended family. My aunts and uncles all lived on the ranch or close by. Even though my grandfather had lost most of his land before he died, the other members of the family remained and leased land from nearby ranchers. My parents' two-room adobe was close to grandmother's larger clapboard frame house, and I always seemed to be surrounded by uncles and aunts—my mother's brothers and sisters. We all interacted with one another, and it was a close family environment.

I was allowed to mingle freely with the adults as they went about their daily chores. I could watch them chop wood, provided I didn't stand in the path of flying wood chips. Chopping wood was everyone's responsibility, and I was intrigued by the skills the adults displayed: the women could be as accomplished and as strong as the men.

Laundry day called for an outdoor communal effort. Some washtubs were reserved for scrubbing, the washboard adjusted and positioned to suit individual preferences. White clothes and sheets were boiled in soapy water over large wood fires to get them very white. This was all women's work. The clothes were turned and stirred with a wooden paddle. The metal tub would be left charred black on the outside, but a very clean chalky white on the inner side from the soap sticking to the inside, a contrast that appealed to me.

Everyone took care of everyone else. When my mother was in labor with my sister Susan, it was my aunt Aurelia who kept me occupied and out of the bedroom. I was only five at the time and not sure what was happening, but it was reassuring to be with my aunt. She helped soften my unspoken trauma at being displaced as the baby in the family.

There always seemed to be a lot of people around, all family. That's one of my most reassuring images of New Mexico. People loved one another. So many lowly routines were performed *con cariño*—with love.

My older sister, Toni, and I have shared vivid memories of our daily morning ritual, which included paying our respects to our grand-mother. "*Buenos días, abuelita. Déme su bendición.*" (Good morning, grandmother. May I have your blessing?)

The example of quiet family affection was set by my grandmother. I don't remember her using words of overt endearment, such as calling me a beautiful or wonderful child—"*m'hija*" (my child) said it all. I belonged.

I do remember being called Kika or Kikita, short for Francisca. "*Aquí viene la Kika*"—here comes Kika. I was probably four or five years old at that time, and these were welcome sounds to me. And indeed, I was allowed to listen in as my aunts and their friends shared secrets about their boyfriends or some love note that someone had received.

I don't recall much arguing or bickering among my aunts and uncles. Moreover, family members didn't criticize one another but instead focused on the positive. All the relationships in my extended family tended to be of this nature. And my memories of the interactions among family members are of equality between generations.

Children by around age seven—the age of reason—were treated somewhat as equals. I grew up with the belief that by the age of seven, when a young girl makes her first confession and takes first communion, she should know right from wrong. I remember, for example, my father at the breakfast table putting coffee in my milk or eggnog when I was around this age. Being allowed to have coffee made me feel that I could participate with my father at the breakfast table as an adult. In later years I continued to enjoy having my father share his food with me.

I was and still am very conscious of the history on my mother's side of the family. This is not as much the case with my father, Teodoro, who was separated from his world and from his family. Unlike my mother, my father was born in Mexico. He was from the north, from Santa Clara in the silver-mining area of the state of Durango.

He was the youngest of six children and an orphan by age three. He was raised by his maternal grandmother and a stepgrandfather, who treated him as a stepchild. For example, they did not give him formal schooling like they did their own children. Instead, by age seven, my father was tending the animals and the crops. As a result, he grew up quite independent and left home at the age of about fifteen.

My father talked occasionally about his family background in a way that instilled in me a desire to be like him. I especially admired his sense of independence. My father first worked in the silver mines of Durango and then in an electrical plant in the state of Coahuila. When he was around twenty he decided to join up with an American construction company to work first in Texas and then in southern New Mexico building roads. One of my mother's brothers was also working at the same company and met my father there. It was through that acquaintance that my father eventually met my mother.

My parents never talked about their courtship. My reluctance to ask my mother about this period in her life stemmed both from a respect for her privacy and from an unspoken assumption that such questioning would have breached the bounds of propriety. There were lots of things we didn't discuss, especially those things that had sexual connotations.

In the case of women, there seemed to be a tacit understanding that a young woman just moves from one stage of development to another without necessarily discussing it with anyone. At some point, imperceptibly, she makes the transition from childhood to young womanhood, no longer a child but rather a young virgin. In due time, somehow, outside the purview of her parents, she meets a young man. Marriage is the inevitable and natural consequence. The Church consecrates the union, and she becomes a *mujer*—a woman. In the best of circumstances, her first child will be born within nine months to a year. And the cycle repeats itself. She will have children and will now find fulfillment in her role as wife and mother.

I've had occasion to reflect upon the use of the word *mujer.* "*Ya es mujer.*" Now she's a woman. The sounds of that phrase, the guttural "j," depending on the context, could convey disdain, opprobrium, or even wistfulness—a sense of loss like that which occurred in the Garden of Eden, in this case, a loss of the innocence and luster of virginity. As a trade-off, motherhood would confer on a young woman new honor and respect.

Although my father was from Mexico, he was readily accepted into my mother's family. He proved to be a very valuable worker on the ranch. He also served as a mentor to my mother's various sisters and brothers. Some of them were still quite young, and since they had lost their own father, they looked to my father for guidance. My father taught them, for example, how to perform particular chores on the ranch. I remember my aunts always referring to my father as "*hermano, mi hermano.*" He was an older brother to them.

I recall one incident that marred this nurturing family environment, an incident that I didn't fully understand at the time and that took me a long while to confront. When I was about four or five, one of my uncles fondled me in what I perceived to be a sexual manner. I remember being in my grandmother's house engrossed in my paper dolls. I guess my sister had left the room. My uncle seemed to appear from nowhere, and he picked me up and pressed me close to him in a way that seemed strange. I remember being very conscious of his genital area, but it didn't go any further. Afterward he never said anything about it.

I felt shocked. No one had ever picked me up in that manner—it was totally out of context. Sadly, I told nobody. Certainly, things such as child molestation were never openly discussed. In fact, nothing sexual was ever discussed. It wasn't until I was past thirty that I mentioned the incident to my mother. Throughout those years, I had relegated the incident to an unexamined part of my consciousness.

My mother remained silent when I recounted the incident to her. She looked at me but expressed neither shock nor condemnation. Her silence made it clear to me that she didn't know how to talk about this subject and, of course, neither did I. I didn't know what else to say to my mother other than to add that afterward I never liked this one uncle and never had much to do with him.

Years later, I concluded that this incident had accelerated my awareness of my body and my sexuality as a female. It contributed to my sense that I was maturing very early. It made me wary.

There was no electricity on the ranch, but we were not entirely out of touch with the outside world. My uncles had car radios, and we played records on grandmother's hand-cranked Victrola. Most of my aunts and uncles lived at my grandmother's house. She had a gas lamp in her parlor, while in our house we had only a kerosene lamp—her parlor seemed very bright compared to the dimly lit rooms in our house.

Our house was also much smaller than hers. It had no indoor plumbing, only chamber pots and an outdoor privy. There was no refrigeration. One room served as the bedroom for both my parents and the three children: Toni, my younger sister, Susan, and me. My parents slept in one bed and we in another. I don't remember feeling particularly crowded in the bed. If you think about it, a bed is really mathematical space. You can block out a section of it for each small child so that places on the bed are not perceived simply as parallel to one another. What you do is apportion each section, including the foot of the bed, according to need as determined by the size of each child. I grew up with this kind of arrangement, and it made perfect sense, given the circumstances.

The other room served as the kitchen and dining area. It's true that there was not a lot of space in our house, but then we didn't spend a lot of time inside. The house was more a place to eat and sleep. We went to bed early and got up early.

Despite its starkness, I don't recall our home being uncomfortable. The thick adobe walls kept the indoor temperature pleasant throughout the year. Living in the country at that time was very much like camping. Years later, when I had my own children and they would ask to go camping, I would tell them that I had already experienced my full share growing up. To this day it is with reluctance that I will agree to "roughing it" (unnecessarily).

During the day, my father either worked on the ranch or, like my uncles, went to work on someone else's ranch as part of a lease arrangement. My mother stayed at home and did her chores, which included feeding the chickens and milking the cows. I remember helping to take the cows out to pasture and the feeling that I was in charge, but I couldn't possibly have been, since I was so little. I used to watch the milking and I remember enjoying the hissing sound as the milk hit the pail. I remember scooping the foam off the top. The fresh milk smelled wonderful.

We also had pigs, and I remember the strange snorting sounds they made as they wallowed in the mud. I especially remember the freedom of our horses, particularly their friskiness just before a rainstorm.

Besides her chores with the animals, my mother had her household tasks. Of course she prepared our meals. One-hundred-pound sacks of staples such as wheat flour and potatoes were kept in a partitioned bin along one wall of our small kitchen. My mother made cheese from the fresh milk our cows produced. The cheese tasted like mozzarella; it was very mild and soft. She also made buttermilk and eggnog. She baked bread in our wood-burning stove and made wheat-flour tortillas on the griddle.

We had fresh milk every day. Eggs from our chickens were always served for breakfast, and my mother frequently made pancakes as well. We rarely ate meat such as beef or pork, but chicken was served occasionally. Our noontime and evening meals usually included beans and rice or noodles. While we produced a good deal of our food on the ranch, my father did buy some of our staples such as flour, beans, potatoes, and rice in Artesia. Occasionally the whole family accompanied him into town.

Home production also involved my mother making some of our clothes, such as dresses for my sisters and me. As I've mentioned, she ordered other clothes, such as shoes, stockings, coats, and hats, from a mail-order catalog.

As children, we contributed in small ways to the household economy. I, for example, sold cloverine (an aromatic ointment) at a small profit to earn small amounts of spending money for the family. My mother ordered the cloverine out of a catalog or magazine and I would sell it to my aunts and uncles. Cloverine had a rosewater smell, and was considered a cure-all for all kinds of ailments. My sister Toni and I and some of the younger aunts also sold eggs from our chickens. We walked a couple of miles to the little general store that stood isolated at a country crossroads to sell them. We would give the money we made to my mother. This is partly how we maintained a cash flow.

Living in a rural environment, we didn't have access to many of the things townspeople had. Physicians, for example, were not readily available. If we really needed a doctor, we had to go into town, a distance of perhaps ten miles. Once when I fell and injured my knee I had to be taken to a doctor. This is when I learned about gangrene. There was always concern that, if you neglected a wound, gangrene might set in. The doctor gave my mother some dark ointment to apply to my knee. The smell was obnoxious, and I remember remaining fixated on my medicated smelly knee for days. I would sit under a tree and contemplate the horrors of life, including gangrene, a word that sounded just awful to me. I bear the scar on my knee to this day.

Although life on my grandmother's ranch must have been quite difficult for the adults, especially during the Depression, my memories as a young child there are of good times. Our life was centered on the ranch since, outside of trips to Artesia, we never traveled.

Because I didn't have any commercially produced toys, I played a lot with paper dolls. I think my imagination must have developed as we cut dolls out of outdated mail-order catalogs. I had a large family of dolls, and my sister Toni and I used to play games with them. We constructed our own doll furniture out of paper and cardboard. I had only one real doll, a cute little baby doll, but I don't remember how I got her. She may have been a Christmas present. She was black, an African American doll. I don't know why I received a black doll, since there were no blacks around that I was aware of. I enjoyed playing with *mi negrita*.

Besides providing the material for our dolls, the catalog had many other uses. It served as a picture book and a story book (when my mother read aloud from it as she placed her orders), and it served other more utilitarian purposes as well such as providing reading material in the outhouse—and toilet paper.

We had no stuffed animals, and most of our live animals, including our dogs, were not pets but farm animals. I did have my own live baby chick. Sadly, I caught his little leg in the screen door, and one can't keep a baby chick with a broken leg—he couldn't be allowed to live in that condition. I regretted what I had done, and I felt guilty about it for years.

My sister Toni and I also played outdoors a lot, in the nearby creek and among the cottonwood trees. I loved to listen to the trees. The rustling of the leaves drew my attention skyward, and I would watch in fascination as the shifting wind made the leaves dance first in one direction, then another. If I listened carefully, I could detect the different sounds—sometimes a moaning sound, at other times a sigh that could drop to a whisper. The trees stirred my imagination. They were a live presence for me.

Exploring nature enabled me to occupy my time creatively. Now, many years later, I can still get in touch with the memory of these images and sounds. When I walk along an ocean beach, the sounds of a tide's ebb and flow give me that same sense of timelessness.

Watching the adults and observing what they did both at work and at home was still another pastime. I remember with special fondness those occasions when the men would come together to relax and sing. My father played the guitar, and often, after work or on weekends, he would sit around with the other men who helped on the ranch or who worked on nearby ranches and sing Mexican ranch songs—*rancheras*. My father knew these songs from Mexico and from his work experiences in Texas.

As a child, I was allowed to join the inner circle of men, and I recall being fascinated by their facial expressions as they recounted in song tales of bravery, romantic longing, loss, and unrequited love. They put so much feeling and gusto into their singing that, even as a child, I got a sense of the powerfully emotional attraction of Mexican music. The music had an impact, and the performers fascinated me.

My father had a good voice, and his singing was special. He became powerful in his ability to convey so much feeling in song. He held my hand and taught me proper fingering on the guitar. I sang and danced to the delight of everyone, and I felt very proud.

My father explained and demonstrated harmony to the others in a manner that made perfect sense to me. Now, as an adult, I might call it "training the ear." As a child, I simply admired the men and their ability to create music.

Music came to us also in another way. My younger uncles and the ranch hands or young friends sometimes sat in their cars and listened to a Spanish-language radio station, which played *rancheras*. The young men especially enjoyed the songs of the already legendary Lydia Mendoza, who sang Texas-Mexican border music. She was a singer whose name everyone seemed to recognize. And her ballads were considered standards by everyone. My aunts and uncles spoke of her knowingly, but listening to music on the car radio was very much a male ritual in which the women did not participate. Still, from inside the house, we could see the men in their cars, and I could tell that, from a distance, the women, too, enjoyed the music.

I don't recall that much of our family culture included telling folk stories or legends. What replaced this form of oral tradition were the conversations engaged in by the adults, either at our house or at my grandmother's. These conversations were about real-life stories. The adults talked about family history and about other families in the area, and sometimes those other families would visit and join in on the conversation. For me, this adult conversation was probably the equivalent of other children's bedtime stories. Toni and I were allowed to listen to everything that was being said. We were never shooed out of the room. Sometimes the conversation would be among only the women. My aunts would read to one another letters that boys had sent them. This could be a whole evening's conversation. At about that time, in 1936, my five younger aunts ranged in age from nine to twenty-two. They didn't feel that talking about boys in my presence was a problem. This kind of "intimate" talk was innocent enough. It was just talk about girls liking boys and about who looked at whom. There were no explicit or even implicit sexual references involved; however, by listening to these conversations, I became aware early on of courting mores.

I also remember some things that puzzled me and could be considered superstitions. For example, my father always insisted that his bed had to face in a certain direction. This was either east or west—I don't recall. I remember once asking why this was so and not receiving much of an answer. I could sense, however, that my parents did not want to be perceived as superstitious.

Home remedies involved what seemed to be superstitions. I remember one instance when a baby became sick and an egg yolk in a bowl was placed at the head of his bed. I probably witnessed this at a friend's home, but I do remember that this was done to ward off the *mal ojo*— the evil eye—and to drive away the illness, *para rebajar la calentura* (to reduce the fever).

I also recall my mother telling me that she was once accused of causing the illness and death of a child by casting an evil eye on him. "*La gente decía que uno que tenía ojos podía hacerle ojo a una criatura. A mí me dijo una vez una mujer que yo tenía ojos. Que yo iba pasando, iba no sé para donde, y ella traía a su niño en los brazos y que le dije yo que era bonito, y él se enfermó y se murió.*" (People used to say that someone with the evil eye could cast the eye on other people. One time a woman accused me of having the evil eye. I was on my way to somewhere, I don't remember where, and what happened was she was carrying her baby in her arms and I said her baby was very pretty, and the baby got sick and died.) It was believed that a person who had *ojos,* the evil eye, could harm a child by simply looking at him and saying "what a beautiful child," which is what my mother was accused of having done.

Beliefs of this sort were never really explained. If I asked questions, the response would be *"Es una creencia. Así dice la gente."* (It's a belief. That's what people say.) The focus would be on purported remedies: an egg yolk to dispel the evil eye. A blessed palm or a heated rock or a splash of cold water thrown at the face of a sleeping person to rid him of fears and phobias.

Home remedies also included the use of *sobadores.* These were particular men who had the skill and the touch to deal with *empacho,* which is a vaguely defined illness and perhaps an evil or unhealthy wind that enters your body and is quite painful and immobilizing. I once complained to my parents about my legs hurting, and I remember their diagnosis being that I had contracted *empacho.* I was taken to a *sobador.* He rubbed kitchen fat all over my legs and then massaged them in a manner similar to that of a Japanese massage. The massaging was from top to bottom and out through the toes. After he did this for a while, he finished the process by grasping my toe and moving my leg with a whipping motion. I'm not sure what all this was supposed to do, but my legs did feel better afterward.

Another example of superstitious belief is that people in New Mexico feared lightning. During any lightning storm we would cover all the mirrors in the house, since it was believed that lightning was attracted by mirrors.

I don't recall birthdays as being particularly special occasions. This probably had to do with the Depression. Somber times had set in. I've been told that, before the Depression, birthdays or *días de santo*—saints' days—were celebrated quite lavishly on the ranch. Entire animals were butchered, and family and friends would be invited for a barbecue. But this didn't happen when I was young. We didn't receive gifts but rather became more of a focus for attention and praise on that day. Christmas was also not a time for gift giving. It was more strictly a religious celebration.

While my memories of growing up on the ranch are happy, I have memories of stern discipline as well. Although my mother did not use corporal punishment, she exercised a quiet authority at home, and a rebuke from her could be devastating. My father, on the other hand, did use the rod or his hand on us. I don't think that my mother approved of us being punished physically, but I don't think she protested to my father in a direct confrontational manner. It would be many years before she would learn to stand up to my father and oppose him. Yet I knew that she could protect us from his wrath. She was the person to whom I could go for refuge.

Though my father spanked us, he never injured us. Still, at the time I saw it as a physical punishment and therefore hurtful. This only inflamed me and intensified my growing sense of rebelliousness. Yet I would never characterize my father's discipline as a form of child abuse.

Religion, of course, was very much a part of life in rural New Mexico. My mother's family was very devoutly Roman Catholic. Catholicism defined us as much as our surname defined us. There was the church and there were the saints. Catholicism—New Mexican Catholicism— permeated the environment, and we just accepted it as part of who we were. Although I was aware of "right and wrong," I was not conscious of guilt or sin. Religion retained its benign aspect for me in these early years. Place-names like San Patricio were not merely geographic realities, they were the names of saints, part of the iconography that made up my world. San Ysidro was carried in a religious procession through the *surcos del sembrado,* the fields he was asked to bless as the patron saint of *los labradores,* the tillers of the soil. Santa Rita was a beautiful lady and the saint who healed wounds. Religious pictures and statues were visually appealing. One could speculate endlessly about details of saintly dress and demeanor.

Whereas my mother's side of the family represented to me simply being faithful Catholics, my father was much more intense and dramatic about religion. It was my father who introduced to my mother's family elements of Mexican Catholicism that had not been part of their culture. He was especially devoted to the Virgen de Guadalupe.

It was he who initiated the practice of praying novenas in our home in early December to celebrate the feast of Our Lady of Guadalupe. These nine-day novenas were filled with special prayers and rituals to the Virgen. My family set up an elaborate three-tiered altar topped by a picture of her. The picture was surrounded by green flower vases and paper flowers and lots of candles. Neighboring people joined us in our home, especially for the evening prayers.

One could almost say, respectfully, that the December novena to the Virgen de Guadalupe was intimate theater in the privacy of our own adobe—but in dramatic effect a match for the solemnity of the Roman Mass. I remember watching the adults, particularly the women, fingering their beads, their bodies swaying as they knelt on the hard floor. For me, trying to remain upright in this kneeling position was a form of suffering for what seemed like an eternity. I occupied my mind trying to understand what all this meant. I remember being very impressed by the devotion and the fervent praying of the Ave María and the Padre Nuestro in unison. The ritual was mesmerizing. The light from the flickering candles cast eerie shadows about the room and upon the faces of the worshipers. Facial features stood out in strong relief. I remember how people would kneel close to one another while at the same time respecting one another's space. This compactness and unity gave me a sense of community, although at the time I don't think I was conscious of the impact of this ritual. There was a trusting, fervent religious piety here that I did not yet fully appreciate. I now understand that what I was observing was the dignity inherent in the genuine expression of simple, religious faith.

What I did enjoy about each novena was that hot chocolate, or *cafe con leche,* was served afterward.

My concept of religion developed partly as a response to what I observed as my father's dramatic devotion to the Virgen and to Christ, her divine son. Religion was not so much an awareness of God but rather a perception that Christ and the Virgen were central in our lives.

Besides observing these rituals in our home, we attended the closest Catholic church which, though modest, evoked reverence with its icons and pews that defined ritual. The church was a bit of a distance from our house, and we couldn't walk to it. We had to go by car. We attended frequently, but not every Sunday.

I don't recall being baptized or confirmed but I learned later that these sacraments were administered simultaneously shortly after I was born. They were done at the same time to take advantage of the infrequent times when the bishop visited our area.

∽∾∽

We, of course, lived in a Spanish-speaking world. Everyone spoke mostly Spanish, although some English was also spoken. I remember my uncle Vincent having to deal with businesspeople in town and having to use English. My mother knew some English, since she had learned it in school. She used to read to us in English whenever she ordered from the mail-order catalog. These uses of English, however, represented the exceptions. For the most part, we spoke Spanish on a daily basis. My father especially insisted on this and was very conscious of our use of language.

His angry assertion that *"aquí en mi casa se va hablar español"* (here in my house Spanish is spoken) was delivered with a menacing look, more in the direction of my mother than of anyone else. My mother, clearly, was held accountable for our behavior. These scenes were likely to occur at dinnertime when my father returned home from the fields tired. *Mi papá mandaba.* He was the boss. We would look at my mother and take our cue from her response. She always acquiesced. Silence would descend for the time being, and there would be no more English that evening.

Many years later, when I was married and had a much easier relationship with both my parents, my father was able to tease my mother by saying, "*No, pues tú hablabas puro inglés.*" (You used to speak English all the time.) He was referring to the tension that choice of language created in our family.

My mother enjoyed speaking English as well as Spanish, and my father, too, exerted himself in public to express himself in English and to understand it. Although he didn't know much English when he arrived in New Mexico, he had taught himself along the way. As he sought out jobs, he had to exert himself to speak English and he was conscious of both the pitfalls and the humor inherent in the struggle to master a new language. But at home, he was in control, and language lent itself well as a control mechanism.

For my grandmother, speaking Spanish was the norm. What else would she speak? She knew absolutely no English, and she tuned out any language she didn't understand. But although Spanish was my grandmother's language, she did not object to the use of English by others.

I think that perhaps my father had experienced some bad encounters over language in Texas and that he therefore was more adamant in his "there shall be Spanish in this household." He stressed Spanish that was as "correct" as possible. Slang was frowned upon.

In his normal speech he would lapse into language common in that part of New Mexico. "*Es lo que dicemos, pues pa' que lo v'a negar uno.*" (That's what we say.) But in reflective moments, sometimes after dinner when he might be counseling us about our behavior, for example, he would clear his throat and muster up his best Spanish. *Pa'* would become *para* and *dicemos* would become *decimos*. This was our clue that he was trying to teach us a lesson about some important matter. "*Y así viene siendo la historia de la vida, m'hija, así.*" That's the way life is, daughter, he would say. He was philosophical about the fact that he had become an orphan at age three and had not been favorably treated in the home of his maternal stepgrandfather. "*Quedé huerfanito de tres años, pero toda la gente me quería. Tuve buena suerte, gracias a Dios.*" (I was an orphan at three, but I'm thankful to God. I was fortunate. I knew that the people in my little village cared about me.)

I admired my father in this didactic role. On occasions such as this, he would say to me, "*para que sepa, m'hija, lo importante qu' es la buena educación.*" (I want you to understand, daughter, that to get along in life you need to be polite and have good manners.) He would tell me that a good education didn't come just from textbooks. Attitude was also important.

I, like my mother, learned to speak English when I started attending school in New Mexico. Spanish was absolutely forbidden in school. I was about five when I started a variation of kindergarten called primer. My older sister, Toni, and I walked to school, which was close enough. It was a small wood-frame building. I don't remember more than a couple of rooms. The playground was a tiny yard with a little merry-go-round, a teeter-totter, and a slide. Only Hispano children attended this school. I remember seeing Anglo kids, just like my mother remembered, being bused to another school as we walked to our school.

Although no Spanish was allowed in our school, I don't recall that this was particularly traumatic for me. I already knew some words in English, and it helped to have an older sister who had gone to school two years before me. Toni paved the way. She was the older sister who had a sense of responsibility and looked after me. As *la mayor,* the older one, she had status. She could tell on me if I misbehaved.

One time when I stole pennies from my mother and bought candy to give to my friends at school, Toni went home and told my mother about it. I was neither conscious of my motives nor aware that Toni was going to tell on me. My mother took me aside in the kitchen and, with Toni watching, confronted me with the report that my sister had given her. I felt trapped. And worse yet, my mother looked more than angry. She looked worried.

"*M'hija, ¿por qué hiciste eso?*" (Why did you do it?) she asked. Clearly, we had a problem on our hands, and I was the problem. "*No quiero que lo vuelvas a hacer,*" she said, with a definite stress on the word *quiero,* making it clear that she didn't want me to ever do it again.

I think it would have been easier for me if she had just swatted me. Instead, I was left to ponder the significance of my actions. I was only about five years old and had scant knowledge of "right" or "wrong," but it was evident that my actions would lead to unimaginable consequences. This proved to be a learning experience. I got the message: "You don't steal pennies from your mother's cookie jar." But more important, I learned that discipline need not be accompanied by physical punishment.

I really don't have any specific memories about my early schooling, at least not lasting or warm memories. I especially don't have any fond memories of my teachers. I do recall that once, after getting a finger on my right hand caught in the teeter-totter at school, I was taken home by the school principal, who also happened to be my teacher. She was an enormous lady, the type of woman I would in later years visualize as a Nordic type. She was also not very warm or solicitous. I remember contemplating her large facial features as we were driven to my house by someone. In the back seat she and I sat in silence, my bandaged and injured hand on her lap, motionless.

I didn't realize it then, nor did I think about it for many years, but my New Mexican background had a profound influence on me. It gave me a sense of belonging, a sense that I could count on family acceptance and total support. In later years, even in the worst of times and no matter how hostile the environment, I always knew that I could trust my family. It was a given. I hardly had to even think about it. Yet, now when I reflect upon it, I realize what an incredible support system I had. It involved nothing more than their acceptance of and their pride in me. It was good to know that they were always happy to hear about me, to hear that I was doing well. I was one of many, but I was made to feel that everything I did was important.

Later, in my adolescent years, as I acted out my growing sense of rebellion against my parents, I intuitively trusted that my immediate family would continue to be there for me. I became aware of this sense of trust when I returned to New Mexico many years later. I was still *m'hija*. In my case, it wasn't true that I couldn't "go home again."

New Mexico also provided me with a certain sense of ethnic identity. Even when she knew she would not be leaving California any time soon, my mother continued to identify with her New Mexican background. She identified with other Hispanos from New Mexico. My mother would say, "*Es de Nuevo México.*" (So-and-so is from New Mexico.) This is how she defined people with whom she could identify. I myself still retain that affinity for Spanish-speaking people from New Mexico. New Mexico means family and roots.

TWO

Moving on to a New Life in California

My parents' decision to leave New Mexico and go to California was not spontaneous. The Great Depression worsened as the thirties progressed, and my father, along with my aunt Zenaida and her husband, my uncle Jess, decided to go to California in search of economic opportunities. This was in 1937. The decision on my father's part was totally based on economic factors. Although we were not starving, times were difficult in New Mexico. Uncle Jess was seen as the instigator, but my father, of course, had a previous history of migrating. For my father, going to California was just another instance of seeking out opportunities.

My dad's intent was to go to California first and look for work. He went to southern California and found work in a factory near Bakersfield. My mother's family was prepared to face both the harsh economic realities and the fact that my father had left. However, within less than six months, my mother's older brother, my uncle Vincent, asserted his authority and directed my mother to write to my father demanding that he return at once to his family.

This father did. Again, it was made clear to everyone that unity was of paramount importance. A man had a moral obligation to care for his family. "*Un hombre casado ante Dios tiene que responder. No debe pa-*

garle mal a su esposa porque jura ante Dios. Allá está Dios." (Through the Church, marriage is sanctified in the presence of God, and a man is ultimately answerable to God if he fails to live up to his marriage vows.)

As a child, I was not fully aware of the economic difficulties surrounding us in New Mexico. All I knew was that we always had enough to eat. We grew our own vegetables. We had our chickens and cows. We were comfortable, at least from a child's perspective. But I guess that as the family started to grow, prospects for the future did not look good. The ranch had to sustain a large group. The entire country was in an economic depression. My father had acquired sheep, but he had difficulty selling them and their wool because times were hard.

I don't remember the decision to go to California being a problem for the other family members. My grandmother and my mother's family accepted it. The potential move didn't elicit jubilation, but they weren't traumatized by it either. This acceptance was remarkable, given that New Mexico was the only home that generations of this family had ever known. It was also felt that this was probably going to be a permanent move. There was no talk about returning at any future time. Instead, there was a sense that we were going on to a new life.

My mother took it all very well, even though it meant selling her prized cows and her chickens. And more important, it meant leaving her mother as well as her brothers and sisters. My mother was devoted to them, but she now had her own family to take care of. This meant going with her husband and her children to California, a natural decision for her. It was something that was expected. I don't think that she ever saw it as anything other than taking care of her own family. My mother's family understood this and supported it. They expected that my father would take care of my mother and the children, and this expectation was conveyed to my father.

Taking care of us didn't mean acquiring lots of material possessions. My parents never seemed acquisitive in this sense. They wanted a good life for us, and that meant having enough to eat and a decent place to live. A good life to them also meant having some level of economic self-sufficiency. Home ownership remained a goal. In New Mexico, it was said of a good husband, *"Le puso casa."* He provided a home for his spouse.

We left New Mexico in 1937. I was six years old. My father had acquired a pickup truck, and six of us piled in with a few pieces of furniture, clothes, and whatever other possessions we could take. My father drove, and my mother rode in front with my baby sister, Susan, and with Sotera, a member of my father's adopted extended family in New Mexico. This was the family with whom my father had lodged when he originally came to Artesia and with whom, over time, he developed familial ties.

Toni and I rode in the back in the covered truck bed. I remember feeling crowded and cold. Somehow now I always associate being cold not with New Mexico but with California. We drove straight through, only stopping to rest here and there.

We traveled for what seemed a very long time. I remember stopping at state borders and hearing "this is the border." I remember struggling with the concept of a geographic border and wondering, "Is there a line or some kind of physical demarcation?" Later still as a child, I would look at a map in school and at what I was told were border lines and again wonder if those lines on the map existed, somehow, in reality.

The end of our journey was Corcoran in the rich agricultural San Joaquin Valley in central California. What I was yet to learn was that we were substituting one rural experience in New Mexico for another starkly different one in California. For me the difference was profound. The labor camp we moved into was unlike anything I had ever seen. The tents (*carpas*) on elevated wooden platforms were crowded together, and the people in them were an undifferentiated group to whom I couldn't relate. My dad started working by picking cotton there.

I no longer retain clear images of Corcoran, except for some memories of my new school. Unlike my school in New Mexico, this one had both Mexican American and Anglo students. But initially I was bored. The work was slow and didn't interest me. I was surrounded by strange faces—both the faces of the Spanish-speaking and the faces of the others, who were equally alien.

There is one spelling test that I remember. The teacher was taking forever to dictate the spelling words as she walked around the room from one student to another monitoring our performance. Spelling came easily to me. I would write the word as soon as I heard it, and then I had nothing to do for minutes while other students seemed to struggle, and the teacher repeated the words over and over, exaggerating the vowel sounds.

"ALL ways," she might say, stressing the "a" sound in the first syllable of the word *always* and then adding a sentence such as, "We 'ALL ways' do our best work." This she would repeat two or three times with long pauses between repetitions, which seemed unnecessary. Her illustrative sentences were deadening.

I started to shade in the vowels on my paper to occupy my time. As I recall, I warmed up to my little game by shading in the vowels first, in this case the "a." Then I began a little debate with myself as to whether or not I should shade in the loops of letters such as "l" and "y." Visually, the possibilities were endlessly intriguing.

I was busy doing this when the teacher unexpectedly came up behind me. If she said anything, I have blocked it out. What I do remember is that she yanked me out of my seat and whacked my little derriere, and I wet my pants. She then shoved me toward the coatroom, and I remember being very shocked and very hurt. I stood there alone in the long, dark, skinny coatroom—ashamed and confused, tears streaming down my face. I felt a deep sense of injured pride, because I didn't think I had done anything wrong. This negative experience taught me to observe teachers carefully to decide which ones could be trusted and could be my friends. I was becoming selective.

But I also had some positive experiences in Corcoran, thanks mostly to my mother. I remember to this day, with a lot of fondness, a lovely outfit that she made for me for a school performance. My school in Corcoran had some kind of school festival, perhaps for May Day, and we had to make our costumes at home. This must have been a challenge for my mother, because whatever stores there may have been in this area must have been at a great distance. I certainly don't remember seeing any. My mother somehow got to a store and bought crepe paper, out of which she made me a little aqua-colored costume. She invested an extra effort in the project and also made me a little crepe-paper purse and braided a handle for it. I remember that day as probably the first time I became aware that my mother related to my schooling and wanted me to do well. That day I felt good about myself.

From Corcoran we migrated to the Tagus Ranch, which was situated between Visalia and Tulare, still in the San Joaquin Valley. I was now about seven years old. We lived there for about three years. I remember vividly our housing situation at Tagus. It was a farm-labor camp, and families were designated to live in particular sections identified by the coloring of the frame shacks. There was a white camp, a green camp, and so on. I don't know if those distinctions had anything to do with race or ethnicity, even though overall it was quite a mixed community of people: Mexicans, a few African Americans, and many whites—the so-called Okies and Arkies.

The shacks were one-room wood-frame dwellings all in rows facing one another. There were no sidewalks or hard-surface walkways, and during and after a rain there would be lots of mud. Undoubtedly there had been mud in New Mexico, but for some reason I was more aware of mud and dirt in the Tagus Ranch, where for me it grew to be an insidious presence.

Each of the dwellings was sparsely furnished. There was electricity, and I remember the single naked lightbulb hanging from the center of the little room when we first moved in. Just the way it hung there, with its exposed wiring, made it seem unfriendly to me. Indeed, the whole camp at first seemed unfriendly and strange—an unfamiliar array of small shacks with little space in between them. Each was about twenty feet from the next one, space enough for parking a car or a pickup truck with room left over for personal items such as work gear.

There was no running water in the house, and we had to get water from an open spigot outside the structure. We bathed in a tub near the stove, where my mother heated the water. There was only an outhouse available. Heating was a problem since there was no insulation, and the only source of heat was our tiny wood-burning stove.

While we couldn't hear conversations from our neighbors, we were quite aware of sounds from one building to another. There was the hubbub of a community in close quarters. None of the houses was furnished, so it was fortunate that we had brought with us from New Mexico some of our furniture and the like.

We were clearly more crowded than we had ever been before and we seemed to have little privacy. I remember my father, shortly after we arrived at Tagus, making friends with one of the few black people there, a man who sometimes poked his head into our doorway to talk to my father. It shocked me that someone outside the family could so easily intrude into our space. I remember feeling an overwhelming loss of privacy. Our home in New Mexico was not much larger, yet intrusions didn't seem to be a problem there.

My guess is that as I was growing older space within the home mattered more to me. I became conscious of the fact that there were other people—family members—sleeping in the room. My sisters and I slept on one side of the room on the floor while my parents slept on the other side on their bed. I began to feel constricted not only physically but psychologically. I think too that I began to resent how difficult the economic struggle was for us and that, because of this, we had to live in the restricted way that we did.

The way we acquired our food and other provisions was also something new and strange to me. While in New Mexico we were generally self-sufficient on our ranch, here at Tagus we were at first totally dependent on the wages my father earned as a laborer. He was actually paid mostly in scrip, which was only redeemable at the company store. We now bought everything there. We no longer had fresh milk or eggs. Groceries were mainly dry foods and canned foods since there was initially no refrigeration. Eventually we acquired a small icebox.

Part of my image of this strange new environment includes a memory of experiencing hunger and deprivation for the very first time. I certainly missed fresh food. I don't know if I was bothered more by the fact that we weren't able to secure enough food or the circumstances under which we were living. We were cramped in our house and I may have been associating mealtimes with these other material discomforts. There was now an unpleasantness associated with eating that possibly affected my appetite.

I didn't look forward to mealtimes. I focused on what I didn't like. Condensed canned milk diluted with water, with its overly cloying taste, was particularly distasteful to me. Furthermore, I was also having to accustom myself to eating cafeteria food at school, some of which I ate with revulsion. The "buttered" bread would sometimes get soaked in the juice from the canned spinach, and I had to eat the soppy mixture before I could raise my hand to request fresh bread.

Usually, out of everything on my meal tray, this "buttered" bread tasted best, but even that was questionable. I had seen the ladies in the cafeteria stirring large vats of white margarine to mix in the little packets of orange coloring that would give the margarine a butterlike appearance. The margarine looked like lard to me, very unappetizing.

At home, the only meal I really continued to enjoy was an early morning egg breakfast, which I became obsessive about. If I hadn't had eggs by seven o'clock in the morning, I became ravenous.

The crowded conditions at Tagus continued when my first brother, Severo, was born. Not only was he the first boy in the family but he was also the first of my siblings to have been born in a hospital. My parents and others expressed delighted surprise and joy about the fact that the new baby was a boy. It was evident that a male child was highly prized. His birth made us all happy, even though it meant less room in the house.

I remember when Severo was baptized. His godfather was a very proud man from Mexico who had become a good friend of my father's. He was tall and handsome and presented the stereotypical image of "macho." He personified male assertiveness to me—chauvinism, we would call it today. This was also my first encounter with what I would in later years recognize as the stereotype of the Mexican who leaves a common-law wife and children in Mexico and sets up housekeeping with a new woman in this country. The phenomenon puzzled me, but my parents did not discuss it in their children's presence, if they discussed it at all.

Certainly one of my most vivid memories of Tagus Ranch (and of our subsequent migrations) is of working in the fields with my father. During the school year, Toni and I worked after school, on weekends including Sundays, and on holidays. We did this to add to the family income. My sister and I didn't receive wages; they were added on to my father's. My mother usually didn't work in the fields but stayed home to take care of the younger children. I don't recall many other neighboring children working, but this may be because I wasn't that conscious of other children. Outside school, for my sister and me, there was primarily the world of work. Working in the fields made me more aware of the day-to-day life of my dad and other adults than of the activities of other children.

Working in the fields also meant getting up very early, before sunrise. I remember on Sundays attending seven A.M. Mass before going to work. I actually enjoyed the early morning hours when the stars were still quite visible and the air was fresh. We could see lights that weren't visible at other times of the day. The sounds were also special. There was an absence of familiar sounds, and instead you listened for the unexpected. There was a sense of anticipation and adventure. The world was out there waiting for you, full of possibilities.

Depending on just where on a ranch we would be working, we either walked or drove to the fields. In some instances, we were picked up by labor contractors at a specified location along with other workers. These contractors were Mexicans usually from Mexico, or at least I had the impression that they were from Mexico.

We worked in groups. While the workforce was ethnically diverse, I remember being aware primarily of other Mexicans. This was probably because we—certainly my father—had more in common with them. African Americans and Anglos were not people I socialized or identified with. I was vaguely aware that they were out there working with us, but the Mexicans were the people with whom we most interacted.

My sister and I had no previous experience with some of this type of field work—picking peaches, for example—so we learned by observing our father and others. I learned the differences among types of peaches and why some were considered more valuable. Cling peaches were suitable for canning and brought a higher price on the market. Some peaches were tastier than others, but they didn't ship well, so they were not commonly grown. When we picked cotton, we learned the manual dexterity required to pick it out of its brown, hard shell with maximum speed.

"Mire m'hija, así se agarra, con las dos manos, a montones," my father would explain. He would point out that a dry plant laden with the downy white cotton could be quickly picked if you started at the base of the plant and you used both hands, fingers separated and extended, to grasp the cotton and draw it upward in one continuous motion. Where the picking was more sparse, the trick was to maintain speed by coordinating the alternating motion of your arms, to the left and to the right, as you picked two rows at a time.

Picking cotton was particularly difficult. The pointed ends of the dry shell were hard on the cuticles. Gloves were for finicky women, so I didn't use them. You needed to be dexterous, focused, and alert to pick a plant clean at a profitable pace. At the end of a row, you could look back to see who had picked the cleanest. If your row wasn't clean, you had to go back for a second picking—less rewarding and less profitable. Speed was called for because we were paid by the pound.

But we were fast learners, and pretty soon I was competing with the adults—both men and women—and being treated almost as an equal. The more proficient I became in picking cotton, for example, the more praise I received from my father and from the other workers.

"M'hija no s'entretiene. Es muy empeñada." Using my formal name, Francisca, for example, my father would point out to others, "My daughter, Francisca, is not one to dally. She is an eager worker." This made me feel good. I liked the feeling of being a good worker and not being treated as a kid.

Working in the fields was demanding but it taught me the value of hard work. My father valued it, and he remained a very physical and active man even later in his life when he had crippling arthritis. He saw dignity in his work and took pride in it. I shared that pride. I don't recall ever hearing my father complain about having to work.

Field work likewise produced a type of work culture that became more and more familiar to me. Part of this culture involved how we dressed for work. Toni and I wore men's clothes such as blue denim shirts and pants, the best option for working in the fields. We also wore a kerchief around our necks to protect us against peach fuzz and to wipe the perspiration off our foreheads. In addition, we wore another kerchief around our heads and under our hats. We didn't wear men's shoes, but we did wear relatively heavy oxfords.

The Mexican men and women who worked alongside us would distract themselves from the hard labor and the hot sun by singing as they picked. Some would whistle. The songs were *rancheras* and *corridos,* some of them tunes with which I was familiar. I wasn't conscious of it then, but over time, as I listened to these songs, I learned to recognize certain themes.

There was the melancholy of leave-taking:

Mañana me voy, mañana.
Mañana me voy de aquí.

(Tomorrow I bid you good-bye.
Tomorrow I bid you farewell.)

or

No volverán mis ojos a mirarte.
Ni tus oídos escucharán mi llanto . . .

(Never again will I gaze upon you.
Nor you hear my lament.)

There was the sadness of loss:

Se me fué mi amor.
Se me fué mi encanto.

(Gone is my love,
my life's enchantment.)

or

Cuatro milpas tan sólo han quedado
del ranchito que'ra mío, ay, ay, ay, ay . . .

(Four barren cornfields remain
of what once I called home.)

Soulful love songs could be happy but were more likely to be expressions of heartache and pain:

Alegres se ven los campos
por las mañanas del mes de abril.
Aún se ven más alegres si mi ranchera anda por ahí.

(Happy fields on an April morn.
Happier yet when my love is come.)

or

Tengo un amor
qu'en mi vida dejó para siempre amargo dolor.

(It's a love I carry
ever in my aching heart.)

Drinking tequila was associated with one form of passion or another:

Mira como ando, mujer, por tu querer
borracho y apasionado no más por tu amor.

(Woman, look at me now,
in a drunken passion for your love.)

or

Borrachita de tequila traigo siempre el alma mía
para ver si se mejora d'esta cruel melancolía.

(Ever seeking comfort in tequila
to gladden my sorry heart.)

The woman seemed frequently at fault and was likely to pay the price:

Tú, sólo tú. Has llenado de luto mi vida
abriendo una herida en mi corazón.

(You and you alone cast my wounded heart
into eternal mourning.)

or

Y tú vas a saber que siempre gano.
No vuelvas, que hasta 'ti haré perder.

(It's a game I always win,
and you have everything to lose.)

Jalisco, more than a geographical location or state in Mexico, represented the essence of machismo, the type of vigorous male assertiveness
that was so much admired.

En Jalisco se quiere a la buena
porque's peligroso querer a la mala . . .
Ay Jalisco, no te rajes . . .

(A woman runs risks when
trifling with love.
For a man it's a question of honor.)

The *corridos* told wonderful stories and sometimes ended with a
moral—a cautionary note to young women regarding matters of the
heart:

Popular entre la tropa era Adelita,
la mujer qu 'el sargento idolatraba.

(Adelita! Adored by the troops,
idolized by her sergeant.)

or

Decía la güera Chabela cuando estaba agonizando,
"Mucho cuidado, muchachas, con andarlos mancornando."

(In breathing her last,
she cautioned all girls
against the temptations of lustful desire.)

I felt free in the open air, away from the constraints of my crowded
home environment. I enjoyed working with my dad. After hours of
working under a hot sun, I looked forward to resting in the cool shade
of a tree or a vine, away from the other workers. The lunch hour was always welcome. The food that my mother packed for us tasted delicious.

This was usually flour tortillas wrapped around whatever we had at home such as beans, scrambled eggs, or leftover rice. My dad would bring a thermos of coffee, while Toni and I drank the water available in the fields. My dad loved his coffee and he would always let me have a sip. Since we generally worked in the hot sun, thirst was a problem. Sometimes the managers or contractors provided water in large lidded metal containers. At other times we brought our own containers. We'd put them at the end of whatever row of fruit or cotton we were working on and then go back as needed for a drink. Everyone shared the same container. But people were considerate of one another. They drank only what they had to, and they were careful to wipe the rim of the drinking cup that we used in common. There was a sense of community sharing.

There were no bathroom facilities in the fields. We just used the outdoors. I didn't like relieving myself where others might see me; I was too self-conscious. I controlled the urge as best I could, but sometimes I just had to go. This was inconvenient, but then life at that time presented many inconveniences.

While I don't recall during this time any particular labor conflicts in the fields, I do remember that part of the work culture was learning how to cut corners. For example, in picking cotton you were supposed to separate the cotton from its open dry shell and leave behind the heavy, closed green "balls." But some workers added these balls to their sacks to give them more weight, since the weight of the sack determined how much you got paid. Putting in the whole shell also meant you worked faster and could conceivably get more pay. Some workers undoubtedly saw these practices as a legitimate way of trying to make a living wage. But I knew it was dishonest, and my father did not encourage it.

Although my sister and I didn't receive wages, one of our rewards came at the end of the workday when my father would take us to the company store or some small general store at a crossroads and buy us cold sodas. He called them *sodas—una soda.* This was a real treat.

By the time we got home, generally by sunset, we were exhausted.

After some supper, my sister and I usually went right to bed. Needless to say, I slept very soundly on the days I worked.

While field work was a challenge for me and I came to respect physical labor, at the same time I also came to feel alienated from it. Even though I was still only a young girl, I sensed that this was not what I wanted to do for my life's work. I had also begun rejecting—probably unconsciously at the time—the idea of being merely another breadwinner for the family. Toni took easily to this supportive role, but I didn't. I started to think about what I wanted to do for myself. I knew that my mother thought it was important to be *hermanal,* to express brotherly and sisterly love toward one another—to think of the family first. Toni seemed to take this dictum to heart, always willing to take care of her little sister. By contrast, my focus was elsewhere. I tried to communicate to anyone within earshot, particularly my parents when I dared, "I don't want to let anyone take advantage of me."

I think that seeing my parents burdened with so many family problems over time reinforced my determination to avoid a similar fate. When I became particularly aggressive in asserting my determination to do no more than my fair share of kitchen duty, for example, my sister would say, "I don't worry about it. I know all I have to do is tickle you, and I can make you laugh." She preferred to avoid confrontation.

Rather than giving me a sense of subsuming my identity for the family good, working in the fields instead provided me with a sense that I could take care of myself, that I could work and provide for myself. This would not necessarily be work in the fields. I had no notion of what my choices might be in the future, but I did believe that I could look forward to some kind of work that would allow me to further my education and to make something more of myself.

Schooling at Tagus Ranch represented an important new experience for me. I began to recognize school as a distinct institutional process, becoming conscious of the neat rows of desks in my classes and that we raised our hands to recite. I recognized the teacher's formality in front of the class. And I grew more aware of the other students.

I was becoming increasingly adept at producing right answers. While this approach initially provided positive reinforcement for me, it ultimately became problematic, as I would later discover. I remember an arithmetic question in one of my classes that none of the students was able to answer successfully. The teacher finally said, "Well, I guess we'll have to ask Frances." I gave an answer, and it was right. I was very proud of myself. I was probably not as conscious of this at the time, but I was beginning to see education as a process that contained "right" and "wrong" answers. This was interestingly consistent with how I had been trained in religion, so my religious background reinforced my approach to schooling.

I grew up with the concept of life as an ideal closed system. My religion represented that—there's heaven and there's hell. Our destiny is, or should be, heaven. In this life we strive to earn a place with God after death. For me truth was knowable and ultimate, and it came from a higher authority. In my early years, my formal schooling did little to dispel this notion of absolute truth.

Although I came to appreciate school more at Tagus and to be interested in what was going on in the classroom, at the same time I also began to experience a certain alienation that came from my sense of otherness. This took different forms. One way in which I was conscious of being different involved the content of some of our books. For example, I remember that one story read to us in either second or third grade was *Heidi of the Mountain.* I detested that story. Even though I had grown up with animals, I couldn't identify with this Heidi at all. We had no goats when we were growing up, and worse, I couldn't imagine any little girl being so interested in them and clambering up and down hills in Switzerland, a land that seemed so alien to my experience.

I had no clue as to what the story was about and I could have cared less. I remember deliberately not listening and instead occupying my mind with observing the teacher's behavior and that of the other pupils. The teacher was oblivious to my existence as a person. I hated Heidi, and I didn't want to hear my teacher droning on about her.

I also resented the Dick and Jane stories. Spot's "woof woof" was unreal to me—I had never heard a dog go "woof woof." Nothing about this family, from the manicured yard on up, matched my reality. It wasn't entirely that I objected to reading about something new or different. That was all right, in a sense. I accepted the fact that I was learning new things in school, but at the same time I knew that this was not me. I was dealing with parallel realities. In time, I became even more aware of this parallelism in my life.

I existed in two worlds, which I perceived to be divided by a distinct line of demarcation. On one side there was the sphere of experiences at school; these experiences had little, if anything, to do with my real life. Alongside that sphere but apart from it was what I believed was actually real about me, my family. As an adult, I've allowed these spheres to merge more, but as a young girl I was more sensitive to or aware of their separate existences. But I wasn't rebellious in school. I just had rebellious thoughts.

One additional source of alienation had to do with language and how it affected my relationship to my parents and their relationship to my schooling. I was becoming more proficient in English, while Spanish remained our language at home. This also felt like functioning in two worlds simultaneously, two worlds that rarely coincided. Although my parents supported our education and reinforced it as best they could and taught us to respect and obey our teachers, they couldn't help us with our school work, whether in reading or in mathematics.

This was particularly true of my father, who spoke even less English than my mother. My parents, of course, were also busy working and raising younger children. There was little, if any, contact between my mostly Spanish-speaking parents and my English-speaking teachers. What my parents conveyed to us was more abstractly ethical than practical.

"*Depende de la criatura, el empeño del niño,*" my mother would say. (It's up to the child to cooperate and demonstrate a willingness to learn.) It was clear to me that it was my responsibility to adjust to the shifting realities and demands of schools, classrooms, and teachers that were continually changing as we moved from one place to another. It was also clear to me that my parents had their own difficulties that appeared to have little to do with my needs. I knew that my father worked very hard.

For my mother, every day was a struggle—to get food on the table, to respond to the demands of living with a growing family and of my father, who could be autocratic. My parents were preoccupied with many daily problems, and school remained my world and apart from my parents' world.

By the time I was about eight or nine, I started being conscious of the fact that these worlds didn't exist in a state of harmony. The more my school world became an English-speaking one, the more I resented having to speak Spanish at home. Whenever we could, despite my father's insistence on speaking Spanish at home, Toni and I spoke English. Moreover, my resentment about speaking Spanish at home became wrapped up with what was becoming my natural inclination to oppose parental authority.

An atmosphere of tension and stress was not uncommon at dinnertime. Sometimes my mother set the tone by scurrying about fearful that she wouldn't have the meal ready when my father arrived home from work. Because farm work is seasonal, my sister and I didn't always work after school. At such times, my father might work long hours doing solitary work such as pruning orchards. He would come home tired and preoccupied. Any childish banter, particularly in English, would upset him, so we rushed through the meal in silence.

These intricacies of language, school, and parental authority were somewhat exacerbated when, at a certain point in my early school years, I began to recognize, to my surprise, that my parents were perceived as being foreigners because they couldn't fully function in English. This phenomenon was particularly puzzling and distressing to me, since I knew that my mother had been born in this country, as had her ancestors before her. But then, if Anglos saw my parents as foreigners, I, in my own way, was beginning to do the same, certainly with respect to school.

This growing awareness that I was living in separate worlds affected my personality as it developed. Actually, in many ways, there were more than just two worlds. There was my world at home, my world at school, and then there was the world inside my head as I tried to negotiate or mediate these different spheres. But I was too young to really do this successfully. Consequently, I wound up expressing my feelings and insecurities in the most familiar environment: my home.

For one, I began to develop a temper—an inclination to quick anger. I think I inherited this proclivity from my father, who could display an awful temper. We witnessed this volatility and felt his wrath especially when Toni and I spoke English in his presence or whenever I talked back to him. There were times when anything other than model behavior would set him off. Despite his temper—and because of my own—I challenged his authority. Looking back on this, of course, I recognize that I was quite childish and stubborn. I didn't appreciate how hard life was for my parents then. If I had, I'm sure I wouldn't have behaved as defiantly as I did.

For better or for worse, I was becoming preoccupied with my sense of isolation at home. I was coming home and finding fault there. I blamed my parents, sometimes my mother, sometimes my father, for these faults. As I did this, I began to develop a sense of looking out for myself. I compared myself, for example, to Toni, who unlike me, appeared more placid and was more comfortable accepting responsibility at home and for the family. I, on the other hand, questioned any parental demand that I viewed as an imposition.

This was the case, for example, when we moved to a ranch in Goshen. One of my responsibilities was to "pump" my younger sister Susan to school on my bicycle, and the school was a long distance away. I resented being required to assume responsibility for others when there was so much I needed to do for myself. Some days it was very hard to pump against the wind. Besides, my bicycle was a girl's bicycle without a center bar and very difficult to control with a weight behind me. At times I would feel so frustrated by the difficulty of the task that I would be close to tears. But Susan was cooperative and a good sport, so we managed somehow.

Still, my inclination was to rebel at home, at least against my father's authority. This took the form of speaking English at home or defying him in other ways. Sometimes this only took the form of defiant eye contact or other defiant body language. But I paid for this. My father was not about to abrogate his authority at home. He both scolded me and punished me physically. Although Toni sometimes felt my father's temper, she felt it much less than I did. It was I who incurred his wrath most violently, and it was I who refused to be cowed.

I remember dinner scenes when he would walk into the house, slamming the door as he entered, with angry eyes, intense and alert, surveying the room.

"*¿Ya está la cena?*" Is dinner ready? he would ask.

This was an irrelevant utterance, given that my mother had already leaped into action and was noisily moving pots from the stove to the table to prepare his place. We children were also presumably supposed to fall into line. Instinctively enraged by the effect of his behavior on my mother, I would lift my chin, hold my body very still, and give him a defiant, hard stare before beginning, slowly, to move toward the table. He would spring from his chair, aiming blows in my direction.

"*¡Teodoro, mira lo que estás haciendo!*" my mother would shout, cautioning him. Be careful!

He would retreat as I fled, arms raised to fend off his blows.

A dark corner somewhere in the house would be my refuge. There

I would have the time to think about my dilemma, but there never seemed to be a solution. My father couldn't or wouldn't seek me out in an act of conciliation, and my mother was too frightened to take any further action in my defense. I was hungry and didn't relish the thought of going without dinner, but I had no intention of making a move. Asserting my stubbornness was more important than a meal. I was vaguely conscious of the irrationality of my position but incapable of doing anything about it.

Toni, unlike me, inherited more of my mother's even temperament. I don't think the term *long-suffering* could be fairly applied to my mother, but she did display very little emotion regarding our situation. She rarely cried or spoke in a loud voice. She never engaged in name-calling. And, as I've mentioned, she never punished us physically.

However, her gentle appearance belied a flinty stoicism. Externally, she was a gentle person but that persona was accompanied by an unspoken inner toughness. She represented stability in our family. She didn't work outside the home much during the years when she had small children, but she was never idle around the house. She ultimately raised seven children, but she did it in a way that made it seem easier than it actually was. Life was hard for my mother with so many children, but she didn't talk about it much. For her, difficulties were just part of life. She rarely complained in our presence. In fact, I don't recall her customarily chatting with me about a great many things.

I remember one time telling her what a neighborhood lady had recounted to me. This was before I had even reached puberty. The neighbor had said, "I believe in having my daughters watch the birth of a baby so they'll see the pain and they'll learn not to have babies." This was probably the woman's way of frightening her daughters out of sexual experimentation.

My mother expressed surprise and puzzlement at hearing this account. She would never think of telling us anything like that. She never told us horror stories about childbirth or menstruation or about any aspect of life, for that matter. In fact, she never told us anything of a personal or intimate nature. Her characteristic silence on these kinds of subjects conditioned me to avoid questioning her about sex or marriage. Instead, I remained observant and frequently found myself drawing conclusions about what I saw.

I tended not to share this accepting side of my mother's personality, and as I sensed my own development, I believed I was heading in a different direction. Furthermore, she was accustomed to noting that my older sister resembled her, while I was more like my father. In spite of myself, I was identifying increasingly with the inequity in my father's situation as I observed the disparity between how hard he worked and how poorly he fared.

As I grew up, I became more aware not only of myself but also of those around me.

I began to see my parents changing physically in a way that I didn't like. I had brought with me to California a memory of my parents in New Mexico dancing to the Zacatecas, a sprightly marching tune from the state by the same name in Mexico. My father especially loved to dance. He had been young and light-footed then. But now he and my mother seemed more weary, probably because they were.

I remember that look of weariness especially on my father. My parents were both quite slender, and perhaps their slimness sometimes exaggerated their haggard look. My mother called herself *la flaca*—the skinny one. She didn't take pride in being slim; she just knew she was thinner than some of her sisters, but this didn't seem important to her. Weight wasn't a topic of concern in our home, but I was conscious of it.

The more I observed what was happening around me, the greater was my need for a sense of individuality. Our crowded circumstances at home required that we accommodate to one another's needs. But I think that these conditions actually made me more individualistic. As our family size increased, the demands placed on me to surrender space to others made me resistant. I felt my need for personal physical space intensifying. Perhaps, unconsciously, grappling with the question of where I belonged in my family was an expression of my need to identify where I belonged in the "other" world, outside my family. I began to identify how I was different from people at home. This was one way to assert my sense of who I was.

Yet while searching for individuality, I couldn't escape the reality of my ethnic identity. As a young girl at Tagus, I was aware that I was of Spanish/Mexican background. I experienced this awareness in different ways. Certainly my language experience was one way. Even though I was becoming more proficient in English, I still spoke Spanish at home. But the contention over language at home—English versus Spanish— was distancing me from my parents. The more I asserted my right to use English, the more I began to reflect the attitude that my parents were "different." I was becoming ashamed that my parents were Mexican, a stigma whose full weight I was yet to experience. Ironically, my sense of shame only seemed to emphasize my own ethnic identity.

Part of my anger about these issues concerned the fact that I had begun to link physical appearance with ethnicity. I was probably beginning to confuse ethnicity with biology and environment. I don't know if it was clear to me where one ended and the other began. Probably at that point I was aware that most Mexicans were different in appearance from Anglos. I certainly could see that I was different. While I was not particularly dark, and nor for that matter were my parents, I had jet black hair, similar to my father's, while some of the Anglo kids were much lighter in both hair and skin coloration.

This difference bothered me and even caused me some anguish. I knew or felt that I couldn't match the Anglo model of hairdos and clothing. The Anglo model was highly visible in school and the only model among teachers and in our school books. Hence, the alternative models for me were other Mexican girls. But other factors made the choice more complex. While a part of me might have wanted to emulate the Anglo girls, another part of me rejected this notion.

I tended to agree with the Mexican girls that there was something "wimpy" about the *gueras,* light-complexioned Anglo girls. The Anglo girls didn't wear any lipstick or earrings, and they generally looked very pallid. They seemed childish, and I preferred to think of myself as more adultlike. The world of work as I had experienced it was an adult world.

I was also conscious of and uncertain about emerging physical changes in my body. I had no concept of early adolescence—childhood in the usual sense. Growing up meant going from babyhood to more adultlike behavior. In this respect, perhaps I reflected a cultural aspect of the Mexican community.

My school attire consisted of a skirt and blouse or sweater. Sometimes I vacillated in selecting a blouse or sweater to wear. I wasn't sure that I wanted anyone to notice my early breast development. I also wore a moderated pompadour that was much less exaggerated than that worn by some of the other Mexican girls. However, unlike some of the other girls, I didn't wear lipstick or nail polish, since my father forbade that, and my mother, of course, concurred. I challenged my parents' authority, but I knew the limits.

This attire and look were in direct contrast to the Anglo look, which consisted of a loose-fitting dress and straight hair worn with little barrettes. Differences in appearance didn't seem as pronounced among the boys. The Mexican boys my age dressed pretty much like the Anglo boys and retained a young boy's look.

My parents, besides not allowing me to wear nail polish or lipstick, never objected to the way I dressed for school. However, I was careful not to draw undue attention from my parents for fear of their objections. Moreover, my attire wasn't particularly different from that of the other Mexican girls. Up to a point, my parents were less interested in our outward appearance than in how we conducted ourselves.

They gave us a lot of latitude, especially at school, to work out our own social relationships and solve our problems, as long as we demonstrated that we were doing all right. They were very rigid about such things as attendance at church, and I knew that boy-girl relationships were forbidden, but in terms of day-to-day details of attire or doing homework, for example, there was an unspoken expectation that we would make our own appropriate decisions. This lack of day-to-day direction or monitoring I later came to resent. While I may have wanted to be accepted as an individual and as an adult, something within me also desired more guidance and direction in dealing with the new experiences that were bewildering me. Clearly, those first years in California were not easy for me, but if I had known how my adolescence would develop, I would have been even more daunted.

THREE

Migrant Souls

In 1941 we left Tagus Ranch, where we had lived for approximately three years, and moved to Visalia, which was about ten miles northeast of Tagus. I wasn't sure why we were moving again, but by then I had internalized the fact that lack of permanence was a way of life for us. Even the three-year stay at Tagus had been interrupted by brief periods in the summer, when we lived in tent camps on a grape or cotton ranch where we were a part of large migrant-worker crews.

It wasn't until years later, in retrospect, that I began to understand the pattern of those years—a continual search for more stable work for my father and better housing for the family. With the birth of my brother Severo and my sister Nieves at Tagus, there were now five children in our family.

Visalia represented my introduction to barrio life. We were no longer in company-owned housing; we were renters. This was now a more urban or at least semiurban experience. Visalia was a town rather than a big city, but it certainly had separate and different residential areas. I understood, in a very general way, that there were two sides of town: the Anglo side and the Mexican side. We lived in the Mexican barrio.

Until we moved there, I hadn't known that such a thing as a barrio existed. I didn't even know what the term meant. All I understood was that it meant more housing, a greater variety in housing, and definitely more Spanish-speaking people. Our barrio consisted entirely of other Mexicans, as far as I could determine.

Terms used to identify people were acquiring new meaning. In New Mexico, Spanish-speaking people had been Spanish Americans; a *mejicano* was a foreign-born person from Mexico. In the barrio the people were *la gente mejicana*. The others were *los americanos*.

I also knew there were "Okies" and "Arkies" who had come to California during the dust bowl migration. Except for hearing such terms, I don't recall any discussion of the Great Depression of the 1930s. But it was not an abstraction for me; it was a reality that had altered my life.

Although we lived in the barrio, my father continued to work as an agricultural worker in the surrounding ranches. Sometimes he would travel as far as the Fresno area to work and return the same day. My older sister and I continued to accompany our dad to the fields on weekends and on holidays. The surrounding area had become somewhat familiar to me, and I have some memories of a tent camp near Fresno where we spent some time during grape-harvest season. At Tagus we had picked mostly apricots and peaches. Now we were picking cotton and grapes.

Instead of living in cramped row houses, as we had done on Tagus Ranch, in the barrio we were able to afford a somewhat larger two-room house—one room used as sleeping quarters for the family and the other room as a kitchen/dining area. We had electricity but no indoor plumbing. The sewer system had not yet been installed in the barrio. Years later, I was told that, despite the fact that the barrio was within the city limits then, the Anglo side of town had opposed extending the sewer lines to our side of town. Consequently, we had to use outhouses.

Some of these discomforts were familiar and similar to the rural conditions we had encountered at Tagus, but I don't recall being nearly as uncomfortable as I had been on the ranch, where the winter rainy season was a time of unrelieved cold and mud. I think that my mother appreciated the new house because she had a small yard where she could cultivate a garden. It was here, also, that the sixth child, my brother John, was born.

In the barrio, we had a sense of living in a real neighborhood as opposed to a workers' camp. I remember being more aware that some of the kids in the neighborhood were also in my school. This feeling of community had, for the most part, been missing at Tagus, where I don't remember having any neighbor children to play with—in fact, there had been little time devoted to play or recreation. In addition to going to church services, my older sister and I primarily occupied our time with school and work throughout the year. We saw school friends only at school.

It was probably for this reason that I remember how important Valentine's Day had been at Tagus. If someone really liked you, you received a store-bought valentine from that person; otherwise you received a simpler one probably made during an art period in the class. All valentines were placed in a beautifully decorated box prepared by the teacher, and at midafternoon the box would be opened and the valentines distributed. It was a time of anticipation and sometimes heartbreak, and we would all talk about it in the school yard later.

I still remember hearing snippy remarks from one or two girls about other girls to whom they had or had not given a valentine. I don't have any recollection of having been snubbed by any particular girls, but I do know that I felt especially vulnerable on Valentine's Day. What I do remember well is that I knew with confidence that Albert liked me. He had told me so. I was about nine at the time and didn't know the word *boyfriend,* and *novio* would have been too serious. I just knew that he liked me.

Now in the Visalia barrio I had new situations with which to contend. Part of the maturing process for me was the beginning of my menstruation. I started quite early, at about age ten. My mother had never discussed with me either sexuality or the expectation that I would begin menstruating when I entered puberty. The fact that I started early and before my older sister started her period was a shock to my mother, judging by her facial expression when I told her.

I remember the incident well. It was early in the morning when I discovered that I had my period. I ran to my mother's bed and awakened her by simply exclaiming, "Mother!" In her initial startled response, a surprised "huh!" was all she could muster. But she knew why I had come to her. Her look of surprise became an intense gaze scrutinizing my face. Then, very quickly, she composed herself. In a manner that seemed both mechanical and wooden, she pushed back her bedclothes, raised herself off her bed, and walked toward where she kept her personal clothing.

"*Aquí están los trapos limpios,*" she said, showing me the clean pieces of fabric, rags, really, that I would be using as the necessary sanitary protection. It would be about six years before I would be introduced to Kotex and even longer before I would discover that in English a girl's menstruation was referred to as the "curse" or as "being on the rag." In Spanish, the reference was to an illness. "*Le vino su enfermedad,*" they would say.

I had expected reassurance but instead encountered my mother's silence. She was a rather shy, reserved, and circumspect lady, and we did not discuss what was happening. The effect of this silence was to distance me from her. I probably felt a little lonely and afraid, but I was not shocked. After all, having lived in crowded conditions in the camps, I had observed and overheard other women talking about "female problems."

Actually, I had first learned about menstruation from my aunt, who had accompanied us to California. One time I saw the menstrual flow on what she used as a sanitary napkin. She giggled and said, "Oh, you're surprised, huh? Oh, that's one of those things." What she meant was, "It's one of those things that happen to women." That's how I learned that "it" happens to women, and the knowledge wasn't threatening, since my aunt treated it very casually and comfortably.

Religion, of course, continued to be an important part of our family life, as it had been all along. The difference was that here, too, in the barrio, I began to see that our family functioned in two worlds. There was the regular, big Catholic church that all Catholics in town presumably attended, but I was also aware of religious practices and customs unique to the people in the barrio.

For example, I was aware that devotion to the Virgen de Guadalupe was strong here. I also remember one occasion when a religious procession of some kind was organized in the barrio, possibly by the Sociedad de la Virgen de Guadalupe, and my dad organized a group of young boys to march in the procession. The boys were dressed in white trousers and white shirts with kerchiefs at their necks. They wore straw hats and carried miniature *huacales hechos de varitas* on their backs. The *huacales,* miniature Mexican-style crates, probably contained religious images or icons.

In any case, I remember being awed by my father's skill in fashioning these small crates out of *varitas,* very thin matching tree branches, which he had probably selected very carefully somewhere out in the countryside. This was an unexpected view of my father. He rarely talked about his experiences as a boy or young man in Mexico, and the skills he displayed on this occasion were a surprise to me. The image of those young boys remains with me today, a reminder of my dad's religious devotion, which he brought with him from Mexico and retained his entire life. In church, for example, my father would kneel down with arms extended in the form of a cross, like the crucifix.

I had not yet learned the extent to which, even in matters related to a common, shared religion, Visalia was divided between the Spanish-speaking world that was my world and the "other," dominant world that was out there somewhere and still largely unknown to me.

When we moved to Visalia, I entered the fifth grade at the largest school I had ever attended. It was a two-story red brick building with imposing hallways and rooms. There was a sense of permanence to the structure as if it had been there a long time and would remain there forever. I especially remember being impressed with the indoor flush toilets, which were unlike any I had ever seen before.

My school was not in the barrio but adjacent to it. It was close enough to our home that I could walk there. Since the school represented a type of border school serving both the barrio and a portion of the Anglo side of town, the student body was mixed. Yet I don't remember being impressed enough with the other kids that I can recall much about them. What sticks in my memory the most is the school building itself.

While no particular experiences in that first year of school in Visalia remain with me, I do recall some of the attitudes toward education that I was assuming. In terms of formal learning, school for me at that time was still a kind of neutral experience. I was alienated in that I still couldn't see much in the learning process that was directly relevant to my condition or that of my family. Much of this bridging of cultures and experiences would come in later school years. At that point, I was not making these connections consciously.

But I do remember being observant—perhaps almost to the point of being vigilant. I think that, at that point in my life, I had become aware of being a watchful and alert person. By this I mean that my life seemed to be a series of new and unexpected experiences that I somehow had to incorporate into a useful construct that would enable me to function. Of course, I didn't think of my life in these terms. Rather, I always seemed to find myself questioning everybody and everything, trying to make sense of who I was and what was happening to me. Undoubtedly, what did sustain my interest in school or at least my faith in schooling as a valid institutional process was the faith that my parents had in education.

Even though they maintained only a distant connection to my school and to my teachers, my parents believed in the validity of formal education, and they conveyed to us their faith in the educational process just as they conveyed to us their faith in the Catholic Church.

"I don't care what people say," my mother would remind my father.

"It isn't true that a child's only obligation is to add to the family income while she lives at home. A person needs an education to improve her lot, *para ver si un día cambia.*" For years, as her children grew up, my mother expressed in various ways her determination that we receive the education she had wanted but had been denied.

I had come to believe in the value of education, even though I wasn't sure yet what that implied for me specifically. I still couldn't see, for example, the connection between schooling and a better life, certainly not in economic terms.

It wasn't that I had no interest in learning. I did. But this stimulus was coming more from my own curiosity abetted by my parents' encouragement than from my teachers or my school. I was doing fine with regard to grades, but it was I, more than my school, who was responsible for these good grades. My excitement about school hadn't come yet. Part of this conflict between my own self-motivation and my lack of enthusiasm for school was due to the types of materials that were available. I was interested in reading but had little to read other than school textbooks, which weren't particularly interesting to me. Unfortunately, I had not yet discovered libraries, because they had not been part of my experience. They simply did not exist in migrant camps.

At this early age, I was fascinated with languages. One way in which I fed my appetite for learning languages was by immersing myself in my church missal. I was intrigued by this missal, which was written in both Latin and English. It was in the missal that I discovered the joy of the printed word. I loved the sound of the Latin that I heard in church on Sundays, and I loved identifying the similarities and differences between Latin and Spanish or Latin and English.

For example, the priest's introductory or prefatory "Dominus vobiscum" and the server's response, "Et cum spiritu tuo," had a comfortable and familiar sound to it. The Lord be with you. And with your spirit. *Y con el espíritu tuyo.* Years later, I would receive formal instruction in matters such as cognates, but here, throughout the missal, were the sounds of languages clearly related. Through studying my missal I was acquiring a sense of language and a sense of its power as a vehicle for conveying ideas.

While my school lent a sense of permanency to my existence, my family life did not. Since our migration from New Mexico, my family seemed to be ever on the move, not having yet put down roots in California. In addition to the places where our family was specifically based (such as Corcoran and Tagus), over the years we stayed at many camps for brief periods of time as we followed the crops in the broad San Joaquin Valley and further north toward San Francisco. Some I remember quite well; others are fleeting images.

The crop seasons varied—peaches, apricots, grapes, apples, pears, walnuts, cotton, tomatoes, green beans, and "prunes" (plums picked for drying). But there were some constants as we went from place to place. The tents were familiar. And usually there were wooden packing crates of one size or another that had to be filled, lifted, and stacked. We developed a good sense of balance as we scampered up and down ladders with fruit-laden buckets. An entirely different skill was required to balance a fourteen-foot ladder or a two-hundred-pound sack of cotton on your shoulder.

For green Thompson grapes there were the large wooden drying trays, eventually replaced by brown paper trays, that were laid side by side and required a long reach to fill fully and properly. Later in the raisin grape season, we worked in teams of two flipping the trays to turn the underside toward the drying sun. And always speed was important for it was all "piecework."

In the camps, the familiar sight was the ever-present packing crates that doubled as tables, benches, and beds. For the early riser, such as I was, the sound of women somewhere in the camp rolling out tortillas at four o'clock in the morning meant that it was time to get up. By five, the day's early light would be just right for heading out toward the fields.

Although I was not conscious of this at the time, I believe that this lack of a more permanent home and the shifting from one place to another plus migrating to work with my father to still other locations had a lot to do with the alienation and other tensions I experienced as a young girl and as a young woman.

The summer after that first year in Visalia, my older sister and I, along with two of my father's adopted sisters, traveled north with my father and other migrant workers to pick apricots and plums. We were transported by truck, bunched together with our bundles in the tarpaulin-covered rear of a truck. I had no idea where we were going as we set out, late in the day. I remember being aware that we were on Highway 99, but it was dark. The overhead canvas cover isolated us even as we huddled together. The sounds of the highway were relentless and discordant, making sleep difficult.

Truck stops served as our rest stops, and we could get out to stretch and look around. There was not much to see in the starkly lit expansive parking areas except the immense trucks parked in no particular order. There were trucks of all sorts, most of them overpowering in their sheer size. The garish neon signs were intrusive, dimming the stars in the night sky. A few men at meal counters were visible through brightly lit cafe windows. If someone had asked me how I felt as I contemplated these scenes, I probably would have said, "lonely," wanting to cry.

Eventually, we turned off Highway 99 onto what, undoubtedly, was Highway 152, and I learned new place-names—Los Banos, Pacheco Pass, and Gilroy. We were headed for San Jose.

In San Jose we lived in a temporary labor camp consisting of tents in the foothills. It was not a large camp, but there were several families there. We cooked outdoors on open fires. My sister, my two adopted aunts, and I slept inside the tent with our bedding spread on top of wooden packing crates. My father slept outside, alongside our tent. My mother had remained in Visalia with the younger children.

Besides working in the orchards, my sister and I also worked in the cutting shed adjacent to the orchards. Here the workers, almost all Mexican women much older than we were, cut apricots in half, pitted them, discarded the pits, and laid apricot halves on trays in an orderly pattern. These trays were then stacked and put on carts, which were wheeled into large, walk-in ovens where the "cots" remained for several hours in a sulfurous steam. Afterward, they were set out to dry in the sun.

Working in the sheds was easier than working in the orchards, but it was also very boring and tedious. I preferred the more physical labor of the fields to the monotony and mindless work of the cutting shed.

What was boring in the sheds was having to listen to eight hours or more of conversation among the older women. It was absolutely numbing. To lighten their work, they engaged in swapping what I considered to be dumb jokes and mindless trivia. Perhaps my alienation had more to do with the age difference between me and these women. It had nothing to do with the women themselves who, I'm sure, were wonderful people. It was the setting and the work that I was rebelling against. I knew that this was not what I wanted to do with my life.

One particular experience that I recall during this summer migration to San Jose concerned a little transgressive foray into San Francisco. The daughters of the Portuguese ranch owner where we were working invited me to go with them to Playland at the Beach, an amusement park in San Francisco. It was probably during a weekend. These girls were older than I, about eighteen, while I was then about eleven. They had access to their father's car, so we took off for the city. What was particularly risqué and daring was that they picked up a couple of young sailors on the way who then accompanied us to Playland.

I had never been to San Francisco before, and as we approached the city I was immediately struck by the fact that this was a city the likes of which I had never seen or imagined. It seemed colossal. I had thought Fresno was a metropolis, but San Francisco was something else. It was unreal.

We drove around the beach area, and the girls and the sailors talked, joked, and played the car radio. I didn't really participate much in all this. I enjoyed listening to the music, but primarily I think I was scared, apprehensive, or just overwhelmed by the experience.

Finally, late in the day, we drove the sailors back to their base and we returned to San Jose. I think my father knew that I had gone off with the girls, but he didn't know where we had gone or what we had done. I certainly didn't tell him, and fortunately for me he didn't ask. I was at an impressionable age, but as a result of this episode I realized that joyriding was not something I was ready for.

After that summer in San Jose, my father decided to take a foreman's job at a small ranch in the Goshen area, a farming community near Visalia whose one identifying mark was Goshen Junction, a Greyhound bus stop on Highway 99 at the juncture of Highway 198. My father was responsible for much of the work on the ranch. But he also was able to use some of the land for cultivating his own vegetable garden. I remember that garden with a great deal of fondness. We now had an abundance of fresh vegetables to eat, including tomatoes, string beans, squash, and corn. What we didn't eat, my father was able to sell, and herein lies a memory that is still painful to recall.

My father was especially proud of the first crop of tomatoes from our garden—beautiful, large delicious tomatoes that he picked carefully with the expectation that he would be able to market them to some local small grocery-store owners. I remember the joy with which he left the house with that prized first crop, and I remember how crestfallen he was when he returned. He had been unable to sell the tomatoes to any local store owner. He had not been well received, and the quality of the produce didn't seem to matter.

I realized that what my father was really saying was that he had been rejected because of who he was rather than because of what he had produced. He had been judged by his ethnicity. The thought generated an explosive feeling within me. I was enraged. I identified with and internalized the experience, silently vowing never to allow myself to be similarly crushed. I was eleven at the time.

What was really involved here was that I had begun to develop my own patterns of reaction and action, separate and apart from my parents. Neither of my parents was accustomed to speaking ill of others. To the contrary, they taught us to be polite to and respectful of other people. I was accustomed to seeing them being deferential. I can't recall ever having heard at home any phrase or expression that conveyed the notion of discrimination either for racial or cultural reasons.

And in relating this account of rejection, my father expressed neither anger nor rancor, merely disappointment. And, in fact, in his usual undaunted manner, he devised other ways of selling his crop, from the back of his pickup truck, for example. It was I who felt the anger. And equally devastating for me was the fact that I couldn't express this anger. My father believed in what he taught. He believed in "turning the other cheek." And in matters of this nature, even I didn't dare defy him.

Goshen represented more stable work for my father, compared to the seasonal labor that he had engaged in since our arrival in California. Besides a better work environment for my father, Goshen was also a better and healthier place for us to live in. In a way, living there reminded us a bit of being in New Mexico. It was a feeling akin to a sense of owning the land we were on. Our home was still a small frame house with no indoor plumbing, but we certainly thought of it as being more our home than the houses we had occupied in Corcoran, Tagus, or Visalia. As in New Mexico, here we were surrounded by fields and trees.

Almost everything now in my young life represented a new experience of one sort or another. I was at an impressionable age. Goshen presented more experiences. In New Mexico, I had been intrigued by geography and nature, and here those feelings of fascination were refreshed. As I bicycled on country roads using no hands and feeling the wind blowing through my hair, I sensed a wonderful freedom. I didn't feel the physical restrictions that I had experienced at Tagus or in the Visalia barrio. In the countryside in Goshen, I felt free to move about.

Some incidents involving the external world, the "dominant" society, I was even able to view with detached amusement. I remember, for example, that our existence evidently came to the attention of some well-meaning, charitable group, and we were sent some used clothing. The clothing was clean, and the gesture was appreciated, but it only heightened my sense of the incongruities in our life. Most of the clothing consisted of exotic or party-type dresses or outfits made of impractical fabrics such as rayon.

I don't recall what we did with most of this clothing, but I do remember the short-sleeved sweater, white with pastel-colored trim, and the green and white one-piece shorts outfit, which I wore for a long time—reminders of the kindness I sensed was in the community even when the communication was less than perfect.

Clothing for me at that time consisted of simple skirts and blouses or sweaters. My shoes were sturdy oxfords worn with bobby socks. By age eleven, I no longer worked so hard to hide my developing body, which at ages nine and ten I had attempted to cover up with loose-fitting blouses.

It's with a sense of irony that I now think back to the fact that, throughout my growing years, I was not allowed by school authorities to wear any type of trousers to school. This regulation governed my life even in winter, when I wanted so badly to wear warm slacks to school to try to alleviate my menstrual cramps. However, after school and on weekends and summers, I exchanged my school skirt and blouse for a pair of boy's pants and a denim work shirt, appropriate attire for my work in the fields.

My world was expanding. I was developing a stronger sense of other people, becoming increasingly aware of their reactions and relationships. For example, one morning when I took our milk bucket to the ranch owner's house, where the owner's wife daily filled it with fresh milk, I remember being very embarrassed because the owner and his wife were engaged in an argument. I was particularly embarrassed because they were Anglos and hence authority figures to me. They represented the dominant group, and I was seeing them at their worst, "with their hair down," literally looking disheveled early in the morning.

I just didn't know how to react or whether I should flee the scene I was witnessing, which would have violated my sense of propriety. My parents had inculcated in me a sense of having a "proper" place as a young girl. I had been taught not to be forward. I knew I wasn't supposed to meddle in other people's business, and yet here I was in the middle of a family spat! Fortunately, they must have sensed my dilemma and so quickly ceased arguing. I, of course, did not tell my parents about the incident. We simply didn't talk about other people.

School at Goshen furthered my maturation. It was an ethnically mixed country school, and for the first time I developed a particularly strong relationship with one of my teachers. I believe her name was Mrs. Johnson. She was a very large lady with twinkling blue eyes, a nice smile revealing a row of very white teeth, and a comfortable laugh.

She communicated well with body language. When I sought her out, early in the morning before school, she had a special way of putting down her work either at the chalkboard or at her desk. There was something nonthreatening about the slow manner in which she would turn to face me. It was clearly mutually understood that I was interrupting, but her warm smile sent a message that it was all right. She granted me time and in fact indulged me. For the first time, I became comfortable talking to a teacher. She was very responsive and allowed time for our conversations.

I found myself looking for opportunities to talk with her rather than with the other kids. I would stay after school and discuss class lessons with her. With the support and attention of Mrs. Johnson, I found myself gaining more confidence in myself and in my ability to engage with others, particularly my teachers. I don't recall very much about my schooling at Goshen except for Mrs. Johnson.

What I do recall is that I had now become aware that learning doesn't always come out of books. It was in our home in Goshen that I first saw, graphically, a married couple in conjugal embrace. It happened quite by accident, and I was therefore all the more startled. The walls of our little house were covered with newspaper, and I was accustomed to lying in my little cot randomly reading headlines, ads, captions, sentences, or whatever attracted my attention. I would concentrate on the printed material, mentally withdraw from my surroundings, and let my imagination take me wherever it would.

It was during one such moment of reverie, on a warm afternoon, that I heard unusual noises coming from the adjoining room. Some people had been visiting us, and I guessed that this had to do with what I was hearing. I sat up, startled, and sought out the source of those sounds. It required a little ingenuity on my part, but not much. Our little house was really a frame shack, and the planks that formed the inner walls were not well aligned—cracks between the boards gave access to the adjoining room. I stood up on the cot, peered into the next room, took one quick look, and was dismayed.

I saw two people, a jumble, in disarray—a scene I knew I had no business witnessing. I felt guilty about what I had done, and, worse, I had no one I could talk to about it. I would now have to carry this burdensome information unaided—another piece of the big puzzle, and no deliverance in sight.

My frustration and anger mounted. I lost my appetite. I became surly and more defiant at home. I challenged my mother's authority. My poor distraught mother's response was to attempt to control me by blessing me with holy water, which she sprinkled in my direction. I viewed this as an act of attempted exorcism, which exacerbated my emotional turmoil. I vowed to be even more defiant if necessary. I would just have to be strong until I could figure things out for myself. I hadn't a clue about what to do and didn't think in terms of options. There seemed to be none. I didn't think things could get worse.

But the scenery would continue to change. Our stay in Goshen lasted only one year, and our family moved again. My parents decided to return to Visalia, but first we spent the summer in the tomato fields of Tassajara.

The tomato fields were located in the northern part of the state, east of San Francisco. The land looked desolate to me. There were no trees, and I missed the peach orchards to which I had become accustomed. Camp housing consisted of tents as well as small cabins. There were new people to get used to. There was a new crop to learn to harvest. This was different from our vegetable garden in Goshen. We had to work fast, with little attention given to the quality of the tomatoes we were picking. It all had to be harvested.

It was in Tassajara that I learned about the existence of Filipino farm workers in California. For the first time that I could recall, my mother spoke about people who were perceived to be different. Apparently she had learned that men from the Philippines were allowed into this country to work in agriculture but that women were excluded. That explained the fact that we saw no Filipino families.

My mother also spoke about the fact that hurtful stories were told about the men—"*que tienen cola*"—that they had tails and were less than human. I was horrified and repelled by that kind of information, and I couldn't understand it. Although the word *prejudice* was still not a part of my vocabulary, I was beginning to get a very definite sense that the world was a very unfriendly, if not a downright hostile, place.

I remember speaking with the Filipino men in the fields and that they were friendly. But primarily I remember that by this time I was very conscious of needing to keep my distance from men. I did not have any specific distrust or fear of men; they were undifferentiated. I just knew that I was to keep them at a distance somehow. My focus was on my own body, the discomfort I felt with every indication of oncoming puberty.

One young Filipino man was particularly attentive to me, and as I recall, I didn't do anything to encourage him. But I lacked the social skills I needed to deal with this. I have forgotten the specifics of how I dealt with his attention. I just remember that I knew I had to be careful. Over the years, at one time or another, I have been reminded by my mother or my older sister that this young man had offered my mother gifts and a diamond ring for me. He was requesting my "hand in marriage." My mother had politely declined the offer. I was about twelve years old at the time.

At that age, I was also probably still puzzling over the memory of "el señor Wences" who, at Tagus Ranch, had proposed to my parents that I be allowed to go with him and his wife to live in Los Angeles. There he wanted to put me in a convent school. His bulging eyes gave him a Diego Rivera look, and his strange full lips, split on one side, had the look I associate with cleft palate. He was a very religious man, a fanatic I thought, who quoted the Bible a great deal. This was not religion as I understood it, and I didn't trust him.

So it seemed that in Tassajara I was again experiencing my world as an environment of unwelcome sounds and sights. There was the time, for example, when I returned from the fields to the camp on an errand in midafternoon. It was a hot day, and as I walked along the narrow path separating individual living quarters, I could see that tent flaps were open.

I glanced in the direction of one tent and noticed a young married couple embracing. They were lying on their bed, which, as was common in tent camps, consisted of wooden packing crates covered with a mattress or quilts. The couple seemed to notice me, and I hastened on, not wanting to see any more. I had a feeling akin to disgust at the circumstances. I was unintentionally invading their privacy, and I was being forced to be part of a scene that was not to my liking. The thought of married life as furtive embraces in this bleak environment did not appeal to me.

Some time later, when this young couple invited me to go to the movies with them, I agreed—more out of a sense of wanting to reciprocate their gesture of friendship than out of any real desire to be with them. As I watched the young woman literally counting her pennies, I felt sorry. For them, a good time meant counting their coins to see if they had enough money to take in a show.

I had been taught differently. Starting at about the time when I was in second grade, my mother had regularly counted out coins for me to take to school to deposit in a savings account, a savings program sponsored by the schools in conjunction with a local bank. Coins meant savings. I enjoyed seeing the transactions recorded in my small green deposit book—the dates neatly stamped alongside the deposit amounts, giving it all a very official look.

❦

After that summer in Tassajara, our family returned to the barrio in Visalia. I didn't know why. I had never known, for certain, why we were continually moving. My parents never consulted us or discussed their plans with us, and it never occurred to me to question them. By now I had grown accustomed to life as seeking work—going from one job opportunity to the next. Seasonal work was clearly just that.

In retrospect, it occurs to me that, at this point in their lives, my parents were not only continually seeking economic stability but were also probably considering their children's schooling. In Goshen, I had been responsible for transporting my younger sister Susan along with myself to school on my bicycle. My older sister, Toni, was being bused to school in Visalia. The schools seemed very far from the ranch where we lived. Since the younger children were reaching school age, transportation would have been a problem had we remained in Goshen.

In any case, for whatever reasons, we were back in the barrio. Our return to the barrio remains significant to me, because it was at this time that I got the first inkling that my parents were going along with or supporting my desire for independence. They sent me back from Tassajara to Visalia ahead of the rest of the family so that I would not miss the beginning of the school year. For two to three weeks, I stayed in the home of my father's adopted sister, Sotera.

I enrolled in Sierra Vista, the town's only junior high school. There was a parish school in town, but I did not want to attend a Catholic school, and my parents allowed me to make that decision. Though only dimly aware of the implication of my actions, I was beginning to feel responsible for my future.

This second time in the barrio, my parents rented a two-room house comparable to the one in which we had previously lived. It was here that my parents' seventh and last child, Teodoro Faustino, was born. There were now seven children at home—the oldest was about fifteen years old.

I was now more conscious of the town as a community, or rather, as two communities. I walked to school, which was located in the Anglo part of town. The dividing line was "the oval," a small, oval-shaped public park that separated the two worlds, one, a world with sidewalks, paved streets, and relatively uniform architectural patterns, the other, a world with no sidewalks, some asphalt streets, and mixed groupings of houses, some little more than shacks constructed by inexperienced hands. In the barrio, architectural symmetry was uncommon. Outhouses were not. The one grocery store was owned by a Mexican family. There were no other public services. A Catholic church in the barrio had not yet been built.

One of the things that stands out in my mind about our return to Visalia was being conscious that there was a war on. I remember the optimism, the gung-ho spirit, and the patriotism. I recall people giving servicemen a lift in their cars. This was considered the patriotic thing to do.

I remember the ads in various publications and the trailers at the movies (commercials, we would call them today), all reminding us that we should be proud of our fighting men and informing us of how well we were doing in conducting this global war. Then there were the billboards with images of the enemy: Hitler with his mustache, Tojo with his big teeth, and Mussolini with his big cap. We knew who the enemy was—the "Japs" and the Germans.

I also remember my mother collecting the fat after she cooked. My mother and the other women of the barrio would turn over this residue to the local butcher, who in turn would send it to the military. We were told that the grease was somehow used in making munitions.

Another memory of the war involved our landlord's daughter, who married a young man just before he left for military duty. Almost immediately after marrying and after her husband left, this young girl acquired a new status in her family. She now had her own room. She no longer had to obey any family rules. Being the wife of a young soldier carried a new, elevated status.

Although I was quite young myself, I was aware of some young men in the barrio who were going off to war. I remember how young they looked in their uniforms. There was also a young woman in the barrio who joined the WACS (Women's Army Corps). This was considered unusual and unladylike, at least in the barrio. Only men went off to war. But her decision impressed me. I wasn't attracted to the idea of joining the military—I was too young anyway—but what appealed to me was the courage this young woman demonstrated in doing something that went against the norm.

I remember that, early in the war, one of the ranches in which we were working was owned by a Japanese family that disappeared suddenly. It was not until years later that I would learn about Japanese internment camps. What I do remember is walking through the large empty house that the family had vacated and observing someone ripping fixtures off a wall. The mindlessness of this act somehow made me feel a little guilty.

One thing in particular about the war that struck close to home had to do with overhearing my parents talk about the discrimination that some Hispano soldiers from New Mexico faced in the army. These were young men they had known in New Mexico, and their families and my parents had kept in touch. My parents were especially upset about this discrimination and the fact that these young men had to stress that they were "Spanish Americans" to avoid various forms of ethnic or race discrimination in the military. Being Mexican was not desirable.

While this obviously bothered my parents, it didn't affect me directly, because I was still not fully cognizant of how this type of discrimination applied to me. At the same time, there was no bitterness or rancor on the part of my parents but more a sense that this was a fact of life. They didn't talk to us about this, but we did overhear it.

From time to time at the dinner table, my father would also mention some of his views about the war. Not that he was particularly political, but he did have certain reactions to these events. He once explained to me that Germany had desired an alliance with Mexico and that this had resulted over the unfair treatment that the United States had given to Mexico over the years. My father didn't really draw any conclusions from this, but it was one of the few times that I can recall that he suggested that the United States had been less than fair in its treatment of Mexico.

Yet he never vilified or reviled the United States. And he never glorified Mexico. He wasn't rabid about the subject, but I did sense that he perceived unfairness in U.S.-Mexican relations and that he even felt some pride that Mexico, as a nation, could have other allies besides the United States. Unfortunately, we never had a chance to develop these ideas. I never knew what other political views my father had, since he rarely, if ever, discussed politics.

Where my father did continue to be involved was with the church. His major activity outside the home, besides work, was with the Sociedad Guadalupana, which he helped organize in Visalia. In fact, it was through the Sociedad that the barrio church ultimately was built. My father was dedicated to the Sociedad and to the church. In later years, long after the family had moved out of the barrio, my parents continued to attend Mass and other services in the barrio church.

Upon our return to Visalia, my father resumed working in different fields picking crops at different seasons. One thing that was different, however, was that by this time he knew many of the big ranchers and farmers in the area, and they knew and trusted him. This enabled my father to obtain employment more easily.

My older sister and I continued to help my father in the fields on weekends and on holidays, and by this time so did my mother, when she was able. There were times when she worked in the fields, taking her newborn baby with her. There she nursed the baby or placed him in a playpen that my dad had constructed out of packing crates. My mother worked willingly, because she saw it as a way of adding to our income, allowing us to receive an education and ensuring that we would never have to be pulled out of school to help support the family.

Despite the scarcity of affordable housing, within one year of our return to the barrio my parents were able to purchase a home, which would remain the family home for the remainder of my parents' long life together—a home outside the barrio but close to the church.

During those years when Toni and I had worked in the fields with my father, we had accepted the reality that our earnings were part of family income. We did not receive an allowance, and spending money was rare. Frugality was a way of life consistent with goals that my parents, evidently, had shared from the start. And this pattern would continue as the younger children grew.

FOUR

Discovering the Limits of the Barrio in Junior High

Our return to Visalia made me more aware of it as a specific place. Like the rest of the San Joaquin Valley, Visalia's most evident physical characteristic was its flatness. Except for the Sierra Nevada, which was sometimes visible in the distance to the east, there were no hills or mountains. In all directions there was just flatness, composed of either irrigated green fields and orchards or barren terrain. Visalia was clearly an agricultural town, the county seat. Farmers represented the dominant group, seemingly more important than other businessmen.

The retail businesses were relatively small. J. C. Penney's was the largest retailer. There were no big buildings. Other businesses included a hotel, a feed store, a couple of drugstores, two or three banks, the restaurant in the Hotel Johnson, a few cafes, and three movie theaters. At least those are the ones I remember.

With a few exceptions on the side streets, all the businesses were located on a four-block stretch of Main Street, the main artery in Visalia. I don't know what the population of the town was at that time, but it was still small. Growth would begin much later.

The Mexican barrio, which we returned to, was situated in the northern part of town. Main Street ran east to west. Mexicans lived north of Main Street, to a distance of about a mile and a half beyond the oval, and Anglos lived closer to Main Street on the north side and in the residential area to the south. Each side was clearly discernible.

The Anglo south side and the area close to and north of Main Street had nicely constructed homes with architectural unity and generally well-kept front lawns, paved sidewalks, and streets. The sewer system was also in place here. The layout and cohesiveness of the homes provided a sense of neighborhood. On the west side of the Anglo part of town was a specific neighborhood called Green Acres, which was considered the most upscale section. This is where the wealthier townspeople, including rich farmers and some businessmen, lived. It was the Beverly Hills of Visalia.

On the other hand, the north side had no uniformity in its houses. There was a more haphazard arrangement. Most were frame houses, but each was built differently. There was a heterogeneity to the more dilapidated nature of this housing. Instead of planting lawns, most Mexicans used their front yards either to grow flowers and/or vegetables or to park their cars. There were no sidewalks. Some streets were paved, but others were not. The sewer system had not yet been extended to the barrio, and outhouses were a visible part of the landscape.

I became more aware of the ethnic duality of Visalia's geography. I began to recognize where people lived. At the end of the school day the Anglo kids walked home in one direction and the Mexican kids, including me, walked in another.

Sierra Vista Junior High School was the only junior high in Visalia, and along with the one high school—Visalia Union High—it was located near the center of town and drew students from both the Anglo and the Mexican neighborhoods.

Junior high school, like elementary school, was not particularly significant for me. I did well—quite well, as a matter of fact—but schooling as education didn't affect me in any discernible way. Part of the reason for this lack of inspiration, as I reflect back on it now, was the tracking system that I was placed in, even though I had no awareness of it as tracking at the time.

Mexicans were put in less academically oriented classes, where the teachers had lower expectations of them, while Anglos were placed in a more enriched program. There were some exceptions, but on the whole the school was segregated in this manner. Although I didn't recognize then the ethnic or race divisions in school, I did become aware that some school practices didn't seem to make sense. My classes were not challenging me. Some classes were absolutely irrelevant.

I remember being assigned to a homemaking class, where we learned to make applesauce. This to me was a minor and trivial activity. I already knew about homemaking, about cooking for a large family, about budgeting. Or more precisely, about making ends meet. You have to be resourceful to provide for a big family. My mother was my model in this respect. I didn't have to go to school to learn about this. And yet here I was, stirring a little pot, making a cup of applesauce. It was a waste of my time.

The sewing class was not much better. I bought fabric and made a dress, which I hated and never wore. I felt frustrated because this was not the learning I desired.

I also remember my music class and how useless it was. The teacher didn't know what she was doing and couldn't even control the class. It was chaotic. All she could do was play records. I loved the Strauss waltzes, but all I did in that class was daydream and talk to my girlfriend. She and I would sit in the back of the room talking quietly, occasionally glancing at the teacher or at one student or another who might be shouting or throwing something.

Listening to the waltzes, my friend and I pretended to be ballerinas. That's all we could do in that class. It was a disaster. At the end of one class period the teacher just broke down and cried because she couldn't maintain control. I felt helpless and frustrated.

I liked my homeroom teacher and she liked me, but in homeroom there was little intellectual challenge. I was assigned to a study hall supervised by an elderly teacher, but there was very little that I needed to study. I was bored most of the time. One day I began to talk quietly with another student. I was shocked when I was reported for this.

Mrs. Clark, my homeroom teacher, called me in during one recess period and very gently said to me, "Frances, this isn't like you. You don't do things like this." I lowered my head as tears streamed down my face. I cried because I felt I had let my homeroom teacher down. But I also cried because I was being perceived as a problem, when in fact the problem was the class, where I had nothing to do.

Besides the more vocational classes, I must have had some mathematics and science. But I remember very little about these subjects. What did interest me was anything to do with languages because of my love of words and because language was a subject that was familiar to me. But overall during junior high I had little appreciation of my classes as representing particular academic disciplines. This appreciation would come later.

It wasn't until almost the end of junior high that it began to dawn on me that what I would only years later recognize as tracking had affected me. This realization was sparked by my problematic music class. I found out that, in addition to the class that I had been assigned to, another type of music class, in which the students were taught to play instruments, existed. These dual music classes represented a clear bias. The instrumental class was reserved for mostly Anglos, while the chaotic, record-playing class I was in contained mostly Mexicans, with one or two exceptions.

Tracking and segregation were also occurring in other subject areas. Anglos attended their English classes and Mexicans attended theirs.

At the time none of this stood out very clearly in my mind, but my discovery of the other music class gave me a clue that tracking existed. While I may have been ignorant then of the ethnic implications of this practice, I couldn't help being aware that the results were quality learning for some students and a lack of quality for others.

Toward the end of the eighth grade, I also became vaguely aware that testing was used to identify students somehow. One day I was standing in the lunch line waiting to enter the cafeteria when a teacher, accompanied by the school principal, approached me unexpectedly, touched me on the shoulder, and said to the principal, "Here she is. This is Frances."

Smiling, he said, "Hello, Frances."

I said, "Hello" back.

The teacher didn't explain why I was being introduced to the principal, and I had no idea why I had been given this attention. After lunch when I returned to class, my teacher, looking flustered, took me aside and gave me a special piece of paper—heavier stock than I was used to. She wanted me to recopy, in my best handwriting, some of the work I had done in class.

"The principal wants to post your work," she said.

Of course, I became more flustered than the teacher, smudged the first two pieces of paper, and had to ask for fresh supplies. I still didn't really understand why I was being selected, but I was happy that my work was being appreciated.

At the end of the day, when I had time to think about it, it occurred to me that whatever was happening was somehow related to a test I had taken a few days earlier. The test, a kind I had never seen before, had been long. The explanation for the test, whatever it may have been, had not registered. However, the test itself had intrigued me because it contained questions and vocabulary I wasn't used to encountering in school.

I had actually become engrossed in it and had enjoyed it somewhat. I did not understand that it was an aptitude test of some kind, but I knew that it was hard. I assumed I had done OK on it. Then I promptly forgot about it, because it had no significance for me. Now, some days later, school officials were apparently recognizing that I was a capable student, and that was a gratifying thought.

Tracking, a system of grouping students, became more evident in high school. It was when I entered the ninth grade that, due to my junior high record—I had received better grades than other Mexican American kids and, I guessed, had done well on that test—I was placed in the college-preparatory classes. I was one of the very few Mexican American students on this track at my high school.

When I myself became a teacher years later, the insidious nature of tracking became even more obvious to me. It begins in the early years, when kids are grouped and there are high expectations for some and minimal expectations for others. I can go back now and look at my high school yearbooks and see the evidence of tracking based largely on race or ethnicity. Anglos are pictured as members of particular classes and activities. Mexicans are shown in classes consisting almost entirely of other Mexicans, and they are all but invisible in the photos of extracurricular activities.

Despite the lack of stimulating classroom experiences in junior high, I was fortunate in discovering a new treasure: the library. If I learned anything in junior high, it was that there was something called a library, and our school had a good one. I don't remember ever having seen one in any of my other schools. For that matter, I don't remember having seen many books besides textbooks. Books were scarce commodities in rural areas.

Nobody taught me how to use the library or the Dewey decimal system. I simply went to a shelf, discovered fairy tales, and fell in love with them. I reveled in these stories. My favorites were those about the princess and the prince with the white horse—the stereotypical romantic stuff—but I loved them.

Later, when I entered high school, my love affair with library resources continued to grow when I made still another discovery: the public library. It was here that I began to shift from fairy tales to heavier tomes. I stumbled upon the writings of the economist Adam Smith and recall being fascinated by the weight of these books and reading some passages thinking, "Wow, there's a lot of stuff in here!"

I had never heard of Adam Smith—I was just attracted by the size of his books. Books had a visual appeal for me. I understood some of what I read, or at least I thought I understood, and I was intrigued by the amount of reading material that I was not yet ready to digest. I sampled other books in no sequential order. I kind of just dipped into them.

∽✠∾

Junior high and the move back to Visalia brought other changes for me. Even though I still felt alienated from school, I was beginning to realize that one way of breaking out of this sense of alienation was to move more toward the mainstream. This meant further acculturation and identifying more with Anglo models of behavior and appearance.

My way of dressing, for example, started to change. I started wearing more "Anglo" clothes. And though I still continued to wear my hair in a small pompadour, I was becoming more style conscious. I particularly wanted to get a pair of what were called "ski boots." These weren't really for skiing but were more like today's high-top Reeboks. I never got them, but I sure wanted them! Along with these ski boots, some girls—mostly Anglos—wore a particular type of coat with a belt. I desired those outfits and was aware that they represented an "outside-the-barrio" look.

I began to choose clothes that I thought made me look good, even if they were different from the ones worn by barrio girls. For example, I bought a red pantsuit. It was made of rayon gabardine, a synthetic fiber that was in at the time. The war had introduced these new fibers and fabrics. It had a classic look, a Chanel look of its time. I liked it because I was becoming conscious of my profile, and this suit, I thought, made me look trim. Also, it was very bright red, and I loved red.

I reserved this suit, however, for more special occasions. For school, I favored skirts and blouses, but more in the style of the Anglo girls and not of the Mexicans, especially the *pachucas*.

My junior high school years during the early 1940s coincided with the *pachuco* era, which was especially associated with the Los Angeles area. This was the period of the zoot-suit riots in 1943. In Visalia we had our own versions of *pachucos* and *pachucas*. I didn't care for them. I perceived them as swarthy and large and had heard they carried knives hidden in their exaggerated pompadours. Dressed in their defiant style, the *pachucas* looked mean and threatening, their attire consisting of short tight skirts, bulky sweaters, and high-top black shoes with black socks sticking up above the shoes.

I think that my rejection of the *pachucas* was due in part to my father's negative attitude toward them. "*No tienen porqué andar en patrullas,*" he would say. He objected to their roaming the streets in packs. "You stay away from those girls; they're up to no good," he warned Toni and me whenever he encountered them and we were with him.

The *pachucas* and I didn't get along at all. I was afraid of them and they were hostile toward me. They had a reputation for fighting, but I didn't want to admit my fear of them, so I carried myself proudly. This was how I handled my vulnerability—I assumed an air of arrogance whenever I thought I could get away with it.

In crossing the street, for example, I would deliberately make the cars wait. This was one of the few ways I had of expressing my defiance of the barrio style and attitude they exemplified.

Although I never wanted to be like a *pachuca,* I did admire their street smarts and wanted to be equally street-smart and assertive, but in my own way.

When I encountered them on the street, I attempted to avoid them by crossing to the opposite side of the street. They would give me hostile stares that we called "mad-dogging." On occasion they yelled things out to me: "Hey—you. What you looking at?"

Although I worked hard at blocking out their existence, they were hard to ignore, particularly at public dances, which I occasionally attended chaperoned by my father. Fortunately for me, I never engaged in any fistfights with them. Fights were common, but I had enough sense to avoid them.

The male *pachucos* were also visible in the barrio and in school. They, like the girls, had a distinct appearance. They also favored black clothes, which consisted of baggy pants that tightened at the ankles and huge shirts worn outside their trousers. Some wore brimmed hats slightly tilted toward the forehead, the brim rolled up at the back. This was not the complete zoot-suit, which with its long coat was worn on special occasions such as when some of the big bands came to Visalia to play at dances.

My fears and rejection of the *pachucas* reflected the fact that the barrio was not some stereotypical homogeneous community. There were differences and divisions. There were tensions and animosities. We all came from different places. It wasn't as if we were all one people. We did not all know one another, nor were we friends with everyone.

In junior high I began to sense that I was definitely becoming more Americanized. For one thing, I was acquiring some new Anglo friends who introduced me to new experiences.

At first it seemed strange to have Anglo friends. One girl in particular, Deborah, a redhead, sought me out as her friend. I think she was in my homeroom. She came up to me one day during recess and in an excited way said, "Frances, I want you to read some of my stories." I remember thinking, "Why is she doing this? What does she want? What is this?" But she persisted and we became friends. I was fascinated with her because I didn't know that kids could write stories, and here was this kid who had a real love of writing.

I particularly recall the time when Deborah first invited me to her home. Her parents had died, and she lived with her grandmother. This was one of my first ventures into the Anglo side of town and the first time I ate a hamburger at someone's house. We didn't have hamburgers at my house, although I do recall having eaten one once at a carnival. So my reaction to Deborah's house was, "Oh! You can make hamburgers at home?" And she served them on buns, something my parents never bought.

We ate the hamburgers and read Deborah's stories. She was a prolific writer, and I marveled at the confidence she displayed in sharing her creations. I was favorably impressed with her stories, which were modeled on the Nancy Drew books.

On another occasion when I visited Deborah's home, she had invited some other Anglo girls. We ate more hamburgers and engaged in girl talk. All this introduced me to the other part of town and to other kids.

Yet while I was becoming more acculturated—more Americanized—I still at times had to confront the dualities of my young life. I couldn't escape them. These took different forms.

For example, Deborah introduced me to the Nancy Drew mystery series. I remember trying to read them but not being able to relate to Nancy Drew. I thought she was a stereotypical Anglo girl teenager. While I liked my fairy tales because they represented fantasies that I knew were simply fantasies, the Nancy Drew stories were different.

Instead of fantasies, they were supposed to depict real-life situations so that young girls could identify with Nancy—even though she was running around trying to solve murders. Yet this reality—or the lack of it—was precisely why I couldn't accept Nancy Drew. I had never had such adventures and didn't think that I ever would. I didn't think that I could look like Nancy, and I knew that I was totally incapable of solving murder cases. And I was conscious of the fact that I couldn't identify with Nancy Drew because she was an Anglo and I was not.

I was sensitive to these types of differences. Everywhere I turned I was reminded of them. Even language, which I loved, conveyed difference. I became acutely aware of the subtlety of language when, one time at Deborah's home her grandmother, in her warm, sociable way inquired about my family.

"Oh, you have a baby in your home?"

The baby, in fact, was teething, and in Spanish we said *le está saliendo un diente*. So I told the grandmother that the baby's tooth was coming out.

"Oh dear," she responded. "I'm sorry to hear that. What happened?"

She had interpreted my words to mean that the baby's tooth had fallen out. In English a baby's tooth comes in, and in Spanish it comes out. I remember being very embarrassed by that slip and by the confusion that my innocent remark had caused. But this incident served as a reminder to be cautious about how I spoke English lest I commit another blunder. Functioning in two language worlds—Spanish at home and English outside my home—made me very wary and restricted me in my natural inclination toward openness.

I was not helped in this matter by my surname. When I was born, my parents used to spell our name with a "b" (Esquibel), a spelling that was changed to Esquivel some twenty-five years later. I was never quite sure how to pronounce my last name to Anglos, or for that matter to other Mexicans. Should I say "Es-kee-VEL" (Spanish pronunciation) or "Es-KWIB-el" (English pronunciation)? All this was particularly upsetting in English, because most Anglos butchered my name.

I was also embarrassed by and frustrated at always having to spell my name to others and having to explain how to pronounce it, a process that never seemed to end.

"Who are you?"

"What's your name?"

"What's that?"

"How do you spell it?"

This process made me feel that my name was a problem. It would have even helped if my name had been a simpler Spanish one like García.

My Americanization and the tension it produced were further evident in my attraction to Hollywood movies. These movies were also associated with the ever-present movie magazines. I didn't buy the magazines, but they were around. I recall differentiating these magazines from the Spanish-language reading material that my father would, on rare occasions, bring home—newspapers primarily with fine print and names of people and places I didn't recognize.

By contrast, I was fascinated by the colorful Hollywood movie magazines, because I knew who the movie stars pictured in them were. I knew when their films played at the Fox Theatre, and sometimes I went. These movie stars became my models with respect to standards of beauty. Everyone knew who Betty Grable was, and girls wanted to be like her.

"She has pretty legs—long, slim, and straight," my adopted aunt, Rita, had once explained.

I especially loved movie musicals. I loved the fantasies they depicted. I knew that they were fantasies and I reveled in them. It was make-believe. You could be anything. You could dance, fly, be anything. You could lose yourself in these movies.

Betty Grable was my favorite star, even though she was probably not a very good actress or dancer. Still, I could identify with her because, unlike Nancy Drew, I identified her with singing and dancing. I loved to sing and dance and fantasized about being able to sing and dance like her. With Betty Grable I lost that sense of difference that I associated with Nancy Drew.

Another indication that I was beginning to feel more American was my reaction to the death of President Franklin Roosevelt. He was the only American president I had known in my short lifetime. He was a father figure to me: I had heard his voice over the radio, and it was a fatherly voice.

When he died in the spring of 1945, our principal called an emergency assembly and there we were told of the president's death. Many of us, including teachers, cried at hearing the news. I walked home crying. I didn't fully understand the loss, but I knew something would be missing from our lives. President Roosevelt was our symbol of hope. I had the vague understanding that he was doing things for people.

I think I also cried because it was a first for me—the death of someone important to me. No one in our family had died while I was growing up.

President Roosevelt's death impressed me even more than the end of World War II a few months later. I was aware that the war was over and that our country had triumphed, but I have no vivid recollections of any major parades or other festive events associated with the war's end. One day the war was on and the next day it was off. War, in any event, had been only an abstraction to me. At school our teachers did not teach us anything about what war was really all about.

Even before junior high I had already been interested in boys and boys had been interested in me. Some would write notes to me in class: "Dear Frances—guess who likes you?" This was all perfectly innocent and nothing came of it.

This certainly didn't lead to my actually having boyfriends, which was not allowed in my home. My parents had very definite ideas about such things as dating and boy-girl relations. Dating was something Anglos or others did, but my father made no bones about it not occurring with his daughters.

Going anywhere besides church or school required my father's permission, or at least my mother had to account to my father for our whereabouts. Going out with other girls was all right, but all of us girls knew that when we returned home—and it had better be at the appointed hour—our mothers would look anxiously for telltale signs, such as smeared lipstick, that might indicate a forbidden rendezvous with a boyfriend.

Yet, despite my parents' strict rules against dating and having boyfriends, when I was in junior high I did meet a boy whom I "dated" for over a year. This was Peter Nava. He was from the barrio and older than I, perhaps by as much as three years. He was in high school.

I think we met at a movie and someone introduced us or else we met walking to school. He was also from a poor family. In fact, I believe his parents had died when he was still quite young so he had been raised by older sisters.

I don't think it was love at first sight, but I liked Peter very much from the beginning. He was a wonderful, gentle, and sensitive person. He was mature and respectful of me. He was also very handsome but not in a rugged or athletic way. He had brown eyes, a slender face, and light brown wavy hair, with a curl that tended to come down over one brow. He was about five feet nine and slender.

He definitely was not a "macho." I have always felt a certain physical attraction toward the bravado of macho posturing. But although I can respond physically to the macho type, I am more attracted to the gentle and humane side of a man. I look for a man's ability to assert his presence not by physical strength alone but also by his ability to listen and to think. Peter had these qualities, and they were qualities that even after Peter I continued to look for in males.

I began to date Peter without telling my parents. We would arrange to meet at the park or at the movies at certain times like at two in the afternoon on Sundays. I was always certain to be back home at the time my parents insisted upon. This dating subterfuge was not uncommon in the barrio, where other parents also had strict rules against dating. My older sister, Toni, knew I was meeting Peter, but my parents, of course, didn't.

"You're going to be caught," Toni would warn me.

"Please don't tell Mother or Dad," I would implore.

"Don't worry, I won't. But be careful," Toni would respond in her big-sister way.

I often met Peter at the movies. At that time there were three theaters in Visalia. All three were on Main Street, but otherwise, they were worlds apart. On the eastern end of Main Street, beyond the mainstream retail shops, was the Roxy, which catered to the Mexican population. Spanish-language films, along with old Lash LaRue–type cowboy movies, were the general fare there. Midway on Main Street was the Hyde, which featured other standard and older American films. On the west end was the Fox, which showed major new Hollywood films. Peter and I always went to the Fox. There was no strict segregation in the theater like there was at the local public swimming pool. Still, mostly Anglos attended the Fox, and Peter and I were often the recipients of unfriendly stares. But we didn't care. We enjoyed going to the Fox and being with each other.

After the movies, we would walk across the street to a soda fountain where we would have hamburgers or banana splits. We would sit together and talk. Drive-in restaurants were becoming more popular then, but they were frequented by wealthier or more middle-class Anglo kids who had cars. They went to a place called the BQ, or the Bar-B-Q. Peter and I stuck to our soda fountain.

Peter always treated, both at the movies and afterward. The tradition was that on dates the girls didn't pay but allowed the boy to do so. This bothered me a bit because I knew that Peter was poor, but at the same time I was flattered that he would spend some of his hard-earned money on me. Peter, like me, worked in the fields.

There was very much a double standard in dating. Boys took the initiative in all things. Boys paying was one of those unspoken rules.

Despite his poverty, Peter was always nicely dressed for our dates. He was a very neat dresser, although he didn't wear anything fancy, just a sport shirt neatly tucked inside well-pressed slacks, the opposite of the *pachuco* look. He was always well groomed and possessed good taste by my standards.

We dated like this for some months without my parents' knowledge. I think I felt guilty about it, but I couldn't tell them. They would have forbidden me to see Peter. My feelings for Peter were stronger than my fear of disobeying my parents or of punishment.

This, unfortunately, involved lying to my parents.

"Mother, can I go to the movies with Ernestine tomorrow?"

Little did my mother know that Ernestine was dating Peter's brother and that we were all going together.

This lying made me feel guilty, and I even confessed to it in church.

"Bless me Father, for I have sinned. Since my last confession I lied to my parents twice."

After receiving the priest's admonishment about not lying to one's parents and receiving my usual penance of three Hail Marys and three Our Fathers, I left the confessional feeling relieved—until the next time I lied about seeing Peter.

Over the months that I came to know Peter our relationship developed into a very special one. I don't recall the specific things we talked about—probably about school, the movies we saw, our friends, our families.

I trusted Peter. I felt safe allowing myself to experience a physical attraction to him without fear that he would hurt me in any way. I was in blissful ignorance of the fact that this was probably the very kind of playing with fire that my parents had been trying to protect me from. I was also lucky that Peter was the thoughtful and respectful person that he was. I think he reciprocated my feelings entirely, but we acted out our emotions with caution.

In the theater, we sat at the back of the balcony and Peter put his arm around my shoulder. Other than that, he kept his hands to himself. Occasionally we kissed, but we avoided the kind of necking or heavy petting that was going on around us. When we walked home, we sometimes dared to hold hands, fearful that someone would spot us and tell my parents. "Don't do that," I would say to Peter, pretending to resist. But I would let him win, and I was happy to be able to extend my time with him just a little bit more. A stratagem we used was to take the less-traveled streets, where we were less likely to encounter anyone we knew.

❦

Although I was beginning to discover my sexuality, it was not a subject that my mother ever discussed with me. She was very circumspect and, if anything, I grew up guided by a vaguely defined standard of ladylike behavior.

Tomboyishness, for example, was frowned upon. Of course, I performed a lot of physical labor along with men, but this was considered honorable work and not tomboy behavior. In fact, outside working in the fields, I'd never had the opportunity to participate in athletics or competitive sports, and athletic activity was not attractive to me. I had been taught that a girl who participated in sports risked injury to her breasts.

Instead, I was brought up to believe that a woman's main aspiration should be to get married and to raise a family. This didn't necessarily mean that a woman was subservient to her husband, but rather that, once married, a woman stuck it out in her marriage.

I had seen my mother, despite hard times, doing just that. Other women in the barrio did likewise. Divorce was considered shameful and, of course, a sin in the Catholic Church.

A woman accepted her family responsibility even if it at times included dishonor. If a girl in the barrio got pregnant out of wedlock and had a baby, the girl kept the baby in her family. I recall some years later learning about a family that had put up for adoption a baby born out of wedlock. My parents were appalled at this decision. The notion of abandoning your own child was unacceptable behavior. You took care of your own.

This concept of a woman's responsibility within the family carried over to matters of sex. I acquired the sense that sex belonged within the marriage context, not outside it. Sex not only belonged within a marital relationship but it was also considered something that a woman just had to put up with. Sex as pleasure for a woman was not considered or admitted to. There was a general perception that sex was a negative thing. Respectable women didn't actively seek it.

"You know what my grandmother says," I once heard an older girl say. "That God made women have their period so that at least once in a while they don't have to have sex with their husbands."

In the barrio, my notion of sexuality came in bits and pieces. Sex was not something talked about among most of my friends, both Mexicans and Anglos. Certainly most Mexican girls my age were in my situation. Our fund of knowledge about most things related to sex, including menstruation, was sketchy to nonexistent.

I do remember one occasion, however, when a girl whose parents were from New Mexico had gotten pregnant at age fifteen or sixteen, gotten married, and then divorced talked to me and Toni about her marriage. She revealed her experiences to us as we sat in a car parked right outside our house. The whole scene had a clandestine air about it, and I knew she wasn't the best person to be giving my sister and me lessons about anything, but that's probably why we were attracted to her.

"What's it like?" we curiously asked.

"What's what like?" she responded.

"Being married—did you like it?"

"Oh, it was no big deal. I didn't enjoy what he did to me."

We were too embarrassed to ask just what he did. She did say that when her husband was asleep she would take a good look at his body and that this was a good opportunity for her to see it. So we did get a lesson in human anatomy.

Pregnancy and how to prevent it were also something not talked about in the barrio, at least not openly and not to young girls. What you picked up tangentially was that sex outside marriage was dangerous and forbidden—you didn't do it because you got pregnant.

I remember learning some time later that birth control was forbidden by the Church. I didn't know what birth control was, but I knew it was not acceptable. At the same time, I was curious about it and wanted to know why my family had so many children.

"Mother, how come you had seven kids?"

"*Mi'ja,* sometimes it's hard to explain. It's just the way it happens— *la suerte que le toca a uno.* No one plans it but God."

But I still wanted to know why birth control was forbidden, and I remember sitting in church one Sunday watching a very attractive and respectable Anglo couple with their one child and wondering, "If birth control is forbidden and there are so many large families in the barrio, why aren't there more large families seen among Anglo Catholics?" It appeared to me that there was more to the subject of birth control than I was being told.

Although topics like sex and birth control were largely avoided in my family and in the barrio, still I was experiencing my own nascent sexual feelings. I had gone through a difficult time when I was a bit younger when my breasts started to enlarge and I was embarrassed by that. I would wear large blouses over my dresses to hide them. I was very uncomfortable, but by junior high I had come to terms with the fact that I was a girl. I also knew that I liked boys. But I knew that those feelings had to be guarded.

I was aware of my sexual feelings toward Peter. But it never occurred to me that we would engage in sexual activity. Besides the moral issues involved, it was also a practical matter. Where would we have engaged in sex? We had no place. Peter didn't have a car. Visalia was a small town, and everybody soon knew of any "bad behavior."

I don't know whether it was because I was a good kid or because I didn't have the opportunity. But, for whatever reason, I didn't seek out occasions to engage in sexual activity with Peter. The extent of our sexual expression was confined to sitting in the balcony at the movies, holding hands or kissing, typical adolescent activity. Peter reciprocated my guarded feelings about sex. He never made any demands on me. He was in no sense sexually aggressive.

Most Mexican girls, I believe, were like me concerning sexual feelings. I was not aware of any girls in junior high having sex with their boyfriends. Some might have, but it was not talked about. Casual sex was not in yet. You heard from time to time of some girl in the barrio getting pregnant, but this was not a common occurrence, or at least it wasn't well known.

Sexual violence was likewise not something people seemed to be particularly concerned about then. I heard once about a girl, who after a dance, got in a car with some boys who gang-raped her. But this was an unusual episode. I knew that such things could and did happen, but they certainly were not everyday events. Visalia was seen as a safe haven from the illicit activities usually associated with bigger urban areas.

I'm not aware that these repressions concerning sex and related activities such as drinking and smoking were any different among the Anglo kids. Perhaps they were, since more Anglos had cars, but I never heard of Anglo girls having sex or being "sluts."

∙◈∙

I was very close to Peter and, as much as I could at age thirteen and fourteen, loved him. Yet at a certain point in our relationship, I knew that we could have no future. Not because I didn't care for him—I did very much—but because I began to realize that a future with Peter would mean the end of any future for me.

I knew by the time I had finished junior high and was entering high school that I wanted to make something of myself. I began to want more of an education. I was encouraged by having been selected as the graduation speaker of my junior high school class. Success in school made me want something more than marriage and Visalia.

Peter came to understand this. We never discussed marriage, but it would have been the natural next thing, at least in a place like Visalia. Peter, like most other Mexican American boys in Visalia, was not going beyond high school. What was ahead for him was getting married, raising a family, and working.

"I'm sorry, Peter. It's not you. It's me. You're a wonderful guy and I respect you a lot. But I just think I need to concentrate on school. I hope you understand."

He did. Peter and I couldn't continue seeing each other, caring for each other as much as we did, without considering marriage. We both understood this without talking about it. I think we cared so much for each other that under different circumstances it would have been natural for us to get married.

So when we moved out of the barrio, I stopped seeing Peter.

He did try to see me again some time later. It happened one warm summer evening when, apparently, he had been drinking with some other boys. They drove to my house and stood outside on our lawn.

My father heard them outside.

"Who's there and what do you want?" my father demanded in Spanish. "You shouldn't be hanging around. Get out of here!"

Peter and his friends scurried off, no doubt frightened by my father's stern voice.

A few days later I ran into Peter, who told me of the incident and apologized profusely.

"I guess I'd been drinking. I'm sorry. I shouldn't have gone to your house. But I miss seeing you."

"Peter, you don't have to apologize. But we can't see each other anymore. You know that."

"Yeah, I understand. I'm sorry, Frances. It won't happen again."

It didn't, but secretly I felt just wonderful that he had come to my house. I hadn't lost my feelings for him. I missed him a lot too.

The last time I saw Peter was a couple of years later when I was already in high school. I was now working as a cashier at the Roxy after school and on weekends.

"Two tickets, please."

I looked up from inside my booth, and there was Peter. But he wasn't alone. He had a young woman at his side. I knew that she was his wife. I had heard that he had gotten married.

Peter didn't know that I worked at the Roxy. I'm sure that he was as surprised to see me as I was to see him. He didn't say anything else and neither did I. He seemed shy and embarrassed at our encounter. I didn't know his wife, but I instantly disliked her. I was jealous. I felt saddened. Even though I knew that nothing could ever happen between Peter and me, I still felt sad knowing that our relationship had definitely come to an end.

I've often wondered if Peter is still in Visalia.

In rejecting Peter, I was also rejecting the barrio. For me, even at my young age, the barrio stood for despair and a predictable future. I wanted more. I felt there was more.

It wasn't just Peter and what he represented. It was other people as well. There were Mexican girls I liked, but they didn't seem to be future oriented. I don't remember any discussion among them as to what tomorrow would hold. I think they accepted being in the barrio, and that was it. Even if they aspired to more, there were few opportunities for Mexicans in Visalia.

I remember hearing from my parents about two young Mexican women in the barrio. We called them *las coloradas*—the red-haired ones—because they were very fair-skinned and had natural flaming red hair. They were graduating from high school. Because of their fair skin and red hair, everyone expected them to be fortunate enough, unlike most other Mexicans, to get downtown jobs as bank tellers, perhaps. These were considered prime jobs for Mexicans, but you had to be light skinnned to stand a chance of getting them. I thought about this then and how ridiculous and sad it was that, even with their supposedly advantageous appearance, all they could get out of it were jobs as bank tellers.

My sister Toni, who was very fair in appearance and not at all the stereotypical Mexican, remembers that when she went to apply for jobs downtown she was readily given an application. However, when potential employers in department stores or small shops noted her Spanish last name, Toni would be told that there were no job openings.

She remembers vividly one such occasion when she was told that there was no job available, only to learn that an Anglo girl named Jewel from Arkansas had been hired. Jewel had applied for the job a couple of days after Toni.

But it wasn't just Anglo racism that limited opportunities. It was also the barrio. The people there discouraged the idea that one could aspire to a better life. Parents wanted more for their children, but most didn't believe that it was possible. The barrio discouraged change.

I remember one incident that reinforced for me the barrio's limits. I was in the neighborhood grocery store, which was owned by a Mexican family. A young man came in and innocently asked for "American" cheese. That's what we called cheddar cheese. He was another Mexican from the barrio.

"What kind of cheese?" the store owner asked quizzically.

"American cheese," the Mexican said again, but this time with some uncertainty in his voice.

"*¡Hijo'e la! ¡Quiere queso americano! No quiere ser mexicano,*" laughed the other customers in the store. Hey! He wants American cheese! He doesn't want to be a Mexican!

I felt embarrassed by this scene. I quickly left the store angry at what had happened. How dare they make fun of an innocent request? I knew why they were laughing. They felt that the young man was attempting to be more than Mexican. He was trying to be an Anglo. The expectation was that no barrio resident would or should expect to be like the Anglos, even in aspiring to success in school or to any job other than work in the fields.

When this incident occurred, I had already perceived quite clearly that, in the barrio, residents didn't believe they had a right to enjoy the advantages that Anglos enjoyed. Wanting to be like an Anglo meant betrayal of your own culture, and that was an unacceptable option.

I began to understand that whether I liked it or not, Visalia was a dead-end place for me. There were few or no opportunities for Mexicans like myself who believed that our futures held more than working in the fields, being a clerk, or marrying and having lots of children.

I definitely knew that I would be going on if I could manage it. Life for me would have to be elsewhere. But before this could happen, I had to prepare myself for a different life. I had to learn Anglo ways. And I had to do well in high school. I prepared myself for this next challenge.

Left to right: Fran's great-uncle Tomás Pineda; second cousin Ofelia Fresquez; great-uncle by marriage Eluterio Fresquez; great-aunt Teresita Pineda Fresquez; mother, Florinda Flores Esquibel (bows in hair); grandmother Genoveva Pineda Flores, holding Fran's aunt Manuela. El Picacho, New Mexico, ca. 1911.

Fran's grandfather Vicente Flores holding Fran's aunt Reynalda. El Picacho, New Mexico, ca. 1918.

Fran's grandmother Genoveva Pineda Flores and great-aunt Teresita Pineda Fresquez. New Mexico, ca. 1935.

Fran's mother, Florinda. Hagerman, New Mexico, ca. 1924.

Fran's father, Teodoro Camacho Esquibel. New Mexico, 1926.

Fran (left) and her older sister, Toni.
Artesia, New Mexico, ca. 1931.

Fran's older sister, Toni; her younger
sister Sue; and Fran. Artesia, New
Mexico, ca. 1936.

Fran's father, Teodoro, and mother, Florinda. New Mexico, probably early to mid-1930s.

Fran's mother holding Fran's younger sister Sue. Somewhere in Arizona on the way from New Mexico to California, December 1937.

Fran (left) and her sisters Toni and Sue. Corcoran,
California, December 1937.

Fran in first-grade school picture, seated, first child on the left, second row.
Corcoran, California, 1938.

First Holy Communion; Fran kneeling. Tagus Ranch, California, 1941.

Fran (right) and sisters Toni, Sue (in background), and Niva (in foreground). Tagus Ranch, California, 1941.

Fran. Goshen, California, 1943.

Fran and her father, who is pruning trees. Goshen, California, 1943.

Fran's father and her four younger brothers and sisters: Severo, John (on his father's lap), Niva, and Sue. Goshen, California, 1943.

Fran, age thirteen, in junior high school. Visalia, California, 1944.

Fran at Girls State, second row, fifth from left. Sacramento, California, 1948.

Fran's high school graduation portrait. Visalia, California, 1949.

High school graduation day. Fran with sisters and brothers Niva, Sue, John, and Ted. Visalia, California, 1949.

Fran with her sister Toni upon graduation from Visalia Union High School. Visalia, California, 1949.

Fran on her high school graduation day. Visalia,
California, 1949.

Fran at Sather Gate, sophomore year. University of
California, Berkeley, 1950.

Ed Tywoniak, ca. 1948, before he met Fran.

Ed and Fran in front of Fran's Parker Street rooming house.
Berkeley, California, 1951.

Fran. Berkeley, California,
1951.

Fran on her honeymoon.
Catalina Island, California,
1952.

Ed in Durant Street
apartment. Berkeley,
California, 1953.

Ernie Tsang and Ed, after
the birth of Ed, Jr.
Children's Hospital,
San Francisco, California,
1953.

Fran feeding her newborn baby, Ed, Jr., Durant Street apartment.
Berkeley, California, 1953.

Ed's mother, Eva, Fran, and
Ed, Jr. San Francisco,
California, 1955.

Fran and her three children,
Ed, Jr., Richard, and Rebecca.
San Francisco, California, 1969.

Joining the High School Track to Success

My entering high school in 1945 coincided with our move out of the barrio. This was symbolic for me, although not planned as far as I know. My parents, after having worked hard for several years in California, had been able to save enough money to purchase or at least to make a down payment on a house.

The banker in my family was my mother. Besides my father's wages and the wages that Toni and I earned when we worked in the fields, there were my mother's earnings, which contributed on occasion. She sometimes added field work to her child-bearing and child-rearing responsibilities.

From her own early experiences in New Mexico, she knew about generating an income. When she married my father, she had her own prize cows and egg-laying chickens. "Layers" the chickens were called, and the eggs were sold locally. She knew how to generate a cash flow and how to save and manage money.

I wasn't privy to whatever my parents may have discussed regarding the difficulties of life in the barrio. Nor do I remember my parents discussing their plans for moving out with the children. Certainly the two-room rented cottage we lived in was too small, and there were no prospects for anything better in the barrio. I did sense that my mother felt no special attachment to the place.

In contrast to my father, who was friendly with everybody, my mother tended to stay close to home, caring for her children. She wasn't one to engage in *comadreo*. I was very conscious of my mother being reserved and formal compared to Mexican women, who loved to talk a lot, gossip really, calling each other *comadre*. For my mother, a *comadre* was a godmother in the religious sense, a person to be given special respect.

In any case, when we did move, the focus was not on what we were leaving behind but rather on what we anticipated would be a better life. We were now in a real home, our own home. My parents had probably selected that particular house primarily because of its affordability and because a house with indoor plumbing could only be acquired outside the barrio.

The city sewer system had not yet been extended into the Mexican part of town. At that time, city development was being directed toward the opposite side of town. In fact, it was not until several years later that such a sewer project was initiated.

This exclusion didn't make sense inasmuch as the barrio was, in effect, a part of Visalia, an extension of the town's original residential area. The original county courthouse was nearby. It was obvious that the barrio wasn't getting the same city services as other parts of town, but I don't recall anyone in the barrio challenging or questioning these conditions. That's just the way things were.

I don't recall feeling any sadness or nostalgia about leaving the barrio. I had never felt comfortable there. Moving, for me, merely meant a better home.

Our move didn't mean that we were now on the "other side of the tracks." Though our new home was not in the barrio, it also was not in what could be considered an Anglo neighborhood. It was in a transitional part of Visalia, the northeastern section of town, which was one of the older neighborhoods. The railroad tracks ran along that side of Visalia. There were also still truck farms adjacent to it.

I remember the excitement of moving to our new house. Before we settled in, we all helped my mother clean it.

"*Uf, que feo huele,*" I recall my mother saying when we first went to look at the house. It was with a sense of revelation, and some personal discomfort, that I heard my mother pointing out that the smells of prior occupants remained in the house.

"We'll have to use a lot of Clorox," she said. Clorox was the all-purpose household cleaner, and we set about the task of scrubbing the place from top to bottom. It was a happy time.

Besides having indoor plumbing instead of an outhouse, our new one-story house also provided us with more space, which, with seven growing children, my parents welcomed. It was not a Victorian house, but it looked like the type of house that in San Francisco is referred to as "Victorian era."

The dark wainscoting dominated the front room, and the house had no hallways. You went from one room directly into another, which made the traffic flow awkward. It had a front room, a combined dining room and kitchen, two bedrooms, and front and back porches.

What gave us even more room was an accompanying two-room structure that was separate from the main house but in close proximity. It was initially rented out but would eventually give us the additional bedrooms we needed. In time part of the screened-in front porch became still another bedroom. It was an old house, but it seemed like a palace to us.

It also had a very big backyard, as did almost all the homes in that neighborhood. My parents by then were tired of keeping up a vegetable garden, so they planted mostly flowers, and my father cultivated a lawn both in the back and the front of the house. We also had a huge tree in the back where the younger children could climb and play on a swing. The yards were so big that there was plenty of space between neighbors. We had a sense of privacy.

Sleeping arrangements in the new house involved my parents and Toni and I sharing the two bedrooms in the main house. The other children slept in the front porch area and the adjacent structure, once it was vacated by the tenant living there. Although I didn't have a room to myself, I still had enough privacy in the bedroom I shared with my sister.

Toni, who had dropped out of school in her second year in high school to go to work full-time, helped my parents buy a new bedroom set for our room, including twin beds and a dresser. She was working as a waitress and by living at home was able to save part of her salary as well as contribute to the household.

My parents never asked Toni to leave school. She dropped out during her sophomore year out of a sense of frustration. She had been placed in meaningless, remedial-type classes. These kinds of class-placement practices were evidently widespread. At that time, a migrant family's mobility was determined by crop-harvesting seasons, and returning to a home-base school district could be delayed. A child's late entry at the beginning of the school year could result in a placement that was totally inappropriate.

Many years later, after raising a family, Toni returned to school. She entered a community college and resumed the education that had been interrupted. This accomplishment was a credit to her and, in a sense, a vindication of my mother's belief in Toni's inherent academic ability.

Since Toni worked a lot and at different hours, sometimes I would have the bedroom all to myself. When she came home and went to bed, I used the living room as a study area as late as I wanted. That way I wouldn't disturb anyone. The larger house made it easier for me to study as I entered high school.

Living in what was essentially an ethnically mixed neighborhood, we were fortunate to have neighbors who were friendly and helpful. On the corner of our street lived a black family. Actually, it was a single woman and her common-law husband. They had no children. Behind us there was a Mexican family that became very close to my parents.

The parents were somewhat younger than my parents, and they also had young children. The husband was a successful self-employed house painter, and both he and his wife had a lot of formal education by my parents' standards, being perhaps even junior-college graduates. My younger siblings grew up with that couple's children. For my younger siblings our move meant having real childhood friends. These were experiences that Toni and I had never had.

Our move out of the barrio likewise came at a time when my father didn't have to move around as much from ranch to ranch in order to make a living. He continued to pick crops in the surrounding area, and now he was accompanied by the younger children. He was eventually hired primarily as a gardener. This was work that he could do and still stay in one place. Occasionally, he would still hit the migrant trail, but these occasions became fewer and fewer.

We were now permanently in Visalia. It was our hometown and our home. It is where I finished growing up and where my younger brothers and sisters grew up. It is where both of my parents eventually died and where they are buried.

Visalia Union High School was quite close to the junior high school I had attended. It was also on the Anglo side of town. Although we no longer lived in the barrio, the distance to the high school from my house was still about the same. I walked to school every day, a total of about six miles to and from school. The main difference was that as kids came out of school, I no longer was part of the march of Mexican students back into the barrio. I now walked away from the barrio.

I usually walked to school by myself. But sometimes I was accompanied by a girl whose family had moved into our new neighborhood shortly after us. I wasn't sure where Loretta was from, perhaps from Los

Angeles, but in any case, I knew she had been a *pachuca* before moving to Visalia. She no longer considered herself a *pachuca,* but she seemed knowledgeable about life among this subset of Mexican youth, who were identified by their exaggerated clothing and hair styles and had gained notoriety for their involvement in gang violence. "You should see these guys," she said to me, explaining what it was like on the streets. "They wear these big hats down low over the forehead, and you have to peer under the brim to see who they are."

She amused me when she imitated the *pachuco* gait, the rhythmic way in which they walked, as if on springs. She seemed to enjoy enlightening me on this subject, and though I suspected she might be embellishing her story, I saw no harm in listening to her.

She herself retained some of the *pachuca* look, with her pompadour and brightly painted lips that had the trademark heart shape extending well above her upper lip. Lacking a concept of life in the big city, I couldn't picture her as part of the gang violence that *pachuco* life in Los Angeles was supposedly all about.

She seemed like a nice girl, and we became friends. She always had spending money for treats, which she bought on her way to school and offered to share with me. I usually declined her offer, feeling a little guilty about impulse spending of this nature. I had never been given spending money by my parents, and I guessed that Loretta's mother must have worked hard as a waitress to earn the tips that Loretta was spending so easily. It bothered me.

Sometime later in our high school years I lost touch with Loretta as I moved toward the idea of going to college. I doubt that she ever graduated from high school, because my last memory of her is of the time she appeared on our front yard early on a hot summer evening.

My father had lit a *fogata* in a bucket, a small fire intended to drive away the mosquitoes that could force you indoors if you failed to surround the front porch with a smoke screen. The porch light was turned off as a further precaution. I remember being surprised to see her standing there holding a baby. She looked wistful, and I didn't know what to say to her. She said that she had gotten married, and I let it go at that. I do recall feeling dismayed as I observed this young girl with her baby. How many times had I been warned by my parents: "Don't get involved with boys. It can only lead to one thing. Trouble." It made me sad and a little scared.

One of my first impressions of high school was of its physical layout. Unlike the junior high, which was one large building, Visalia Union High was a number of large buildings on a spread-out campus. The size of the campus was at first intimidating. I felt, as I'm sure other freshmen did, almost lost in what seemed to be an immense complex of buildings. The physical plant and the large number of students impressed upon me the idea that high school represented something very different from junior high. I anticipated a big change for the better.

Because there was only one high school in Visalia—as there was only one junior high—everyone attended it. It was a form of de facto integration—although not completely. Still, there was quite a diversity of students. There were Anglos, Mexicans, and a few blacks and Asians. There were those of us who lived in Visalia, including Mexicans from the barrio. There were those who were bused in from the surrounding farms. The banker's daughter went to school alongside the farmworker's daughter. Yet I didn't fully grasp this diversity at the time.

I became conscious of the Portuguese who spelled their last name "Lopes," a one-syllable pronunciation, as compared to the Spanish spelling of "López," a two-syllable pronunciation. I didn't know where they came from; I just knew that the Portuguese all seemed to own dairies in the outlying areas. And I didn't identify with them as fellow Latinos. The Armenians likewise were a puzzle to me. I was conscious of their dark complexions and the fact that their last names seemed to have a characteristic "-ian" ending.

I recognized a number of the Mexican kids from junior high. Although Anglos formed the majority of the student body of about a thousand students, many Mexicans also attended. It's hard to say what percentage Mexicans represented, but they were a visible presence.

Visalia Union High was ethnically mixed but there was also ethnic separation. Anglos by and large stuck together. Mexicans did likewise. There was very little mixing. Mexicans were largely concentrated in noncollege-track courses, while Anglos and a few Mexicans like myself were in the better classes.

I remember one black girl and one Mexican girl who really stood out because they were quite involved in student activities. But they were the exceptions among the minority students. Not only was there ethnic separation in the classes, but it was also quite noticeable at lunchtime. Anglos ate among themselves and so did the Mexicans. In any congregation of students—assemblies, clubs, sporting events—there were clear ethnic divisions.

While there were a number of Mexicans at Visalia Union High, one difference between high school and junior high was the absence of *pachucos* in high school. Although there were still *pachucos* in town, they were not a presence at Visalia Union High. I don't know why. Perhaps many of them had already dropped out of school or perhaps, like the girl I walked with to school, they had ceased being *pachucos*.

I don't remember much about my first day in high school, but I do remember my freshman year. More than anything, this year was one of adjustment and of getting to know how high school operated. It meant beginning to understand the meaning of different academic disciplines and coming to have a greater appreciation for knowledge and understanding.

Part of my adjustment in my freshman year included escaping from a noncollege track. Although I was still not fully aware of the tracking system in high school, it didn't take much to understand that some kids were not being oriented toward college while others were. I wasn't that definite yet about college in my freshman year; I wasn't even sure what college was. But I did know that I wanted to make something of myself. And I knew that this would mean not only studying hard and getting A's but also being in the more challenging and stimulating classes. I didn't want to be in boring classes with boring teachers. I had had plenty of those in elementary school and in junior high.

At this point I wasn't sure whether I was part of the college track or not. Even though I had been selected as graduation speaker of my junior high school class, that first year I was given a mixed schedule of classes. Some, like algebra, were clearly college prep. But others definitely were not, for example, bookkeeping. I wasn't sure what all this meant. It seems clear to me now that I was partly in what is called a vocational track, a discriminatory placement of the type that, sadly, continues to this day in some places.

I was also confused because, for a language class, I was placed in a Spanish class, which was composed of other Mexican kids. The Anglo kids were all taking French. I certainly had nothing against taking Spanish. I loved languages and had a total comprehension of Spanish, even though by now I was clearly more English speaking. Still, I was confused and resented the fact that I was being excluded from French.

On the other hand, I was placed in an English class with Anglo kids. I also learned that first year that there were agricultural classes and shops. I was glad that I was not in those classes, because they seemed set apart. I never looked into the shops, nor was I even sure who was placed in them.

My freshman year represented unknown territory, but it also represented a challenge for me to try to figure out what this place was all about. I found myself actively asking a lot of questions both of my teachers and of other students. Little by little I became familiar with the patterns of student life. High school no longer seemed overwhelming.

But the more I asked the more I discovered new opportunities for students. During my freshman year I became aware that there was such a thing as CSF (California Scholarship Federation).

"What is this?" I asked one of my teachers.

"Oh, it's an honor society to help you go to college."

"What do you need to do to get into this?" I responded.

"You need to get good grades in certain classes that prepare you for college."

By asking and observing I began to realize that algebra and English counted, while bookkeeping did not. I knew I wanted to be part of CSF.

I did very well my freshman year, and by my sophomore year there was no question but that I was in a college-track curriculum. I started to get a better sense of school and of formal learning. I began to distinguish among disciplines, whereas before almost everything seemed to be lumped together. I began to have more of a sense of control in my classes.

I had always been good in languages, but for the first time I began to enjoy other subjects too. I loved my biology class. It was fun. We had a lab—a real lab! We dissected an earthworm, a sheep's eye, and a frog. I had an excellent teacher. He showed a lot of interesting science films. Audio-visual equipment was new at the school at that time, and my teacher was very proficient at using it. He would whip out the film projector and throw images on the screen. He would also use charts and lots of live demonstrations. I learned about anatomy, physiology, genetics, and a host of other topics that fascinated me. Compared to subjects like bookkeeping, biology was very much alive for me.

Although I became more interested in other subjects such as physics and mathematics and did very well in them during my four years at Visalia High, I still was more attracted to and stimulated by my language and literature classes. For me language was a natural. I had grown up conscious of language and its use, both English and Spanish as well as the Latin of my church missal. It was easy for me to deal with this subject, whether it was literature or grammar or writing. I felt comfortable in these classes and derived great personal satisfaction from all aspects of language study.

I especially remember my English classes with great affection. Part of my excitement about these classes had to do with my teachers. My freshman English teacher, for example, was very lively. She was a round-faced twinkle-eyed woman who seemed to care about her students. For instance, she noticed that at first my mind would sometimes wander. I would daydream a bit because I was still getting over Peter. When she observed this, she would gently bring me back to reality in some wonderful, creative way without making me feel guilty. "If I could just have your attention, Frances," she might say. Startled out of some reverie, I would look in her direction to find a knowing but gentle look of understanding on her face. Her smile made it seem all right.

In this way she won my trust and thereby won me over to her love of literature. In her class, Shakespeare came alive. Portia was a real person. So was Shylock. Even grammar was exciting. Grammar clarified and refined language. There was a reason for it. Adjectives and adverbs had a purpose. That purpose was the beauty of language.

I found that I was responding to both close teacher direction and to being given latitude to work on my own. One teacher to whom I responded very well and whom I very much admired was Miss Julien, another one of my English teachers. She was rumored to be a Communist. I didn't know what a Communist was. What I did know was that she was a wonderful teacher. She ran her classes very differently. She would have us do our work independently and look up the answers and figure things out on our own. She didn't spoon-feed us. Grammar drill sheets with correct answers didn't count.

"Teach yourselves," she would say. "Learn how to learn."

She wanted to know what we were thinking. What counted, she said, was our ability to write with clarity.

I responded to her encouragement, as did the other students. There was no fooling around in Miss Julien's class. She was a very stern teacher but caring at the same time. There was a sense of energy and purposeful activity in her class.

It was during my sophomore year, when I was in Miss Julien's class, that someone accused her of being a Communist. I don't know why this happened or even if she was one. All I know is that she left the following year. I was so upset and angered at what was happening to her that I decided to write a letter of support to our local newspaper. I stated that she was a very good teacher and that I admired her.

To my surprise, my letter was published. I don't know where the motivation to write it came from, and I was not conscious of performing a public act of protest. I just knew that I really liked Miss Julien and wanted to do something to help her. I was angered that somebody who was that good a teacher could be maligned. I don't remember Miss Julien denying being a Communist, but I do remember that she thanked me for my letter.

It was in her class and in my other English classes that I was introduced to more challenging and stimulating readings. I remember one particular essay we read in Miss Julien's class that spoke to me very directly. It was an essay entitled "The Paradox of Poverty and Plenty," which I believe was written by E. B. White. I loved the sound of the title, the alliteration. I loved the sounds of the words and the juxtaposition of the two concepts. I identified with coming from poverty but desiring something better. It made no sense to have poverty in a land of plenty.

We read a variety of authors, especially in anthologies. I loved Jack London. I could actually imagine myself freezing to death in the far north. I no longer had the kinds of problems that I had earlier experienced with *Heidi of the Mountain* in trying to identify with images that were unfamiliar to me. I was learning the fun of imagining places and things that had little or nothing to do with my reality.

I found my Spanish class as interesting as my English class. To me, Spanish was just an extension of English and vice versa. Language was language, and there were more basic similarities among languages than there were differences. The manipulation of words was all the same, regardless of the specific language.

My Spanish teacher was an Anglo. I thought this was an interesting phenomenon. Here was a Spanish teacher who didn't really speak Spanish in the sense that it wasn't her native language, yet she had very good pronunciation (though not Mexican) and was a fine teacher. I learned many things from her. She had traveled to both Mexico and to Spain, and she would enthusiastically describe what she had discovered in those countries.

I was always aware, however, that the other kids didn't seem to be as excited about this Spanish class as I was. It seemed unfortunate that so many of the Mexican kids were not taking the class seriously.

"OK, Frances, go ahead!" the teacher would say, gesturing to me with a shrug.

I would read several pages that I had translated the previous night, very conscious of the fact that I was the only one who had bothered to do the homework. It may have been that the other students were turned off by the grammar and translation activities that occupied most of our class time.

I, on the other hand, had no trouble doing translations. I had a good time. I was interested in the stories, and I loved reading what I considered to be a wonderfully rich Spanish language. I was also pleasantly surprised in this class by how good my Spanish, or at least my comprehension of Spanish, was. I had never previously had the opportunity to test my formal knowledge of the language.

It was the teachers more than anything else that made a difference. Many of them were superb, especially the ones who seemed confident about themselves and comfortable with what they taught. They exuded excitement in sharing knowledge with students and had the ability to use subject matter in ways that were challenging and fun.

I respected and responded to teachers who could communicate with me as an individual and also run an organized class that seemed to have some kind of purpose. These were teachers who loved to teach and who cared about me and the other students.

It was not just these teachers and their classes that helped make me a good student. It was also the fact that I was learning to become competitive. I worked and competed to be one of the best students in my class. I received a lot of A's in high school. I felt very good about being able to compete effectively.

Regrettably, this competition was with predominantly Anglo students. Being in the college-track curriculum, I was in classes with almost all Anglos. In fact, in most of my classes I was the only Mexican student. The Mexican kids were largely in the noncollege-track classes. Although I was not very aware of it at the time, my effort to compete, to succeed, and eventually to prepare myself for college meant that I had to remove myself or, in fact, be removed from other Mexican kids.

I became the exception. I was the female equivalent of Richard Rodriguez's "scholarship boy." I was the "scholarship girl."

Although I didn't have much contact with other Mexican students in my classes, this didn't lead to any kind of animosity or jealousy that I was aware of on the part of other Mexican kids. Occasionally, some of them would kid me about being a good student, telling me that I was smart. But this was more in jest than anything else.

Most of the Mexican students didn't do well, if one can judge by the relatively small number who graduated from high school. This was tragic, but at that time I could only concentrate on my own goals.

Because of my relationship with Peter, one of the things I was particularly sensitive about in high school was the condition of the Mexican boys. I felt sad that they could not be where I was academically. I lost an opportunity to ever really grow up with any Mexican American boys. Certainly my father was a role model, but he was my father. He was not a peer. Academically inclined Mexican American males were unknown to me. It didn't seem that the system had any expectations of them. They were the first to drop out of school, as Peter had done. At least many of the Mexican American girls finished high school, even though they were not in the college-prep classes.

❧

As I distanced myself from other Mexican students, I developed a small circle of Anglo girlfriends. This had little to do with the fact that they were Anglos, but more to do with their being kindred spirits. They were girls like me who wanted to do well and whose main interests in high school were not social activities—as was the case with many other students—but learning and preparing to go on to college. At some point during my sophomore year, as we began to identify one another, we began to meet over lunch. This was a small group of no more than about a half a dozen girls.

Our group did not study together, but we exchanged information— about classes, about teachers, about what we wanted to do in the future. We networked. We didn't talk much about boys and that sort of thing. These girls were not social butterflies, and neither was I.

For me, perhaps the most important thing our group did over the course of our high school years was to talk about college. One of the girls' mother had gone to college. So this girl would share with us what she was learning from her mother. I knew the least about the subject. I had almost no notion of what college implied. But I learned from our group.

I learned that there were different types of colleges. There was the local community college. There were state colleges such as Fresno State, which was the closest to Visalia. We didn't talk at first about the University of California system or of Stanford, universities that did not seem included in the experiences of anyone in our group. It would not be until my senior year that I would learn about the U.C. system.

Occasionally, we would hear about other colleges.

"Did you know that Beth is going to Smith?" one of the girls asked us. Beth's family owned the local drugstore, as I recall.

"What is Smith?" I asked in my ignorance.

By networking, by exchanging information, by serving as a kind of support group, we encouraged one another in our studies. I did homework every night even after I got my job at the Roxy, which required my working early evenings during the week and long hours on weekends. Because I worked, I had little time for social activities.

My socializing was pretty much confined to extracurricular activities that were scheduled during school hours or at lunch time. I didn't go to school dances. I didn't go to rallies. I didn't go to games. My relationship with the Anglo girls in our support group was not social. We were drawn together by our common goals of achieving academic success.

And we did. By my sophomore year I was invited to join CSF because of my good grades. As I recall I was the only Mexican in the group.

The first club that I joined was the Spanish Club. I didn't really choose to join it. Rather, it was an extension of the freshman Spanish class to which I had been assigned along with many other Mexican students. I was in this club for two years but was no longer participating in club activities by my senior year.

In addition to their participation in the Spanish Club, some of the Mexican kids also performed in the schoolwide Pan-American Assembly. This was an annual talent show featuring some of the Mexican students who performed Mexican songs and dances in traditional attire. These were great shows, but I didn't participate since I didn't feel that I had any talent to showcase.

My interest in language and writing led me to join the student newspaper staff. I was on the staff for a couple of years and served as a news editor. I enjoyed my journalism class a lot, probably as much as any of my academic classes. I especially enjoyed learning about the process of putting together a newspaper. Having grown up without much printed material at home, I was intrigued by the idea of actually helping to create a newspaper. We visited a printing company and learned about the use of a linotype machine. I remember the noisy, hot pressroom and being fascinated by how the galleys were produced and then proofread.

Besides helping to edit our newspaper, from time to time I also contributed some articles that were innocuous but nevertheless earned me a byline.

While languages were my main interest, I also became quite interested in political and social issues. This led me to join, some time in either my sophomore or junior year, our school chapter of Junior Statesmen of America, a club that dealt with contemporary political issues.

I think what interested me was government as an institution. I was familiar with the Catholic Church as an institution, and I wanted to learn more about how government worked. At that time, I did not connect the political process with the promotion of justice. I didn't know how these two things came together. I had them separated and compartmentalized in my mind. It would take me years to appreciate the extent to which issues of justice are intrinsically linked to the political process. In Junior Statesmen I learned the rudiments of the American political system in action.

Belonging to Junior Statesmen helped me broaden my experiences. Along with other delegates from our school chapter and one of our teachers, I took a trip to San Diego for a Junior Statesmen convention. I had never been on a trip of this kind and certainly not without an accompanying family member. But my parents supported me and did not object to my going. They saw it as an extension of my education. It was my mother to whom I explained these kinds of school activities and from whom I sought approval.

"Mother, the school is planning a trip," I would say, knowing that the magic word was *school.*

My mother always gave her unswerving support to any school-sanctioned activity. I trusted her and expected her to take care of getting my father's approval.

Unlike other Mexican families who, I learned, prohibited their children from participating in certain school activities, my family never did so if they felt they would further my education. My mother always spoke fondly about her brief school experience. She was an advocate for education.

My participation in Junior Statesmen probably led to my being selected, in the eleventh grade, as my school's representative to Girls State. This was a statewide convocation held in Sacramento and sponsored by the American Legion Women's Auxiliary. Delegates from a number of high schools throughout the state were invited.

The purpose of Girls State was to provide an opportunity for the delegates to learn more about the political process by creating a mock state government. Over the course of one week, the delegates performed the functions of the various executive, legislative, and judicial positions. We also elected representatives to a Girls Nation, where delegates created a mock federal government. I was not elected to the Girls Nation but was selected to perform some role in the mock state government.

About the process, I remember best the sophistication and creativity shown by some of the delegates who arrived fully prepared with placards and slogans intent on capturing some particular elected office. These kinds of political skills I knew I didn't possess. I was impressed.

Some of the more strident candidates surprised me, as did the girls who seemed primarily interested in lying in the sun in their skimpy bathing suits. It was up to each of us, individually, to find a niche in which to function. For those of us who got involved, the pace was hectic.

Attending Girls State was an honor, and the recognition gave me an even greater sense of personal responsibility. I was not sure exactly how I had been selected by my school, but I assumed it was for a combination of reasons such as scholarship and citizenship. I think that the teachers who performed the selection considered me to be a good citizen, and my parents, of course, were very proud of me.

One of the added attractions of going to Girls State was the opportunity to travel by train to Sacramento. I had to find a way to get to Hanford, where I caught the train, which already was carrying a number of delegates for the event from points farther south.

I didn't have a chaperone from my school, but there were statewide chaperones on the train who supervised our activities when we arrived in Sacramento. I had a wonderful time on the train trip. I especially remember the beautiful white table linen in the dining car where we ate. The service was impeccable, and it all seemed quite opulent to me.

In Sacramento I recall being very impressed during our visit to the governor's office. He wasn't in, but we got a tour of his office. His desk was beautifully carved and imposing. We learned that it had been made by prisoners at San Quentin.

These were impressive and powerful experiences for a kid like me from Visalia via Goshen Junction, Atoka, and the other small farm-working communities I had grown up in. It was pretty heady stuff.

As with my experience with the student newspaper and with Junior Statesmen, I don't recall many other Mexican girls participating in Girls State. There was one Mexican girl I met at Girls State who was from Los Angeles. I particularly remember her because she played the piano for us at one of our meetings. I remember thinking how privileged she was to be taking piano lessons. She told me that she had been studying the piano for several years, and I can recall thinking how much I would have liked the opportunity to do the same.

It was through my participation in the activities of groups such as Junior Statesmen and Girls State that I came to recognize what amounted to political heroes. Besides admiring Franklin Roosevelt, I also developed great respect for Eleanor Roosevelt. I thought of her as a humanitarian who cared about the welfare of all people.

By that time in high school I had also gotten into the practice of reading our local newspaper, the *Visalia Times-Delta* and of resenting the vicious attacks on Mrs. Roosevelt by Westbrook Pegler, the archconservative writer whose column appeared regularly in the paper. He hated her, and I enjoyed hating him, or feeling like I did.

Although I had very few opportunities to participate in purely social group activities, I do remember one particularly disastrous experience. For a reason I no longer recall, I attempted to join a Y-Teen club, which was a social group affiliated with the local YMCA. I was probably invited to join by some of the girls I knew in school. I had general knowledge of the fact that the Catholic Church did not permit a Catholic to attend a Protestant religious service. But I hadn't thought about it very much, and I was happy to be joining a group of school friends who seemed very nice and like a lot of fun.

I attended at least one meeting and then was invited to attend a dance sponsored by DeMolay, a boys' organization sponsored by the Masons. The dance was held at the beautiful Masonic lodge in town.

It was at the dance that the seriousness of my situation became apparent to me. When I had attended the Y-Teen meeting, I had been conscious that the girls were Anglo Protestants. However, it was a small group, and it seemed all right. But actually being inside a Masonic lodge with a large group of Anglo Protestant boys and girls was entirely different. I was the only Catholic—and a Mexican Catholic to boot!

I began to experience pangs of guilt about belonging to a Protestant group. So I went to confession and told the priest what I had done.

"It's forbidden," admonished the priest. "It's a sin, and you must never do this again."

Reduced to tears and enraged by my feelings of guilt, I said my act of contrition and left in utter confusion.

I dropped Y-Teen, but my anger at being chastised by the priest deepened my resentment against Church authority. I questioned the Church's right to tell me what I could or couldn't do. I had engaged in what I perceived to be a purely innocent activity.

The priest's condemning my action added still a new dimension to my confusion about what was right or wrong. Unable to reconcile my desire to join some Protestant school friends in a social club with the opposing dictates of the priest, I became convinced more than ever that my allegiance to the Church would be conditional. I would have to think about it.

❧❧❧

My high school years only furthered my sense that I was living in two distinct worlds. I concluded that it would be difficult, if not impossible, to reconcile them.

I knew that I wanted to succeed in high school. I desired something better than what Visalia had to offer or at least something better than what Visalia stood for. But to achieve this I knew I had to compete in a world that was really a world of *los americanos.* And I did.

Whether I liked it or not, being in college-track classes filled almost exclusively with Anglo students was, from my perspective, a privilege. It was the key to a future. It was the way out of Visalia. There was no other choice for me.

Although I was a successful student, during those years I was having a difficult time defining myself. Every success in school increasingly separated me from other Mexican students and, I felt, from Mexican culture as I had experienced it in the barrio. Being academically successful meant that I had to accept being different. My school friends became other academically successful girls.

This doesn't mean that I saw myself as an Anglo. You couldn't really do that in a place like Visalia. I knew when the term *American* was used, or when Mexican students referred to the *americanos,* the reference was to the ill-defined dominant others. The reference did not include me. Furthermore, it was never clear to me where the Portuguese fit into this picture. I was even more puzzled about the Armenians, who, with their dark complexions appeared different from the other *americanos.* But this was something no one seemed to talk about.

I was also dimly but painfully aware that early in my high school years I had been assigned to some vocational classes, while other college-prep students had been placed in academic classes such as ancient history. I came to this awareness when I found myself having to overcome gaps in my knowledge in my American history class. I was completely unaware, for example, of what the class was talking about when they discussed the classical origins of American democracy.

I was never told that I shouldn't think about college, but the community support was not always there for Mexican students. Segregation in classrooms reflected a broader reality. It was generally understood that Mexicans stayed in their own part of town, where minimal expectations were the rule. When a Mexican ventured into the Anglo part of town, heads turned. People stared. Even ten years later, when my brother Severo was an engineering student at the local community college, he encountered surprise from Anglo-American professionals in the community who learned of his interest in engineering.

"Where did you get that idea?" he was asked.

Fortunately, Severo was not swayed by those kinds of attitudes. In fact, he was encouraged by his teachers, and today Severo is a successful engineer and city manager.

I was aware of such differences at Visalia Union High School. I understood that the North American history I was studying was really more like northern European history. The literature we read in my English classes was for the most part European, not American. In fact, there was not very much that I could identify as American. And what I could identify, or what was being presented, as American I knew was not my history or that of my family.

I immersed myself in these subjects yet always retained the outsider's critical eye, as if to say, "You know, it's not really my history." I reacted to these subjects sometimes as a person of Mexican descent, sometimes as a Catholic, or sometimes simply as a nonnorthern European. Here and there I went so far as to correct my teachers when they made a statement that I felt was wrong.

"Some of the popes of the Catholic Church actually fathered children of their own," Miss Grant, my history teacher, once said.

I raised my hand.

"Yes, Frances. You have a question?"

"Miss Grant, you can't really say that about the popes."

I shocked myself for daring to challenge the teacher and also because I realized, the moment I opened my mouth, that I was being defensive. I didn't know anything about the history of the Catholic popes. After blurting out my objection, I experienced momentary panic. I felt that my ignorance was palpable and that my vulnerability had been laid bare. But Miss Grant diffused the tension.

"I understand what you mean, Frances. We need to question things like that in order to understand history," was her response. Or words to that effect.

I was both relieved and pleased. Here was an authority figure who didn't bat you down when you dared to question her authority. Furthermore, her kind smile suggested that I hadn't lost favor with her. She was my favorite teacher, and I would have been devastated had I incurred her wrath.

My sense of differences among people in high school extended to my recognizing differences in the barrio, and even differences within my own family. I knew that even though I was Mexican, I was not necessarily the same as other Mexicans.

Although the subject was never really discussed, I was becoming aware of differences within as well as outside the Mexican community. Some Mexicans had fair complexions, while others were dark. And I was aware that the Anglo community favored those with lighter skin.

I remember an acquaintance who was Mexican but was mistaken for Portuguese when she was admitted to the hospital once. She was very fair skinned. She recounted that when the nurses saw her record they exclaimed, "Oh, my goodness! We thought you were Portuguese." This was supposed to be a compliment, and she received it as such. When I heard about this I just registered it as one of many inconsistencies I was becoming cognizant of.

I also had a friend who was Mexican and who today in San Francisco would probably be considered Eurasian. Her eyes looked Asian and she had very fair skin. I knew that she was Mexican, but I also was beginning to recognize the range of differences in appearance among Mexicans.

These differences were not just physical but cultural as well. When we used to visit family friends in the barrio, I sometimes noticed that some of these families had pictures of Mexican heroes or presidents in their living room. I didn't know at the time that they were heroes or presidents; all I knew was that they seemed to represent something Mexican. I couldn't identify with these images. I was learning about other images in school, and what I saw in those living rooms was foreign to me.

I began to react to the fact that, even though my family was from New Mexico, we were being identified as Mexican either from Mexico or from Los Angeles, the great Mexican metropolis to the south. I resented this imposed identity.

It was in high school that I first became fully aware of the notion of being "foreign." I had never thought of myself this way. We understood that my father was foreign in that he was born outside the United States, in Mexico. My mother, however, we never saw as foreign—she was U.S. born. I was U.S. born. My siblings and I didn't know any other country. I resented being considered a foreigner and having my culture considered foreign. And I thought it was ridiculous for Spanish to be considered a "foreign" language.

I reacted by falling back on my New Mexico identity and that of my mother. We were distinct. We were from New Mexico. This meant not only that we were U.S. born and raised but also that we were not like most of the other Mexicans in Visalia, who were from different regions in Mexico or from Los Angeles. We were from New Mexico.

I was grappling with a sense of ethnic identity. Not that it consumed my life or that I obsessed about it. But my integration into predominantly Anglo classes at school, my awareness that most other Mexicans were not in my classes, and my awareness of the barrio's distinctiveness and that we no longer lived there—all these factors did consciously and unconsciously move me to deal with issues of ethnic identity in one way or another.

As I became sensitive to the existence of ethnicity, I began to have various emotions about myself and my family. I knew that I was Mexican. I knew that I was a particular kind of Mexican. I loved the Spanish language, although I was clearly becoming more English speaking. I loved the Mexican songs I had learned from my father. I loved my father's sense of humor, his sociability, and the confidence he displayed in his work skills.

Nevertheless, my alienation from my parents intensified as I grew older. My sense of isolation focused at times on my father's role as the autocrat, and I saw his harsh discipline as an extension of his control of my mother. And yet I could not empathize or identify with my mother's subordinate role. I saw the life of the Mexican woman as an endless cycle of childbearing and child rearing.

"*¡Ay! ¡Estoy que ya no aguanto!*" I can still hear my mother express her sense of utter frustration: Sometimes I think I can't endure any more!

I rejected the thought of a similar fate for myself. This despite the fact that, unconsciously, I accepted that Mother was central to our family life. She was the one we could always count on. My father, by contrast, could be volatile and unpredictable.

And so my resentment was bordering on some sense of shame, although I didn't think of it as shame at the time. I respected my parents, but I knew that I was changing. What I recognized was that there were dual worlds affecting me and that they didn't seem to be able to come together. All I knew was that I would need to work these feelings out by myself.

Between the time of our family's arrival in Corcoran in December 1937, when I was in first grade, and my entry into high school in 1945, my family had moved six times, not counting the numerous times that we made seasonal trips to places like San Jose or Tassajara following the crops.

This migratory existence had a cumulative effect on me. I felt that I was perpetually accommodating to change, the ever-changing scenes as I went from one school to another, never staying in any one school long enough to learn much about my classmates. Increasingly, I focused on myself and how I fit into these shifting realities.

By the time I entered high school, the one thing that I had resolved about my identity was that I was going to have to define myself. There was no one moment that I can point to as having made the difference. Rather, it was a gradual, and at first tentative, allowing myself to question and reject what didn't make sense to me while at the same time allowing myself to imagine other possibilities.

I had an active imagination. I could enjoy a fairy tale or a Betty Grable musical as much as I enjoyed immersing myself in a literary scene that I might be reading at any given time. I loved the images that language had the power to evoke. Reading allowed me to escape into other worlds. When we read in class "To thine own self be true," I took Shakespeare's words to heart. I knew there was a message in there somewhere. When we read *The Merchant of Venice,* I not only read Portia's speech on the quality of mercy, I *was* Portia.

I became increasingly conscious of the use of labels to stereotype people. I rejected, for example, being typed as a teenager. I disliked the term. The stereotype of the mindless and vacuous teenager was portrayed in comic strips like *Archie.* Ponytailed teenage girls in this strip just sat around the local ice cream parlor or drugstore sipping cokes and flirting with boys. They had nothing better to do.

This was not part of my adolescent experience or the experience of other serious girls that I knew. I rejected these types of labels because I was becoming aware of the power of language and becoming especially sensitive to its potential for being hurtful, particularly when associated with visual images.

Although I sought individuality, I was not unaffected by social influences around me. It was in high school, for example, that I acquired what could be called a more mainstream look in clothing and appearance. That look usually involved a skirt, a cashmere sweater, bobby socks, and Spaulding white buck shoes. This is what the best-dressed girls on campus wore. I wasn't Anglo, but I wanted to be part of the mainstream, not in a social sense, but in the sense of wanting to be in style.

I saw acquiring this mainstream look as a way of saying "I'm as good as anyone else."

Of course, my sweater wasn't cashmere nor were my shoes Spauldings. With the limited earnings from my part-time job, all I could afford was Kirby's shoes and clothes from J. C. Penney's or Mode-O-Day. But I did my best.

It was fashionable to wear a block sweater, either your own or your boyfriend's. You could earn a block letter in official school colors with an identifying school emblem by participating in after-school activities such as athletics or band. I had no time for these kinds of activities because I worked, nor did I have a boyfriend. However, a very nice Mexican boy I knew let me wear his block sweater for a while, which I enjoyed. I'm sure I thought I was really "styling."

SIX

Scholarship Girl

Language, perhaps more than anything else, reflected many of the changes I was undergoing by the time I entered high school. Although I had been raised bilingually (Spanish at home and English at school), English became my language of choice. I was not unusual in this. Most of the other Mexican students also spoke better English than Spanish. I retained a rich passive vocabulary in Spanish, but my active vocabulary was far more extensive in English.

English and my mastery of it, like my clothes, were indicative of my desire to be part of what I perceived to be the mainstream. But the mainstream to me didn't mean social acceptance in the town itself. In Visalia at that time, Spanish-speaking people lived apart and were not visible in places like the major movie house or the one good restaurant.

I understood that. Social nonacceptance was an acknowledged reality, even if it was not discussed. In fact, I probably did not even know the word *mainstream*. What I wanted was an education and its promise of a better life. I had unconsciously internalized my mother's faith and belief in its absolute value. By getting an education, I hoped to make a good life for myself.

To that end I worked at achieving clarity in my spoken English. I did not want to speak it with any pronounced accent, and I was conscious of trying to be super correct in how I enunciated. I was aware that my parents had accents. My father's pronounced accent was particularly noticeable on that rare occasion when he spoke English at home.

My mother's English was much better than my father's, fluent, as a matter of fact. But she had what I regarded as a southwestern accent. I had heard English spoken by people from Oklahoma and Texas, and my mother's accent sounded somewhat like theirs. She spoke English with what I thought was a soft southern sound.

I wondered to what extent my own English was southwestern. I thought that even my Spanish might have a southwestern characteristic. Accents were discomforting to me. I'm not sure whether this discomfort stemmed from the difference they suggested or the notion of not being understood. At the time, I probably did not think about its source, but the unease was there.

By consciously attempting to articulate English with as much clarity as possible, I hoped to avoid being misunderstood as I had been in junior high over the incident of the baby's tooth. I wanted to be understood. I was learning about language as a tool of communication, and losing my accent was a way of being able to communicate more effectively. During high school, aided by numerous opportunities to recite in front of a class, I started to feel good about my facility in English.

But gaining English did not mean totally losing Spanish. There's no question but that English was in ascendancy. Yet Spanish—at least my home Spanish—remained a very important part of my life.

Richard Rodriguez in *Hunger of Memory* writes about becoming aware that English came to represent a public language, while Spanish represented a private language. I can relate to that. I became increasingly aware of my public self, which was English-speaking. Spanish and how we conducted ourselves in it at home were very private matters.

At home I continued to speak Spanish with my parents, especially my dad. But when I spoke Spanish with him, I was acutely aware of the fact that my comprehension was infinitely better than my ability to speak. There was no question in my mind that it was becoming harder for me to explain some things in Spanish. I was conscious of the fact that while I was acquiring an extensive English vocabulary, my active vocabulary in Spanish remained limited. Still, I retained confidence in my total comprehension of the language.

My father, although he had at one time insisted on Spanish being spoken in the home, now expressed no concern over my loss of facility with it. Language was no longer the focus of parental control. He accepted whatever Spanish I could muster and avoided correcting me. He wasn't the kind of person to make his children feel shame over such a thing as language use.

On the contrary, during my high school years I became aware that he understood, as did my mother, that we were changing as a result of our English-language education. He was very respectful of me and the rest of his children as people. He respected my ideas and encouraged me to discuss them with him. I would ask questions in Spanish and he would say, "*Mira mi'ja*"—listen my daughter—and he'd go on to explain in Spanish. "*La juventud ahora está muy trastornada,*" he would say. "*Y la gente mayor también.*" (Young people, today, are in a state of confusion and disarray. Even the adults.)

"What do you mean?" I would ask, curious about what he might have experienced as a young man.

"When I was very little, the people in my village were very united, good people. I was orphaned at the age of three, but I was cared for. My grandmother took me into her home, and in the village I never lacked for something to eat.

"*Me daban frijoles, lo que tenían.*" (People shared.)

I would ask him about his parents.

"*Pues sí, m'hija. Me decían que mi papá había sido muy inteligente, muy empeñado.*" (People would tell me that my father had been an intelligent man and a hard worker.)

Empeñado was a word that was very familiar to me. From early childhood I had been taught that it was good to be *empeñada,* to show initiative and to work hard.

By the time I was a senior in high school, my father and I were more at peace with each other, and we were having adultlike conversations. Language use was no longer an issue for either of us.

My younger siblings grew up speaking more English than Spanish. As they grew up, my father became more relaxed about his Spanish-only policy at home. They did speak Spanish at home, but English conversation was no longer forbidden. Because my younger brothers and sisters spoke less Spanish, their experience with the language was different from Toni's and mine. In later years, though, we did speak English with my dad and he even spoke some with us.

I don't recall ever feeling shame about Spanish as a language. On the contrary, I loved the Spanish literature to which I had been introduced in school. What I did begin to notice was that there was an association between language use and generational differences. More and more Mexicans of my generation spoke English, even though we might still speak some Spanish at home.

Older Mexicans—my parents' generation—spoke predominantly Spanish and, in most cases, a Spanish that was not literate and was heavy with colloquialisms. This linguistic and cultural split meant that I could not readily identify with older Mexicans. Despite my formal study of Spanish, or perhaps because of it, I felt that I had lost my ability to communicate with them and that they could not communicate with me. Language became a form of rebuff or, perhaps more accurately, I used language that way. "I'm choosing not to include you. I'm choosing not to use your language."

This worked both ways. I think my distancing myself from the barrio was not just a physical distancing but a linguistic one as well. I hadn't lived in the barrio long enough to pick up barrio Spanish, and now that we were living outside the barrio, I didn't reach out to "my own people." I actually didn't know who my own people were anymore. In trying to find my identify and to assert myself, I found affirmation in more than one world. I found it in several different worlds—English and Spanish, Mexican and Anglo, home and school—but not consistently. Mentally, I compartmentalized contending areas of my life and I hadn't yet figured out how to integrate them, unaware even that this was what I needed to do.

Although my loss of some ability to speak Spanish alienated me to an extent from the Spanish-speaking community, at the same time this loss was accompanied by my greatly increased facility in spoken English, which empowered me in the English-speaking community. I was becoming aware of the power of language as a communication tool, and I had options—I had an English option and a Spanish one.

At times I seemed to have the capacity to withhold one or the other. Sometimes I would do this unconsciously. I felt that my knowledge of Spanish gave me power in some situations. This was part of the parallelism in my life.

I knew, for example, in dealing with Anglo teachers, particularly those who were not totally sympathetic, that I had a world that they didn't and couldn't share. Language was part of that world, as were concepts conveyed in that language. *Hogar,* the full meaning of "home." Where was that to be found in English? *Humildad,* "humility" or "modesty." Where was *humildad* found in English as a positive attribute? In English it was an attitude to be avoided, but in Spanish it was a desirable attribute. Language—both English and Spanish—enabled me to examine various concepts in a cultural context.

Although I retained some level of bilingual ability, I never used a mixture of Spanish and English in conversational speech—what later came to be called "Spanglish." Many of the other Mexican students used Spanglish in talking among themselves. While I wasn't uncomfortable hearing it, I rejected the mixing of the two languages.

Some girls, for example, might say, "*Se ve muy* handsome." (He looks very handsome.) If I didn't know how to say a word such as *handsome* in Spanish, I might say, "*Me gusta como se ve.*" (I like the way he looks.) Or I might simply say in English, "Handsome, isn't he?"

In my efforts to avoid using Spanglish, I lost both spontaneity and grace of expression. But I did learn new words, because I would look them up later. *Es guapo. Es bien parecido.* Handsome. Good-looking. I focused on what I thought might be subtle distinctions in both languages.

I wasn't comfortable mixing languages because I was working at perfecting my English, and I saw Spanglish as a step in the wrong direction, or worse. Further, I knew that my father did not favor mixing the two languages. He believed we should speak "good" Spanish as much as possible. Although my father called himself unlettered and spoke of his lack of formal education, he attempted to articulate and to express his ideas clearly in Spanish.

I knew that he respected the Spanish language and was conscious of how he used it. It was from him that I inherited a sense of Spanish as a rich language that can and should be used correctly. I was trying to achieve a high standard, and that included the proper use of both English and Spanish.

For similar reasons, I also avoided use of Mexican slang—what was referred to as *pochismos.* Lots of Mexican kids used this language. Often it was a Spanglish version of an English word, but sometimes it was almost impossible to guess the origins of a particular term. Slang expressions included words such as *wátchale* (be careful), *vato* (guy), *gavacho* (Anglo-American), *chota* (police), *chanza* (chance), *jalar* (to work), and *borrego* (stupid). I never heard these words at home. My dad didn't use language like this—he didn't approve of it. Certainly my mother didn't either.

Now, many years later, as I listen to the Spanglish of an artist like Guillermo Gómez-Peña, I can appreciate the power of such language in the exploration of "the territory of cultural misunderstanding."

Identity for me in high school was not only about ethnicity but about gender as well. I became more aware of my identity as a young woman due to the fact that, as I advanced in my schoolwork, I sometimes found myself not only the sole Mexican in class but also the sole girl or one of very few girls.

In my senior physics class, for example, I was the only girl. In that case, being the only girl was not a particularly good experience. For me, the message clearly was that physics was part of a "man's world." Girls simply didn't do physics. We had to have lab partners, two or three, depending on the experiment. I had not acquired the kind of aggressiveness that one needs to assert oneself with men or boys. Consequently, I usually ended up in the secondary position of note taking, while the boys enjoyed the rewards of hands-on lab experience. It was very clear to me what was happening, but I really didn't see myself being able to overcome my disadvantage.

I was not the only girl who was subject to the attitude that girls are not equal to boys. I remember one boy who did very well academically but who had a brilliant sister. In fact, I thought she was a genius. I remember her brother, however, putting her down. He would say, "My sister is not a woman."

What he was saying was that because his sister was exceptionally smart she was not a *real* woman. This view coincided with similar views expressed in the Mexican community about the proper role of women. Women had a role, but it was not as a brain.

"*Que lástima. Tanta educación, y ¿ pa' qué? Siempre se casó.*" (What a pity! All that education, and then she got married anyway.)

Why, I would ask myself, was it a waste for a married woman to be educated? Was education really intended only for men and for unmarried women, women who, somehow, had no sex lives?

Some of my teachers, regrettably, reinforced this gender bias. My algebra teacher, an older woman, clearly favored the boys. I didn't regard her as an especially good teacher, primarily because she keyed in on the boys and neglected the girls. She was very obvious in directing much of her chalkboard demonstrations to specific boys. While she worked with the boys on solving problems, I felt that I was left to work out problems on my own. Unlike many of my other teachers who were mentors to me, this teacher was neither a guide nor an inspiration.

Despite my inability to do anything about this gender bias at the time, I rejected the idea that girls were restricted to certain secondary roles. I don't know how gender conscious I was altogether, but I knew that I wanted to compete at all levels in school—and that included competing with boys. My sense was that there was no reason why I couldn't have access to any opportunities that might be out there. I did not believe that I had to restrict my aspirations simply because I was a girl.

I was supported in this belief by my family, including my father, who always encouraged me to do my best. Despite his autocratic manner, he never insisted that I accept a traditional female role. My mother was also an advocate for me in this regard.

At every opportunity, she would remind us of her dream that her children would receive the education that had been denied to her. I knew that my grandmother and my mother had worked hard, had been productive, and had acted as partners to their husbands in family enterprises. In this regard I drew my inspiration from both of them. I respected their ability to work hard and perhaps, unconsciously, desired to achieve in school what my mother had been unable to achieve.

Despite the many changes that I was experiencing during high school, I was basically a happy person, although I also think that I experienced more than my full share of adolescent anxiety and anger.

I felt good about myself in my ability to do well in school. I had a sense of purpose and of direction. I began to believe that I would go on to college. As I developed self-confidence, I began to soften my earlier more hostile attitudes and to relax.

What anger I had exhibited toward my parents began to subside. I began to appreciate how lucky I was to have the family support that was always there for me. At the same time, my parents seemed more comfortable in allowing Toni and me to make our own decisions, according to certain behavioral expectations. There was never any predetermined career path set for us. We were allowed to evolve for ourselves.

During high school I didn't just devote myself to attending classes and studying. I also worked throughout those four years. While occasionally I would still accompany my father to pick crops in the fields, this practice became less frequent, especially since my father was less involved in it himself. The family was now settled in town. Work now involved getting part-time jobs in Visalia.

I knew that, despite our having bought a bigger house, my family still faced economic hardship, especially with several growing children. Toni had dropped out of school and had started working full-time. I, too, wanted to do my share. At least I wanted to earn money so that I could provide for my own needs. Though my parents provided us with basic necessities, they did not give us an allowance. The concept of an allowance was in fact unknown to us. My parents bought us what we needed when we needed it, within their ability to provide it.

In my first paying job as a freshman, I was a waitress at the Hotel Johnson, the only hotel in town. Before that, I had done volunteer work at the county Tuberculosis and Health Association. The hotel restaurant was the only fine restaurant in town, and the tips were good. But that job didn't last long.

In my sophomore year, however, I got a job at the Roxy, a theater that featured Spanish-language films and "B" western movies. I worked there for the next three years. At first I worked as an usherette. I was then promoted to "candy girl," and I worked the concession stand. My final promotion was to the position of theater cashier. As the sole cashier, for all practical purposes I had the same level of responsibility as the theater house manager. He just got paid more. But I recognized that this was the best job opportunity I could hope for in Visalia.

On week nights, I worked from five-thirty to eight-thirty, with little time to get home for something to eat after school. It became my practice to eat dinner at a Chinese cafe near the theater. The food was substantial, tasty, and very low priced. After work, I walked home and was able to start my homework by around nine or nine-thirty.

I enjoyed my job at the Roxy. It provided me with an income, a sense of independence, and an expanded view of community life. Although it was predominantly a Spanish-language theater, it also showed English-language films on weekends. These were mostly cowboy movies, along with long-running adventure serials. The audience for the English-language movies were the poor "Okies" and "Arkies" who lived in and around Visalia. The westerns featured stars such as Lash LaRue, Gene Autry, Hopalong Cassidy, and Roy Rogers.

When I worked as an usherette I would catch glimpses of the films being shown. Sometimes, during my breaks, if the film seemed interesting, I would find a seat and watch large portions of it. Occasionally, if it was a really good film, I would stay after work and watch the whole thing.

I didn't much care for the cowboy movies or the serials. I hadn't yet learned to appreciate the westerns as the fantasies that they really were, but I did listen patiently as the customers raved about their favorite cowboys.

The serials were tiresome cliff-hangers. Each week's segment of a serial ended with a highly melodramatic scene that depicted the hero or the heroine facing sure death. In the following week's segment, what had seemed to be an inevitable disaster would be averted, but the conclusion would, again, be a new impending peril.

My favorite movies were some of the Spanish-language ones. I especially enjoyed those with Mexican stars such as Jorge Negrete and Pedro Armendáriz, who were very handsome and chivalrous. Their films, which were really Mexican cowboy movies, I accepted as fairy tales. I knew virtually nothing about Mexico or Mexican history, so I took it all in as undifferentiated adventure. The characters were either all good or all bad. Negrete and Armendáriz might just as well have been knights in shining armor and the women princesses.

These stories were not too different from the fairy tales that I had enjoyed reading as an adolescent. I delighted in seeing Negrete, for example, being so good with a gun, able to put a bullet hole in a villain's forehead, dead center. I accepted it as fantasy, assuming that this wasn't really Mexico. It was good versus evil, with good prevailing.

I also enjoyed the Cantinflas movies. He was the Mexican equivalent of Charlie Chaplin. In his roles, Cantinflas was an ingratiating clown figure who invariably found himself in some incongruous situation. Out of place in Mexican high society, Cantinflas proceeded to use his peculiar logic to deflate the pretentiousness around him. He poked fun at all upper-class hypocrisy. His low-slung trousers, hanging precariously from a single suspender, and his little bowler-type hat were his trademarks. In his comic awkwardness, he got into one jam after another and kept you in suspense as you waited for him to fall on his face. But he never did. He always persevered and emerged a lovable, comic hero. The audience loved him, and so did I.

I probably never would have seen his films if I hadn't worked at the Roxy. It would have been my loss. Unaware of it at the time, I was learning a lot from these black-and-white Mexican films. They pointed to social inequalities in Mexico that I would not have been aware of otherwise. These films were very well-made.

As a theater cashier, I had what I considered to be a wonderful job. The theater hours were short. I opened the theater and sold tickets until the show started. Then I worked on portions of my financial report while I attended to late arrivals. After a short break, I returned to the box office for a while longer to wait for other people who might come for the second show. But because of these short hours, the amount of money I could earn was extremely limited.

Still, I enjoyed the work, especially when I became a cashier. One of the things I liked about my job was watching the different people who came to the movies. I was very conscious of the fact that I was witnessing the community up close as they filed past me. Faces, attire, personal habits—I would contemplate them all.

Like my sister Toni, I helped my family by working. With the money I made I bought my school lunch as well as my meals during the weekend when I had to work. I also bought my school supplies and my clothes. I was even able to help Toni buy a used car that she needed to get to work each day. We called it "our" car, although I never drove it. We both understood the car was needed for work. It was not intended for pleasure.

Working while I was in high school also made me feel independent and self-sufficient. I, of course, was no stranger to work. It had always been a part of my life. But work was different now. I was working on my own and not with my father. I felt more independent from him. I think my parents treated me now as a bit more of an adult since I was earning my own paycheck. I was even able to save some money, which was of some help later when I made plans to go to college.

While I wouldn't say that I had no social life during high school, it certainly was very limited.

I didn't really date. For one, my parents didn't look with favor on the concept of dating. This was in fact true for most other Mexican families and their teenage children. Dating as a social process—going out on dates—was not a Mexican custom. It was something that the Anglo kids did. I think that we, as Mexicans, accepted that there were cultural differences with respect to dating.

To me dating was also a prelude to getting married, and I wasn't interested in getting married. That's why I had broken up with Peter. I wanted something more in my life than getting married and having children. Consequently, boys were a part of my high school life only as friends or acquaintances. The fact that I didn't date, as did many of the

Anglo girls, didn't stunt my social development. There were plenty of other girls in school who also didn't date.

There was one Mexican boy in high school who was interested in me. He was a year or two ahead of me, and sometime during my freshman year, he began to talk to me. We went to a few social events together, but I didn't really see these as dates.

However, he began to get serious. He had joined the armed services, and one time, when he was home on leave, he brought me some gifts, including a ring, which was intended as an engagement ring. Earlier, he had also given me his Visalia Union High block sweater to wear. I had accepted it at first not thinking about the implications. I soon began to realize what I was getting into.

But I wasn't interested in him as a boyfriend. And since initially I hadn't been serious about him, I hadn't felt guilty about not discussing him with my mother. But this time the situation was not me seeing a boy without my parents' knowledge, as I had done with Peter. This was a boy who was intent on marrying me.

It took some courage, but I brought the subject up with my mother.

"Look, mother," I said. "I want to show you all these things that Andrew gave me."

"Oh!" she said, with a look of apprehension on her face. Displaying her usual reticent manner, she didn't ask me for details. But I felt compelled to give some account.

"I think he gave me this ring and these presents because he wants to marry me. I think I should return them."

I felt foolish at the sound of my own words, both knowing and not knowing what I had gotten myself into.

"*Pues sí, m'hija,*" she said. "It's not right to keep any of these things. You should return them."

I must have breathed a sigh of relief at that point. It was extremely rare for me to confide in my mother about anything except the most ordinary school matters. Here I was dealing with a marriage proposal, and I needed reassurance from someone. It's likely that, in those days, almost any young Mexican girl in Visalia would have been happy to receive a proposal from a guy as nice as Andrew.

How should a girl deal with a really nice guy in a situation like this? Did I really know what I was doing? I wondered. So I followed my mother's advice. I returned everything, including the ring and the sweater. He seemed to accept that all we could really be was friends. He understood that I wasn't interested in a serious relationship, but for the rest of my high school years we remained in touch. He would write to me from wherever he was stationed.

One of the reasons I wasn't interested in Andrew was that I still cared for Peter. Neither Andrew nor anyone else I knew could compare to Peter. When I had broken up with him, I had decided that if it wasn't going to be Peter, there wouldn't be anybody else. I didn't see myself dating either Mexican or Anglo boys. I had thought the world of Peter. I thought that he was the most special boy I had ever known. To this day he remains a model to me.

Although I never attended any of the school dances, I did decide to go to my senior prom. Since I didn't have a boyfriend and no one had asked me as the date of the prom approached, I decided to get my own date. I invited a boy whom I had met through student government. He had been president of the student body and had graduated. I thought of him as a nice boy, serious about his work. I trusted him.

When I called him, we simply chatted for a short while, and I told him that I wanted to go to the prom. "I have no one to go with," I said. "I thought you'd like to go with me." He agreed readily, and we had a very casual conversation.

"What time shall I pick you up?" he asked. We agreed on a time, and I was delighted. I looked forward to enjoying myself without having to worry about any boyfriend-girlfriend implications. As it happened, we did have a good time.

Some dances that I did attend were not at school but in the local Portuguese Hall, a public arena. This was the era of the big bands, and some of the more popular bands made circuit stops in Visalia. One big band that I remember was Gene Krupa's. I don't know why, but these bands seemed to perform primarily for Mexican audiences. They also played in nearby Tulare.

I had heard about some of the bands coming to town. I wanted to go, and so did Toni. I talked with my mother, who said it was up to my father. As frequently happened with this type of delicate negotiation, I was the emissary. He agreed but insisted that he would drive us to the dance. He paid for Toni and me and said he would remain outside the hall until the dance was over.

Inside the hall, the girls who didn't come with a partner would line up on one side of the hall and the boys would line up on the other. The girls had to wait to be asked to dance. While you waited you checked out who among the boys were the good dancers. The boys did likewise with the girls. I remember not liking this arrangement. It was like a cattle call for the girls.

At these dances I began to see that the Mexican community was much bigger than I had realized. I saw many new faces. There were many attractive and well-dressed couples. Many were skillful dancers. I remember thinking, "Who are all these people? Where are they from?" I especially liked the really good dancers who were all dressed up. The dancing rage at the time was the jitterbug, and some of these couples were excellent jitterbuggers.

I liked to watch the dancers, but I wasn't just a wallflower. I loved to dance and did so at these events. Even though I had never taken lessons, I had become a good dancer just by observing others and picking up their techniques. I think I also acquired my love for dancing and ability to dance from my father, who was a beautiful dancer. I have fond memories of him in New Mexico dancing with my mother.

Besides the handsome couples, there were also some *pachucos* in their zoot-suits and *pachucas* in their tight black skirts who attended these dances. The *pachucos* were particularly agile and theatrical in their dance movements. They jitterbugged in the same style as everyone else but were more audacious in their gyrations.

Because the *pachucas* always represented a threat, the other girls and I avoided the bathrooms in order not to run into any of them. The exchange of nasty looks was common, but I was careful to avoid confrontation.

However, I remember hearing that at one of these public dances a boy from New Mexico had been stabbed to death by some *pachucos*. The element of danger was always there. My father was aware of this danger, and that's why, even though he allowed us to go to a few of these dances, he always waited for us outside. From time to time he would peek inside to see if we were all right. Toward the end of the dance he was allowed to come in without paying and wait for us at the back of the hall. When the dance ended, he drove us home.

Although I didn't attend many dances, I listened to music at home. Toni and I had purchased a radio/record player console, and we bought ourselves some records. Music was one of the interests that she and I shared. We were curious about different sorts of music, and when we bought albums, we studied the covers religiously.

I continued to love traditional Mexican music—the *rancheras*—that my father used to sing at home or listen to on a Spanish-language radio station. But my musical tastes were also shifting and becoming somewhat eclectic.

When we moved in to our new home, the adjacent little house, *la casita,* was rented to a single lady who was black. She owned a lot of records by black artists, what seemed like a ton of records compared to the small number Toni and I had purchased. She also had her own record player.

"I bought some new 'reckerts,'" Dorothy would say. I was intrigued by the way she spoke. She and our neighbor, Essie, were the only African Americans I had ever known. And like Essie, Dorothy was very quiet. She played her records softly into the late hours at night, and I used to wonder if she was lonely.

But we didn't ask her for any explanations. We respected her privacy, as she respected ours. Of the music, I can remember recognizing very little except the Ink Spots, who were very popular at the time.

I kind of liked Frank Sinatra but didn't buy many of his records. I liked some western music, such as that by the Sons of the Pioneers. I could detect the similarities between what was called "cowshit-kicking music" and the *rancheras* with which my father had so familiarized us. I liked some of the big band music like Glenn Miller. And the easy-listening music of Fred Waring was melodic and soothing to me.

But our favorite albums were European classical. I didn't know much about this type of music but I enjoyed listening to it and learning about it.

Religion continued to be an important part of my life during high school. I considered myself an obedient Catholic, though not devout. And because I loved music, it seemed natural for me to join our church choir. I especially enjoyed singing the Latin hymns. My younger siblings attended Catholic school, and although I had never had this experience, I felt that I was a full member of the church. It continued to define me, in part.

The choir was composed of other Catholic kids from the public high school, with me being the only Mexican. Although we sang together, the association did not lead to particularly strong friendships, at least not in my case. My choir experience was a continuing reminder that, in Visalia, religion did not necessarily bring people together.

Like most other kids in high school, I think I remember my senior year best of all. It was a hectic, confusing, but exciting time. My senior year revolved around the issue of college. Would I go to college? If so, what college? What was involved in going to college? Could I afford it?

At first I didn't really have any understanding of what college was all about. It was an absolute unknown. I had no idea, for example, that college, like high school, was a four-year experience. I had no notion of what a college degree entailed. It wasn't until about my junior year that the concept of college became a little clearer. This was the result of the networking I was doing with other academically oriented girls. Besides becoming aware of the state college system, I also became aware of the U.C. system and of Stanford.

Although the idea of going to college still seemed quite abstract, what was clearer to me than ever was that I wanted to leave Visalia. During high school, I became even more aware that there were few, if any, real opportunities for me in "the valley." In these farming communities I hadn't had the love of the land that I had associated with life in New Mexico.

My younger siblings, whose entire early life, unlike my own, was spent in Visalia, did not understand why I disliked the town. They grew up being happy there. To them Visalia is home. To me New Mexico was home.

I had a very simplistic notion of the world then. I really had known only two places. To me, New Mexico and my feelings for it were very real and very important. New Mexico was my extended family and the warmth and love that I recall there. New Mexico was my sense of place.

Visalia, on the other hand, represented to me the dehumanizing and crowded migrant camps. To me the barrio and Visalia as a whole seemed extensions of these camps. Visalia was an agricultural community and little else. It meant ranches and migrant workers.

These limits particularly restricted Mexicans like me. I knew that there were many places in town where Mexicans were not welcome. I knew that downtown job opportunities for Mexicans were almost nonexistent.

But it was not only that I was Mexican American. It was the economy of the place. There were few professional occupations for anyone in Visalia. There were few doctors and nurses, for example. When you walked down Main Street and looked in storefronts, you didn't see many models of professional advancement. This was true for both Mexicans and *americanos.* At least there were our teachers.

I'm not sure that I was fully aware of what a career meant, much less a profession. I certainly was not aware of wanting to become a teacher at that point. All I knew was that anything of importance, anything of mobility, anything better was not going to happen in Visalia. It had to be elsewhere.

I prepared myself for that elsewhere. And so too did the other girls in my group. By our senior year we looked forward to going away. And we didn't think of it as a particularly radical idea to leave Visalia. It seemed like a natural step forward.

There were advisers in school who were supposed to help us prepare for college. But I didn't make much use of them. My real counselors about the specifics of applying to college were some of my teachers. The most encouraging and helpful was Miss Helen Grant, my history teacher. As I recall, Miss Grant was a U.C. Berkeley alumna. In any case, it was she who first talked to me about the possibility of going to Berkeley.

One of the first things I had to do was to take a U.C. system–wide exam in my senior year. The purpose of this exam was not clear to me, since I already had good grades. It's likely that, like the Scholastic Aptitude Test (SAT), which was introduced some years later, the examination was intended to test verbal and mathematical reasoning skills.

I had no way of knowing how to prepare myself, and there was nothing special that I could do. However, Miss Grant boosted my self-confidence by assuring me that I would do all right. I later learned that the examination included the Subject-A English writing test, which, if you passed it, exempted you from the freshman-year Subject-A English requirement.

On examination day, I took a bus to Fresno, a distance of about fifty miles. My memories of the experience remain shrouded in a fog of uncertainty. The whole process seemed impersonal and detached from reality as I knew it. In the testing auditorium with its tiered seating, I was surrounded by total strangers. The auditorium itself seemed cold. To the best of my recollection, I focused on the task at hand and gave it my best shot.

Some time later I learned that I had performed satisfactorily on the examination. I was admitted to the University of California at Berkeley and wouldn't have to take Subject A. I still wasn't sure what all that meant, but I was euphoric. I felt that a whole new world was opening up to me. My teachers were generous in their praise. "We expect good things from you" was the type of congratulatory remark I received. Suddenly, I somehow felt more grownup. It was really going to happen. I was going to leave Visalia. I was going to Berkeley.

But passing an examination was one thing; actually getting to Berkeley was another. I didn't have much money, nor could my parents help pay any of my college expenses. I had been saving some of my salary, but that alone would not be enough.

"Don't worry," Miss Grant told me. "You can apply for a U.C. alumni scholarship. I'll help you with that."

"What is a scholarship? How do I do this?" There seemed to be no end to my questions.

Miss Grant, in her usual confident and reassuring manner, explained to me what an alumni scholarship was and the process involved. It meant being nominated in a regional competition and submitting my grades as well as being interviewed by local U.C. alumni. It was probably Miss Grant who saw to it that I was nominated by the school.

She also arranged for my interview. I wasn't sure what to expect. There was nothing really I could do to prepare for it. "You have the intelligence and the knowledge to do well," Miss Grant kept reassuring me. I trusted her, and she continued to express confidence in me.

My interview took place at the home of a local physician, a Dr. Weiss I believe, who was a U.C. alumnus. I wasn't the only one being interviewed; there were other students from nearby school districts. I don't remember much about the actual interview. I think the panel of three or four alumni asked about the classes I had taken and about what I wanted to do in the future.

What I most vividly recall about the occasion is the get-acquainted hour just before the interviews. We were all seated in an attractive, spacious living room. Someone to my left began passing around a full bowl of white cheese dip, and I was the first person they passed it to. I had never seen a cheese dip before in my life.

It looked like soft, creamy gruel to me. I can still see myself sitting there, transfixed, with this bowl in my lap. I had a moment of panic as I sat there thinking, "What do I do with this?" I remember looking around the room trying to make eye contact with someone who might rescue me. Completely bewildered, I passed the bowl on to the next person and avoided making a fool of myself. I don't remember getting a taste of that dip.

Other events of that evening remain hazy in my mind. For the rest of that evening, my entire body felt obvious and clammy. To my credit, I recovered sufficiently to work my way out of this dilemma, somehow, without committing any major gaffes.

However, greater credit is probably due to our thoughtful alumni hosts, who managed to keep the evening flowing smoothly. As scholarship applicants, we were an awkward and motley group. We seemed to have nothing in common except our social unease.

During the actual interview process, I had no way of gauging the success of my performance. But apparently I did well enough, because shortly thereafter I received the good news that I had been awarded a scholarship to go to Berkeley. I was elated. I was two feet off the ground.

I was to be an "alumni scholar," the only recipient from Visalia Union High School. It was a one-year three-hundred-dollar scholarship and would cover my college fees and the cost of books for the year. That represented a fortune to me! It was everything I had ever dared hope for. I would leave Visalia and go away to college.

I don't recall that at the school a big deal was made out of my receiving the scholarship. However, word did get out, and both teachers and students were generous in expressing their good wishes. I was especially touched by the spontaneity with which fellow students congratulated me. It made me feel good. Miss Grant was delighted and very proud of me. She expressed her delight to my parents at a school open house.

The emotion in this scene I remember well, though the details themselves are blurry. I remember being in the classroom the evening of the open house and seeing my parents walk into the room. I don't remember exactly what was said, but I have this image of my parents entering the room, my looking from them to my teacher, and my sensing that my two worlds were finally meeting.

My family thoroughly supported me. They were proud of me, although at the time they didn't fully comprehend what it all meant. I myself wasn't sure. They understood that the scholarship would mean my leaving home. I'm sure that they thought about it, but they never put pressure on me not to accept it. They supported me in whatever I wanted.

Sometime after it was announced that I had won the scholarship, the school principal actually came to our house. He wanted to know from my parents if they, in fact, approved of my going to Berkeley.

"Were there any problems?" I asked my mother when I learned that the school principal had spoken to them.

"Oh, no," my mother said. "I told him that we were happy that you're going to college. I told him that my dream has always been that my children get a good education."

The school, of course, didn't just hand out a check. The scholarship award was deposited at the university's financial office. At the time of registration, I was issued the first portion of the award.

While I received encouragement and support from many of my teachers, I also had an interesting and puzzling encounter with our dean of students. When she found out that I was going to Berkeley, she called me in and wanted to counsel me.

"You will need a budget," she told me in a stern tone. She was being very formal, because she didn't even know me.

I sat there thinking, "Here's a lady who doesn't understand that I have no money except for what the scholarship will provide." I had no concept of the type of budget she wanted to talk about.

When we had studied personal budgeting as part of our senior problems class, I had done the budgeting exercises, but they had seemed irrelevant. As presented in the textbook, the concept of a "family budget" assumed a reliable source of family income. I had been used to scraping together what I could to make ends meet. A steady source of family income was never taken for granted. What I did understand clearly was that I had to work, and work hard.

The poor woman then added what I thought was insult to injury by saying, "You'll also need to budget enough for nylon stockings." I didn't say anything but I thought, "Oh, lady, I'm going to need a lot more than nylon stockings!" I was polite and deferential to her but didn't give her a second thought after leaving her office. I felt comfortable ignoring her, knowing I still had a lot to figure out for myself.

I began to receive information about Berkeley. Information packets were sent to me from the campus. I also learned a bit more about Berkeley when a former California Maid of Cotton, at that time a U.C. freshman, came to our school to talk about the campus.

She showed a film about Berkeley, or "Cal," as it was sometimes referred to. These were the years, in the mid to late 1940s, when Cal was winning football games, so she showed a Cal Bears film, probably a Rose Bowl game, which wasn't particularly meaningful to me. I didn't go to football games at my own school and didn't know much about football. I was going to Cal for other reasons.

The end of my senior year at Visalia Union High School and my graduation remain poignant memories to me. Everything in my life seemed to be rushing to some kind of conclusion. At that point I was more a bit apprehensive about the future than I was excited.

Preparations for the actual graduation ceremony felt like a rite of passage. As graduating seniors, we were suddenly a group apart. We spent hours in the football stadium practicing what we needed to do. Between practice sessions we sat on the lawns watching the other kids scurrying to their classes. I remember thinking, "I don't have to go to class here anymore." I looked at the buildings that I would no longer be walking through. I didn't have to do anything anymore. I was leaving behind a comfortable routine.

I think that other seniors also sensed, as I did, that we were leaving behind something that had held us together for four years, a link that would no longer be there. It was a kind of separating out. We would have nothing to tie us together after graduation. That's probably why, repeatedly, we wrote in one another's yearbooks, "Let's stay in touch."

Graduation and preparing for it was an emotional time. It was a growing-up time. I had felt pretty grown-up during my four years at Visalia Union High School, but graduation made it seem more real. This time it was a lonely feeling—a scary, lonely grown-up feeling.

"Good luck," we would say to one another. "Best of luck in the future!" But probably very few of us had a clear idea what that future might be.

Nevertheless, it was also a time to celebrate. We had completed high school! I was the first in my family to do so. We were going on. I celebrated with the other girls in our support group. We were all going to college, although no one besides me to Berkeley. Still, we had reached our goal of getting into college.

To celebrate, we organized a dinner for ourselves at a restaurant called Estrada's Spanish Kitchen. We had a wonderful time. We felt like a little sorority. We vowed to get together in a year to discuss our college experiences and to stay in touch. Unfortunately, none of this ever happened. But it was important that we had stuck together through four years of high school and had remained focused on our goal.

Graduation day in June dawned sunny and very warm, typical valley heat. That day went pretty much as usual at home. While it was a special day for me, home activities still had to be attended to. My younger siblings had their needs too. The youngest was barely five. I spent the early part of the day worrying about transportation. I couldn't imagine walking all the way to campus in my new high-heeled shoes, and with my dad and Toni both working, I fretted about getting there on time.

Later that day I began to get ready. I had bought a very nice blue suit and white pumps for the event. It was a bit hectic trying to gather together various members of the family. There was even serious doubt about my father being able to get home from the fields in time to attend the ceremony. But we managed somehow.

The ceremony took place in the football stadium. It was very clear and warm that evening. As we sat in the bleachers, the harsh stadium lights and highly amplified voices drew my attention away from any sense of ceremony. They were soon calling out all the names of the graduating seniors.

Frances Esquibel. When they got to my name, I felt a rush of anxiety, but it passed quickly. We all were now in a hurry to get through the formalities. The ceremony seemed to end almost as soon as it started. Then we dispersed.

Unlike other students, I didn't receive lavish graduation gifts from my parents. Extravagant gift giving wasn't really a part of our family tradition. Love from our parents did not come to us wrapped in fancy ribbons. They had a special way of expressing their love and support. That was very important to me.

The gold-cross pendant and matching earrings from my mother seemed such a natural gesture on her part. Religious symbols were so much a part of her life. "*Que Dios me la bendiga a m'hija*" (May God bless you, my daughter) was my father's blessing, his gift to me that evening. That's all I needed. That's all I wanted.

Toni was, as usual, thinking of my welfare. She bought me a set of attractive luggage as a going-away present. Ever the thoughtful older sister, she included a nice pajama set that would be comfortable for late-night studying.

I remember being conscious of my parents' pride. I also remember that, suddenly, my younger siblings seemed so very young. I had a sense of being older, like Toni, not as a matter of chronology but rather as a matter of relinquishing a position within the family. I would soon be gone.

Imagining myself outside my family circle made that family circle more real somehow. It was a strange feeling knowing that what I had wanted for so long was actually happening. I was leaving. I was happy but somber.

We didn't have a big family celebration or dinner after my graduation. But that evening, or perhaps it was the next, there was a big swimming party at the home of one of the wealthier students. Everyone who was graduating was invited. Although I didn't know how to swim, I went anyway. It was a lavish home and there must have been about one hundred people there.

I said good-bye to many of my classmates, both Mexicans and Anglos. Actually, there were few other Mexicans who graduated. My yearbook shows only about twenty out of almost three hundred seniors. But even the large majority of Anglos, I knew, were not going on to college as I was. I knew that most of them would remain in Visalia or some place like Visalia. I felt sad and even humble now that I was leaving. There was nothing else that I could do here.

I had graduated.

SEVEN

Off to College

After the euphoria of high school graduation had faded a bit, I had to confront the reality of going away to college. My immediate concern was with finances. My Berkeley alumni scholarship was not going to be enough to see me through the first year.

The three-hundred-dollar scholarship would be awarded over a period of two semesters. Of the hundred-fifty dollars I had for the fall, I had to use eighty-five dollars for fees and books. That left me with about sixty-five dollars for other expenses, including living expenses. I had a modest savings account from my high school job, but it still was not going to be enough.

I knew that I would have to work at least part-time while attending the university. Through the University of California at Berkeley alumni in Visalia, I learned about a student placement office on the campus that would assist me in finding a job. What I was looking for, also on the advice of the U.C. alumni, was a job working for a family in return for room and board.

I decided that the best thing would be for me to take a quick one-day trip to Berkeley early that summer to see about securing a job for the fall semester. I'll never forget my nervous tension during this initial trip to Berkeley. I had no clear picture of what I would find there and was anxious to get going. Adding to my nervousness was the fact that I had agreed to let my father drive me to Fresno to catch an early Greyhound bus. The timing was important.

I did not need to take luggage with me for this quick one-day trip to Berkeley. But my father had packed some food for me in a small cardboard box and carried it lovingly as we walked into the station. I may not have been initially grateful for this, but I had to acknowledge that I was still dependent on my father for the simplest things like transportation.

As we walked across the large waiting room toward the ticket window, we saw lots of Anglos standing around with their suitcases. They spotted us, and heads began to turn in our direction. The look of contempt that they gave my father when he appeared with the cardboard box was devastatingly unnerving to me. "If looks could kill," I thought, "my dad would shrivel up on the spot."

I arrived in Berkeley without a map knowing nothing about the city or the campus. All I knew was that I had to find some Quonset hut, where I had been told the placement office was located. I had no clue what a Quonset hut was, but with some help I finally found it. The staff interviewed me and recommended a couple of families who, in return for light housekeeping and help with serving meals, would provide me with room and board.

I was given two addresses in the Berkeley hills. With the staff's help I discovered I could take a bus there, and I was on my way. I got off as close to the addresses as possible and then had to walk a part of the way to my interviews.

The Berkeley hills were more like mountains to me. I had lived in the flatlands all of my life. I had been in the Sierras just once, but otherwise land, as I had experienced, had been flat. The hills were beautiful. I couldn't believe what a magnificent setting they were for the sumptuous homes I saw in every direction. I marveled at the newness of the experience, climbing over those hills scrutinizing buildings as I looked for the address where I was to interview for a job.

I was offered the job at both residences and then returned to the Quonset hut for some advice. There they told me, "No, don't take the first one [with a female politician] because that one works you to death, and she expects you to do whatever occurs to her." This woman apparently was an elected official in the state government. She would also expect me to travel with her from time to time.

The advisers at the placement office instead recommended the second family. So I agreed to accept that job. Bill, the father of the family, was the manager of a department store in Berkeley. Alice, his wife, was involved, I later learned, in Panhellenic activities on campus. She had been a sorority girl, I think in the Midwest, during her college days. They had two sons, one my age who was starting at Stanford that fall and a younger son who was about age nine.

I felt very good and was proud of myself for having been able to negotiate this job placement. I also felt good just being in Berkeley. I think I fell in love with the campus at first sight, the imposing buildings everywhere I looked. I liked the trees, the Spanish tile roofs, and the sounds of the campanile. I was awed by the size of the campus. And the adjoining hills set it apart from any place I had ever seen. It was a discovery.

I returned to Visalia knowing that I had made the right decision.

Even though I had my scholarship and had secured room and board for my first year, I knew that I would still have additional expenses such as clothes and transportation. I knew that I would have to earn some money that summer.

I had my job at the Roxy, but it was only part-time. It was not going to be enough. I needed a full-time job—an eight-hours-a-day, five-days-a-week kind of job and one that hopefully paid more than the Roxy. But I knew I couldn't find that type of job in Visalia.

Visalia was a small town, and in the six years I'd lived there I'd had an opportunity to observe hiring practices. The faces that were so familiar in the vineyards, the cotton fields, and the orchards were not the faces seen behind the neat counters and office desks on Main Street.

Toni suggested that I try my luck in Fresno. She had an Anglo girlfriend who was married and lived there. My parents didn't object since they knew I needed a full-time job and felt I would be safe with anyone Toni recommended.

Toni's friend, Ella, a waitress, was very kind and welcomed me into her home while I job hunted in Fresno. Her husband, a musician, didn't seem to mind, and their ten-year-old son was pleasant enough. Ella's chain-smoking bothered me, and I couldn't understand how she could drink beer for breakfast. Otherwise, I felt comfortable in their home. I tried to show my gratitude by purchasing some groceries and placing them conspicuously in the refrigerator.

Ella and I became friends easily, and she invited me to accompany her to a nightclub where her husband was playing. We all seemed to get along fine, and I was optimistic that things would work out. But it didn't turn out that way.

Finding work in Fresno turned out to be a frustrating experience. I was hoping to get a job as a waitress: besides earning a salary I could get tips as well. Ella did help me find a job in a local restaurant. However, when it was discovered that I did not belong to the union that represented waitresses in Fresno I was let go.

I ran into the same problem in other restaurants. I was told that since I wasn't a member of the union I couldn't be hired. This was all foreign to me since in Visalia I hadn't needed to be a union member to work as a waitress. I knew nothing of unions. I was angry and discouraged.

Ella was resourceful, however. She sent me to a little office somewhere in Fresno to make job inquiries. I found out about a job in a mountain resort at Shaver Lake. It was near Yosemite National Park northeast of Fresno. Through a stroke of good luck I got the job and was on a bus to Shaver Lake the following day. Besides my wages and tips as a waitress I would receive room and board.

I had never been in the mountains before, except for a one-day trip with friends to Sequoia National Park. I had never even heard of Shaver Lake. When I arrived I discovered a beautiful lake resort where people went for boating in the summer and hunting in the early fall. I had my own cabin, and in between my work shifts I was able to enjoy walks in the forest and around the lake.

The resort itself was rustic. It included a series of cabins where guests stayed and a grocery store, in addition to the restaurant where I worked. Some of the guests cooked in their cabins, while others ate their meals at the restaurant. The place was run by the owner and his wife, and their two school-age sons worked there also. So it was a family affair, friendly and relaxed.

At the restaurant I performed a variety of duties. My main job was waiting on tables. Lunch and dinner were served daily. On Saturday evenings the resort sponsored a dance with live music. I learned I had to serve alcoholic drinks besides waiting on tables.

Here I really had to fudge. I was evasive when the subject of my age came up. I mumbled something like "it's my job" when the bartender asked me if I was old enough to serve drinks. I assumed the owner was aware that I was eighteen, and he hadn't brought up the subject of my age. It was only of minor concern to me, since it was primarily families who stayed at the resort and frequented the dining room.

My work assignment was limited to the dining room. If a table asked for beer or wine, I placed my order at a window opening onto the bar. I could check the action in the bar without getting involved, and this seemed all right to me. In addition to waiting on tables, I washed windows and did some dish washing, but no cooking.

There was another girl besides me working at the resort. She worked in the grocery store. She was already in college, somewhere in the east, and her home was in Hawaii. I got the impression that she came from a pretty wealthy family, and so I couldn't understand what she was doing working there. It seemed that she should have been a guest instead. I think that she was just trying to gain work experience in California. And her blond hair and blue eyes gave no indication of her ancestral ties to Hawaii, but she didn't talk about that.

I was impressed by her cosmopolitan demeanor. There was a non-chalance about the way she dismissed the popularity of Honolulu. "I'm from Maui," she said. Whatever subtle difference she may have been referring to was lost on me, something else to add to my long list of things I didn't understand.

Being from Hawaii, she was also a very good swimmer, something I was not. I didn't know how to swim. I didn't even own a bathing suit.

While I worked hard I also had an opportunity to enjoy the mountain setting. It was almost like being on vacation. I particularly enjoyed going horseback riding in the high Sierras, a new experience for me. I had ridden horses before, but never in such a magnificent setting. I was awestruck by the high Sierras. I spent hours enjoying the sweeping and inspiring vistas—trees as far as the eye could see.

One unexpected incident that might have cost me my job but didn't occurred when I accepted an invitation to go riding with an older man who rented pack mules and horses to the resort guests. I knew that he took guests on backpacking trips, so I simply accepted him as part of the scenery.

We went off on horseback and were gone all afternoon. I had a wonderful time. The trails were steep and led to panoramic views of the mountains and the forests. The scenes were magnificent. There were moments, however, when, with some unease, I reflected on how isolated we were, alone in the Sierras.

It wasn't until we returned to the resort complex that I got a sense of the risk I had taken. As I alighted from my horse, I noticed that people were looking out the window at us. I had evidently been seen going off on horseback with this man, and people were worried. The look of concern on their faces when I walked into the building made me feel funny. They were looking at me and then in the direction of the stableman as he walked our two horses back to the stable. They asked me where I had been. My whereabouts had become a matter of concern, and they wanted to know if I was all right.

Initially, going horseback riding had seemed like such an innocent thing to do. Now I felt sheepish, but their concern for me was reassuring. They cared.

One advantage of my summer job at Shaver Lake was that it gave me a chance to catch up on some much-needed sleep in the wonderful mountain air. I hadn't realized just how tired I was from my four years of high school until I got to Shaver Lake. I slept better and longer—sometimes as much as ten hours—than I had for a long time.

Not only was I more rested after almost three months at the resort, but I had accomplished my goal of saving enough of my wages and tips to feel confident that I would have the money I needed for my living expenses at the university in the coming year. Just before Labor Day, I said good-bye to the Sierras and returned to Visalia to pick up my things en route to Berkeley.

I have sometimes been asked, "Was it hard leaving home, being the first in your family to go to college?"

Of course it was hard. I felt an ill-defined anxiety at not knowing quite what to expect even in the near future. Nevertheless, it was always obvious to me that I had to leave.

Economically, we lived a precarious existence. I intended to leave home and put it all behind me. Yet leaving my family also meant leaving the only source of stability I had ever had. I knew that once I left home there would be a real geographical barrier separating me from my family. At that time my parents had not yet installed a telephone in our home—another expense that we could not afford. Separation would be a physical reality.

It was, of course, also an emotional reality. My parents shared my high hopes for new achievements, and I was leaving home with their blessing. But I was leaving them nonetheless. I was the first to leave home. I was going to a university and a place unknown to them, a world totally outside their realm of experience.

In a more literal sense, they would no longer be a major part of my life. Besides, they had other immediate concerns. They had five younger children, ranging in age from five to thirteen, who needed their attention. I was on my own, and they expected that I would do my best. And so I intended.

From the time of my graduation, my family had been very support-ive of my various preparations for my big trip to Berkeley. I treasured the Samsonite suitcase set that Toni had bought me as a graduation present for many years. (Some thirty-five years later, on a trip to China, my old Samsonite started to fall apart, and I gave it to one of our local guides who wanted it and would appreciate it. He was happy, and I was delighted. He would take care of it and give it new life.)

Using my new luggage as well as several boxes, I packed everything I thought I would need in Berkeley. I found out soon after arriving there that much of what I had taken was inappropriate. Things that I didn't normally wear I packed anyway, just in case I might need them. If in doubt I just threw it in my suitcase. I packed a lot of stuff without knowing why. But it gave me a sense of security to be hanging on to as many things as possible—scarves, blouses, whatever—and Lord knows I needed something to hold on to so that I could continue to feel oriented.

But I had no clue about appropriate clothing for Berkeley. The hot San Joaquin Valley was familiar to me, so I remember taking my best cotton dresses, starched, and my polished white shoes and thinking that I had brought my best attire. It didn't take long for me to discover that nobody in Berkeley—at least on campus—wore starched dresses. What was really the thing to wear in Visalia was not so big in Berkeley.

And so I left for Berkeley and my new life. What I remember most vividly is the physicality of the experience. It seemed as if I had packed my entire life into two suitcases and a few boxes. The four years I had spent in the house that my parents had bought in Visalia were the longest I had spent anywhere in California—long enough to acquire a lot of material possessions. Now I had packed it all up and was moving on.

I didn't go by Greyhound. I faintly recall driving there with someone, but I can't recall with whom. It was most likely my father. It's funny how I've blocked this out.

Once I had put a distance of two hundred miles between me and Visalia, the separation was complete. I could put it in the past. I think that at this point I was still pretty much on automatic pilot. By the usual standards, at that time, I had no "right" to expect that what was happening to me should actually be occurring. Finding myself at Berkeley was somewhat of a marvel to me. I had no reality check to rely on. One new experience after another—initially all very much undifferentiated.

When I arrived at the home in the Berkeley hills where I would be boarding, I recall encountering a startled look on the face of my landlady, Alice. She couldn't believe the amount of stuff I had brought. In addition to my two suitcases, I had brought some packing boxes with clothes and some reference books. But it was mostly clothes.

I didn't need to take any household items because the room that I moved into was fully furnished. It had a bed, desk, chairs, lamp, and its own bath. It was a lovely room in a lovely house. Although I had never had a room to myself, at that point it didn't seem like such an important thing. I was too excited and eager to be on campus to think about having my own room.

The room, all of a sudden, was not home. It became more of a physical space rather than an emotional space. There's a difference between a house and a home, and this was not my home. It was a room in someone else's home and I had contracted to perform a job for the privilege of being there.

✥

I was nervous on registration day. I had earlier been sent a bunch of forms to fill out, but actual registration for classes had to be done on campus.

In my confusion getting on the bus to get down to campus, I dropped some of my forms at the bus stop. I didn't realize that I had lost them until I arrived on campus. I then retraced my steps in hopes of finding them.

Fortunately for me the people who lived up in the hills were very friendly and liked university students. Someone had picked up my papers and was holding them for me at the bus stop when I got back there. The people waiting for the bus were very kind. "You're looking for these," someone said. They had been expecting me. They seemed amused and delighted to see me. They were trying to help me, this confused country girl. We all had a good laugh. I think I relaxed after that.

When I finally got back to campus, I experienced my first Berkeley class registration, a mass event. No computers were available then. Everything was done manually. Students registered in alphabetical order. We went through what were called "reg lines" to register for the semester and to sign up for classes.

The process included filling out a multitude of forms such as residence and program questionnaires and a personal directory card. We received counseling from assigned student workers if we had program problems; we signed up for classes and paid fees.

This elaborate process was conducted in one of the gymnasiums. Portable walls and barriers were set up to create a maze—a network of corridors and blocked-off spaces, entrances, and exits where student workers were strategically placed to direct the student flow.

Class enrollment was on a first-come, first-served basis, and it was a mad scramble. In some cases, when there was a heavy demand for a particular undergraduate class, we had to exit and make a dash to another building to check enrollment lists or to track down a professor and plead our case to take the class.

In the reg line, one thing I noticed was how friendly and helpful to one another the students were. They seemed extra kind, clearly recognizing that we were all facing similar dilemmas. It was easy to get information or help. This was important. Negotiating the registration maze required quick decision making, for we were being moved through the process at what seemed to be an inordinately rapid pace.

I was amazed at the apparent sophistication displayed by some students. They seemed to know exactly what they were doing as they selected "cinch" courses to balance an otherwise demanding schedule.

Even though everyone in the line seemed very friendly, there was still a sense of impersonality about the whole thing. Resolving program conflicts was strictly a matter of individual responsibility. But I felt free to work my way through it and even enjoyed the feeling of being unfettered.

One of the conflicts I encountered had to do with a housing form that needed to be signed by one of my parents. Since I was a freshman not living in a campus dormitory or in campus-approved housing, I had to submit this form to indicate my parents' approval of my living in off-campus housing. Without the form I couldn't complete my registration. This seemed strange to me, because my parents were not involved in what I was doing. I felt that I was responsible for myself and for my housing, which I had worked out on my own through a campus referral.

So I fudged. Right there, standing in line, I signed for my parents. I felt guilty about doing it, but I didn't know what else to do. I thought, "My parents don't need to sign this; they don't even know what I'm doing. They've given me their blessing expecting me to take care of myself the best way I know how."

Nevertheless, I believe that I reflected momentarily and wistfully upon the fact that the system was not set up with me in mind. I was not the "typical" student.

I had fewer problems with my classes. I had been sent a course catalog before my arrival in Berkeley. So I had had a chance to study it and had decided what courses I needed and which ones I wanted. All my courses except one were general education courses that all lower-division students had to take. I didn't have much choice. I remember enrolling in an English writing class and an anthropology class.

However, there was one class that I particularly wanted to take my first semester. This was a survey course in world literature. But at the sign-up table I was told that it was reserved for sophomores. Yet I still really wanted to take it. I think the reason that the class attracted me was that I had a perception of myself as not having read enough. I felt that there were so many books to read in the world that I had better get into this world literature class right away. I wanted the course and was not going to take no for an answer.

I decided to go to the professor's office and seek his permission. I found his office somewhere on campus. I don't remember what I said, but I'm sure I believed that reason was on my side. Surely a professor would listen to reason.

I do remember surprising myself with my sense of confidence. I was like a naive country kid who wasn't going to let any obstacles get in my way. I was to approach enrollment in other future courses with the same enterprising spirit. I must have assured the professor, "I can do it. No problem."

To my delight, the professor gave me permission to enroll in the class. I loved the course and did well in it.

Somehow I got through that first day of registration. But it had been quite an experience. Berkeley was a huge campus. It took a lot of trudging over those campus hills to get from one place to another. There was an enrollment of about twenty-five thousand students. I had never experienced such an environment. It was totally different from high school.

At Visalia Union High, the teachers had been parent figures and so much had been predetermined and provided for the students. We had been placed in learning tracks and given a set curriculum and books. We were told what the requirements were. We were assigned to classes with minimal opportunity for informed choice. Attendance was required by law.

By contrast, at the university, as I was quickly discovering, there was a lot of individual decision making. There was very little, if anything, you had to do by law.

✑

My initial impressions of the Berkeley campus were varied. Besides being awed by its immensity, I was struck by how diverse it was. Certainly it was very different from anything I had experienced.

This diversity was visible in the student body. For the first time in my life I experienced foreign students such as East Indians in their turbans. I became aware of what was referred to as the "I House," which was the International House. I also learned that it was known by some students as the "zoo." I became aware that prejudice took this form, and I thought, "How gross."

There were also, of course, the sorority girls. I was surprised to learn that some of these girls had come to Berkeley to earn their "Mrs." degree. My high school teachers, and my parents in their own way, had reinforced the ideal of going away to college to pursue knowledge. By contrast, going to college to find a husband seemed a novel idea.

But even this difference seemed all right in a place where being different didn't seem to be a problem. This variety in the student body is what gave the campus its kaleidoscopic fascination.

All the students at Berkeley seemed talented, but there were many more kinds of students than I had anticipated. There were the "independents" who didn't have that look of sameness that characterized the sorority and fraternity types of students. Then there were the World

War II veterans in their khaki trousers, the frayed-at-the-cuff graduate students, the engineers with their pocket protectors and their slide rules hanging from their back pants pockets, and the foreign students, many in traditional attire.

There were some American minority students that I could distinguish, but not many. I came to know one Japanese American student and would later become friends with some Chinese American girls. But I don't recall meeting any African Americans. Nor do I recall that minority students saw themselves or were seen as "hyphenated" Americans. The practice was to speak of people as being "American" or as being "Chinese," "Japanese," "Negro," or "Mexican."

I assumed that there were other Mexicans like me on campus, and occasionally I would notice a Spanish surname, perhaps in some school publication. However, with the exception of some professors, the only other Hispanic I ever met at Berkeley in four years was an Argentine student whom I dated for a short while.

But I was very busy and didn't have time to worry about group relations on campus. I had lived for many years with what I saw as an overall tacit assumption that Spanish-speaking people were not expected to be achievers. Consequently, their absence at Berkeley was no surprise. Instead, what was a revelation was that this phenomenon extended so far beyond my own painful experience in a small valley town that had receded in importance. On the one hand, opportunity at the university seemed to be limited only by the individual's talent; on the other, the social divisions were clearly evident.

Yet what was different between Visalia and Berkeley was the difference in size, which helped to create in Berkeley a welcome sense of anonymity. Unlike in Visalia, where people made judgments about you based on role expectations, people could and did ignore one another in Berkeley.

I became conscious that no matter what I did it was OK. If I was confused nobody particularly noticed. In fact, it seemed OK to be confused because others seemed as confused as I was. There were thousands of students, and it was like being in a crowd that seemed to be moving purposefully somewhere. But each student had his or her own particular business to attend to.

Of course, what was most impressive to me that first semester were my initial classes. They represented experiences that I had never had before and stressed to me the transition from high school to college.

One of the most revealing experiences I had was in my anthropology class. I remember one of my first lectures in Wheeler Auditorium. I was watching the professor as he stood on stage using the overhead projector, displaying data on a large screen. I had his book with me, the assigned class text. I wasn't really interested in all the details he was going into concerning his fieldwork, details such as the measurements of specific skulls.

Instead, I was focusing on the fact that very quickly I was gaining a sense of why this class and my other classes that fall at Berkeley were so different from my high school classes. The most exciting difference was meeting and observing in action the person who did the research and wrote the very text you were using. I was learning from the researcher himself about the process by which knowledge is created.

It helped in this class that I had some interest in anthropology. By coincidence, I was reading for my English class books by Ruth Benedict and Margaret Mead, two of the great American anthropologists of their time. I remember vaguely thinking that it must have been nice to have been a Ruth Benedict or a Margaret Mead (and I still think that). They had been pioneers, able to work in a field dominated by men.

But I knew that their backgrounds were not my background, and I did not expect that I could be like them. Yet what was fascinating to me was the process that they engaged in, as did my professor, in creating knowledge. This class proved to be a powerful learning experience for me. I liked what I saw as a new experience. I liked what I saw as a new approach to handling academic content.

This awakening about the nature of knowledge was reinforced in my other classes that fall. I also remember sitting in an American history course and experiencing history coming alive. What impressed me was a sense of how big and diverse this country is. For the first time I was seeing not only the United States but all the Americas geographically as one large expanse of land.

I was realizing that there was more to this country and to the world than just Visalia. Before coming to Berkeley, going to Fresno had seemed like a big trip! The idea of traveling for the sake of travel was not something I had internalized, and all of a sudden I could visualize the fact that the United States was and is a finite place.

I began to imagine traveling to other parts of the country and of the world. This became another "aha!" experience, another discovery. I found that very exciting and part of the comfort of Berkeley. So much just seemed to be comfortable, in an intellectual sense.

The world literature course that I had really wanted to take was especially interesting to me because I so enjoyed the assigned books. The number twenty-one comes to mind—twenty-one works of world literature: Goethe, Tolstoy's *War and Peace,* some Dante, *Don Quijote,* some plays by Molière, and so forth. We read all these in translation. It's what I had been looking forward to, this opportunity to immerse myself in the "classics." Today this reading list would, of course, be considered Eurocentric and limited, if not retrograde.

But my reading was very rewarding to me. I could immerse myself easily in Western literature, free to conjure up vivid images of people and places in these "foreign" works. In contrast, much of what I read of American literature was foreign to my experience and, therefore, not much more American than the foreign works. I had difficulty identifying with the works of many American writers. It was a seeming contradiction that bothered me somewhat.

I particularly recall my professor using some novel approaches to engage students in this survey course (later when I became a high school teacher I borrowed some of his techniques). For his lecture on *War and Peace,* Tolstoy's nineteenth-century Russian epic, my professor presented to the class a young Russian woman, who gave us a lesson in Russian history, language, and names.

She explained how inflections are used in Russian to convey familial relationships. An "a" ending on a name to indicate "the daughter of" comes to mind. The diminutives and terms of endearment, such as names ending in "usha," were numerous, but she made it all come alive.

My professor's teaching methods made eminent sense to me. Unfortunately, there were some irreverent students in that class of about two hundred whose jocular response to the class suggested that they were more attuned than I was to the entertainment aspects of the presentations. I, on the other hand, was appreciative, for I needed all the help I could get with *War and Peace.* I was an earnest student and had concluded that I couldn't hope to begin to get through the novel until I made some sense of the names. So, as I read, I drew up a name list with appropriate descriptions. The young Russian woman's presentation was a welcome source of help.

With Cervantes's *Don Quijote,* the professor created quite a stir. As we approached the classroom and began filing into the lecture hall, we first became aware of students snickering, then ripples of laughter as more eyes turned in the direction of the podium and lectern. By the time the classroom had filled, there was a minor uproar.

Our professor was outfitted as the great Don Quijote—his helmet an inverted dishpan, his lance a long stick held sternly in his right hand. He had endeared himself in his impersonation of the idealistic but impractical knight errant, and for his effort he received a warm round of applause.

We also read some classical Greek plays. The professor's introductory lecture to this portion of the course included a very general overview of some highlights of classical Western history, including the names of some of the major Greek thinkers of that time.

Oblique references to Socrates, the manner of his death, and his association with young boys somehow all remained unclear to me. But I did note the snickering coming from the boys in the back rows of the lecture hall. I didn't understand that either, but the suppressed laughter suggested to me that there was a taboo subject at work here.

An instance such as this reference to Socrates' death probably helped me to universalize momentarily the confusion I still felt about things that had been taboo all my life. Sex—and certainly homosexuality—were subjects that I didn't know much about. I didn't even know that such a thing as homosexuality existed. Still, this episode in class helped me to gain some sense that customary prohibitions, as I understood them, were not unique to my personal cultural experience.

I loved this world literature class and thought very highly of my professor. I often sat in the front row with other young wide-eyed female students, who were all probably falling in love with him as he lectured. I liked a lot of things about my professor. He was tall and sandy-haired and had a cute smile. He had these long curly lashes and dreamy eyes, and he had a way of calling students up to the podium and kind of joking with them and making all of us feel close to the literary experiences of the class.

I was never called to the podium, but I did have occasion to talk to the professor after class. He made good eye contact with you when you spoke to him, and he listened intently. He turned literature into a live experience.

Although the amount of reading in this course and indeed in my other classes was much more than I had been used to in high school, it helped me to start building up my own library. Some textbooks were expensive, but you could also buy more inexpensive paperbacks. The Modern Library giant editions cost about one dollar and twenty-five cents at this time. Smaller paperbacks could be purchased for under a dollar, and some were as cheap as thirty-five cents.

In addition to using the campus bookstore, where I bought some of my textbooks, I also became acquainted with and loved the many used bookstores near the campus, on Telegraph Avenue as well as on the side streets.

As I did in my world literature class, I often tried to sit in the front of the classroom in my other classes. I was an eager student. I still had not learned that some considered it "not cool" to be so eager. I think that in many ways I was still like a little kid. My naïveté in this regard took the form of believing that, because I was eager to learn, everyone else was too. I became increasingly aware of this characteristic in me. In my freshman English class, for example, I raised my hand a lot. I was an "I-have-the-answer" kind of student. Although I couldn't readily respond like this in my big lecture classes, I was able to do it in my small classes, such as my English class, and in discussion sections led by graduate teaching assistants.

It didn't take me long, however, to realize that no matter how good I was or how good I thought I was there was often someone better prepared than I. I was surrounded by a whole lot of talent. In some of my classes I was sitting with premed students, for example, who had come to Berkeley with a far superior preparation in science and mathematics than I had received.

But it wasn't just that many of my fellow students were bright. I realized rather quickly how much more knowledgeable and sophisticated many of them were in comparison to me. I became aware that some of these students had traveled extensively, that they were politically aware, that they had done much more reading, and that they were sexually aware. The students who had snickered about the circumstances surrounding the death of Socrates, for example, seemed to know something that I didn't know.

What I was acquiring in these various initial classes at Berkeley was a sense of the variety of forms of knowledge. I'd been taught to have faith in the intrinsic worth and utility of academic learning, and I'd been interested in most of the subjects that I had studied in high school. But I had felt an undifferentiated interest for my various classes in that I did not place a higher value on any one academic discipline. I didn't know how academic disciplines related to one another, and

I didn't think in terms of levels of understanding. To some extent one fact seemed as important as another. It was the exceptional teachers who helped me gain some insight into the significance of the work we were doing in class.

But at Berkeley, differentiation seemed more evident. The very buildings were daily reminders of the university's separate schools and colleges. I enjoyed the walk past the huge life sciences building on the west end of campus, past the campanile toward the beautiful Hearst Mining building. The library seemed a limitless storehouse of books, of knowledge organized and accessible in its infinite variety. There was clearly far more here than I had envisioned.

One of the things that further differentiated Berkeley from Visalia Union High was that I began to see teachers differently—not as authority figures but as individuals sometimes and as scholars at other times. Some of these figures were very fascinating.

I remember, for example, my French professor that first semester. She was a Polish woman who had come to the United States via France. This was the first time that I had ever encountered what I would call a "continental" type of person.

She dressed differently from the other female instructors on campus. This professor frequently wore a skirt slit up to midthigh, which was revealing and provocative. She also often wore a tailored blouse open at the neck with the top button unbuttoned. I don't think I was the only one in class who eyed her up and down when she entered the room. She didn't fit my notion of what a female professor should look like, and I didn't know what to make of her.

If I had known the word, I would have been tempted to call her appearance risqué, which is what I had been taught that a skirt like the kind she wore would suggest. But she was a comfortable, gracious kind of person, very open to students and very approachable—and wearing a skirt with a slit and a blouse unbuttoned at the top, with just a hint of her bra showing. You could tell that she had deliberately left her blouse unbuttoned to convey just a hint of titillation, but she carried it off with remarkable aplomb. She was very different. I saw her style as an option I might consider. Not likely, but an option nevertheless.

Besides getting adjusted to the campus, I also had to adjust to my new living and working arrangements. The work that I had to do was not burdensome. I had to help prepare and serve dinner and then clear the table after the meal, in addition to a few added and related tasks.

Although the work was not difficult, it did circumscribe my time. I had to be on duty from about four in the afternoon to seven each evening, including most weekends. In return, of course, I received room and board.

I did experience some discomfort in my role as a servant. It was a new role for me, and it took some getting used to. There was one instance that particularly brought my status to the fore. The older son in the family, a freshman at Stanford, was home for some brief holiday or a weekend, perhaps. He came into the utility room, which was in the back of the house where I was folding some laundry.

The two of us were having a lively discussion about some casual school matter when his mother called him away. He never came back, nor did he ever engage me in such conversation again. It was apparent to me that his mother did not want him associating with me, even though we were peers in age. I was the employed girl, and he was her son. I may have been wrong in my interpretation of what transpired. I don't know. But that remained my lasting impression.

I thought to myself, "I do have to remember my place." I also became aware that the man who did the weekly housecleaning was called simply (and disrespectfully) the "Japanese man" and that he had to bring his own rice cakes for lunch.

All this bothered me somewhat, but not so much that I didn't eventually get used to it. I accepted the fact that this was what I had to do to earn my room and board. I felt fortunate to have this arrangement, since it made it possible for me to study at Berkeley.

Whereas Alice was more formal about my role in her home, her husband was more liberal. On occasion, he would invite me to join the family to watch television in the recreation room. Del Courtney, a casual low-key talk-show personality was the daily fare. Television was new and few homes had television sets, so I felt somewhat privileged. These occasions were pleasant for me.

Living by myself as a boarder in a strange house at times made me feel homesick. This was particularly true when the fog came in across the bay and reached the Berkeley hills. I became depressed. The grayness made me feel isolated and shut in. I was no stranger to fog. San Joaquin Valley tule fog, however, I associated with working in the fields. Valley fog was seasonal and seemed a natural part of living in the country.

Fog can be beautiful as it collects on and drips from plants. But in Berkeley, the fog seemed unpredictable. It felt like it was intruding on my new urban existence and seemed out of character. It made me feel somber.

Sometimes I also felt homesick when I had my period. I had experienced powerful menstrual cramps for several years. Quite frequently I would vomit on the first day of my menses. I remember times when I'd be in bed curled up in pain and I would suddenly get the heaves. My little brother Teddy would be sent running to get a pan.

To help alleviate my cramps my mother always made me chamomile tea. But in Berkeley I was on my own with my cramps. I had no one to fix me tea. I realized then that I had taken my mother and my family for granted. All of a sudden they weren't there. When I had cramps alone in my room in Berkeley there was nobody I could talk to, nobody noticed. I couldn't allow anyone to notice. I had an image of myself as self-reliant and I didn't want to ask for help.

I missed my parents and my family but I also knew that there was no going back for me, at least not in a literal sense. It was with a sense of loss that I compared the life my parents and I had shared with the life I was now choosing for myself.

So much of what had been an essential part of my life up to that point seemed extraneous to my new environment. There was nothing in Berkeley to remind me of or connect me to my earlier years. But I was so engrossed most of the time with so many new experiences that separation from my parents didn't seem to be a problem—except on those gray foggy days, or when I had my period, or when other students talked to me about their families.

When I heard stories about other families, I became acutely aware of how little I had in common with other students, apart from our shared academic interests. I didn't know where to position my parents in these types of informal discussions. It would be some time before I would begin to understand that I was really trying to figure out where to position myself.

Although I knew no other students at Berkeley when I first arrived, I gradually began to make friends, sometimes in my classes. I learned that students often went to get coffee after class. It wasn't unusual to be invited for coffee by another student, either male or female. It was a casual kind of friendliness. Sometimes people shared tables in the cafes surrounding the campus, and it was not unusual to make eye contact and to start a casual conversation.

In this way I became acquainted with other students, most of whom I found very different from me. I met an Anglo girl not much older than I who was married. She was an undergraduate, and her husband was a graduate student. Although she was about my age, she seemed very sophisticated.

Her husband was getting his degree in either Spanish or Latin American studies and had traveled in Central America. He wanted to go back to work there. He was an activist who thought that the United

Fruit Company, a large American corporation in Central America, was terrible in its exploitation of the people there. This couple seemed very politically aware. I had never heard of United Fruit, but I admired this couple's knowledge and what appeared to be their political sophistication and commitment.

"How did you meet your husband?" I once asked her. "How did you decide to marry him?" I was curious.

"My mother told me," she said, "that before getting married a girl should look at the boy's father. If she likes what she sees, it's okay to marry the boy."

I also became acquainted with Dita, a girl who had lived in Peru and called herself a Peruvian. However, I think that she was actually European, from France perhaps, but she loved to speak Spanish.

She was very dramatic when she spoke Spanish and loved to use French r's and other deliberate, exaggerated guttural French sounds. She also smoked a lot, and she looked very striking as she held her cigarette between thumb and forefinger. She was theatrical, but comfortable in her performance. She had a very distinct personality.

"When I go to parties," she said, "I go to meet different people. I don't worry about what they do. That's what makes it interesting."

I liked her but was reluctant to be friends with her. She seemed to be a risk taker and a little bold for me.

I became acquainted with another girl from France, Emily I think her name was. She also made a particular impression on me. Emily fit my stereotype of a French girl. Among other things, there was an openness and frankness about the way in which she discussed various matters having to do with human conduct, including sex. She had a "let-it-be" kind of openness.

I had heard that the French were open about sexual matters. I recall one time when we were sitting outside the library chatting. Although it was a very nonsexual situation, at one point somehow the conversation turned to sex. I was surprised by her frankness about the subject. To her, sex was simply another aspect of human behavior.

"The woman has as much right to enjoy it as the man," she said.

I was surprised by what she said and recognized that I had grown up a lot more uptight about sex than I realized. Although I was still not prepared to see her attitude as other than "foreign," that is, French, I remembered what she said.

Besides meeting people through classes and in cafes, I also made friends with other students when I joined the Newman Club my freshman year. The Newman Club was the Catholic student group on campus. It was sponsored by Newman Hall, the Catholic chapel and center, which at that time was located on the north side of campus. I attended Mass there and participated in some of the club's social events. Those of us who participated in nonsorority or nonfraternity groups such as the Newman Club were called the "independents."

The Newman Club sponsored a variety of activities such as social get-togethers and lectures, most of which I didn't have time for since I worked. It was at a Newman Club party that was held not at the center but somewhere off campus that I had my first beer. My father had allowed me to taste whiskey, which I liked, but I had never tasted beer, since my father was not a beer drinker at that time.

At the party, I tried to drink a whole can of beer but couldn't. I just remember getting a really sick feeling in my stomach. By the time I got home I was feeling very sick. I developed an instant aversion to beer. To this day I don't drink it.

But it was through events such as these sponsored by the Newman Club that I became part of a small social group of students. Our little group was quite diversified. There was Arni, who was Jewish and was from Mt. Vernon, New York. For some reason that I never found out, he chose to come to the Newman Club. I didn't know anything about Jewish culture. Other than in biblical references, the only time I remember having heard that a person was Jewish was when I worked at the Hotel Johnson as a waitress my freshman year of high school. I remember talking to a male guest in the hotel restaurant who was very friendly with me. I think that he was a traveling salesman who frequently stopped there, and somehow I learned that he was Jewish. I wondered aloud to Toni, who was also working there, just what being Jewish meant.

"I've read about Jewish people," Toni said. "You can tell they're Jewish because they have names like Gold."

"Oh!" I responded. "You go by the last name. That's a clue."

But that was all I knew about Jewish people, and here I was meeting Arni. There was nothing that I could identify as Jewish about him. I simply thought that he was a great person. I liked the fact that he had traveled all the way across the country in his little green MG to attend Berkeley.

In our group there was also Terri, a girl from Turlock in the San Joaquin Valley. She was a friendly, cheerful girl, an unspoiled, thoughtful Anglo kid. She always seemed to have a smile and a kind word for everyone. Terri was not as much of a hayseed as I was but was just a couple of notches above me in sophistication. It was nice meeting another valley girl, knowing that I wasn't the only "country bumpkin" at Berkeley.

There was also Julian, a Filipino student. This was the first time I had ever known a Filipino outside meeting a few in the fields.

Arni and his MG were the center of attention. I liked the fact that he was a graduate student. He was smart and seemed worldly. Arni referred to himself as having been a "legman." I didn't know what this meant until someone said that he had been a legman for a congressman in Washington, and then I kind of got the drift.

Our little group didn't really do much other than socialize a bit after Newman Club activities, but we were friendly and comfortable. On occasion we would go out to eat; a favorite was pizza, a new experience for me. I had never heard of it. There was a college hangout in Berkeley called Bertola's that served wonderful pizza and a green salad, which they mixed to order at your table. I especially remember the wonderful Italian dressing. We would pool our nickels and dimes and order a huge salad and a large pizza, out of which we'd each get one slice.

I also remember one time driving with the group to Holy Names College in nearby Oakland to pick up a friend of someone in the group. I hadn't known that a school such as Holy Names existed and knew nothing about girls' schools. I listened with interest to what the boys said about the school. I particularly remember their commenting that girls who went to an all-girls school like Holy Names dressed sloppily during the week because there were no boys around to keep them interested. They were essentially reinforcing the notion that girls dress only to attract boys.

I recall thinking about this notion and, at the time, reflecting on the fact that women were expected to fit predetermined social roles. I didn't like the practical application of this stereotype, but I recognized that this was how the male-female game was played.

One way that I attempted to participate in campus activities was by joining the staff of the *Daily Cal,* the student newspaper on campus. I had written for my high school paper and thought that I would enjoy a similar experience in college.

I was sorely mistaken. Initially, I neither understood the extent to which my work schedule would limit me nor did I appreciate the time demands of extracurricular activities on a big university campus.

First of all, the *Daily Cal* was a pretty big operation, very professional compared to my high school newspaper. I remember one girl on the staff who admitted to me that she had joined the paper just to meet people, but primarily I remember the staff members being serious about newspaper work.

The *Daily Cal* was almost like a regular city newspaper. It was student run, but the operation looked like what I recalled seeing in city newspaper offices. The paper had its own building. There were real offices. There were editors, reporters, and circulation managers. Reporters were given specific assignments. All this was a far cry from my high school paper, which was under the direction of the classroom teacher, with students relying on the teacher to manage the work.

I don't remember the specific assignments given to me or the stories that I worked on, but I do remember the stress of trying to write a story in a very limited amount of time. We were expected to produce error-free copy the very day that we covered the story. We never had time to write more than one draft—our first and final draft had to be the copy we submitted for someone to review. What happened to copy beyond that point was not clear to me. I didn't have the time to hang around the publications office, where deadlines seemed to be immediate and kept people in a frenzy.

In producing copy, I had some advantage in having learned to type in high school, but my typing skills were modest. The typewriters to which I had been accustomed were old-fashioned manuals with no type-correction features. I had never owned a typewriter and had practiced my typing very little.

It didn't help that, in addition to the pressure of writing under those tight deadlines, I had my own work schedule. I found out that I really didn't have the time to work on the newspaper and do my domestic chores at the house where I was living. I couldn't, for example, cover certain afternoon or early-evening events. I had to be "home" serving dinner.

This experience on the *Daily Cal* impressed upon me that one thing that I would be missing at Berkeley would be the opportunity to participate in extracurricular events. I don't think this realization bothered me a lot that first year. After all, this was a repeat of my high school experience when my ability to participate in functions outside the formal school day had been limited in part by my working hours.

What I did gain, and gained quickly, from my short stint at the newspaper was the added recognition of just how different Berkeley would be from my prior school experiences. The level of seriousness and what I interpreted to be professionalism at the *Daily Cal* revealed to me how much closer the university was to reality.

Students, at least some of them, on the staff were already seeing their work on the newspaper as the beginning of their careers. It became easier for me to see that a student's activities and associations suggested the direction that his or her adult life would take. Course work for some represented only one aspect of this direction.

Given the rigorous nature of my first classes at Berkeley, I found that I had to study a lot. But there was more to it than that. Whereas in high school the pattern of my daily activities had been determined primarily by the routines of school, work, and family life, at the university there seemed to be no pattern at all. Having a place to work that provided my room and board gave me a sense of security but also isolated me from campus life. The Berkeley hills were quite a distance from campus.

Study requirements were fluid. Grades were still the symbol of academic achievement or failure, but the formal feedback from professors came primarily at midterm and finals time. In between, I had a lot of freedom to explore. It was up to me to figure out what I supposedly already knew and what it was I was supposed to be learning.

I still remember the anxiety with which I retrieved my first set of blue midterm booklets, scanning the cover sheet for a grade. I received an A and remember being surprised by how important it was to me. Without that kind of feedback, I really had no way of knowing how well I was doing. Given my circumstances, I had scant basis for comparison. I was delighted with A's. B's were all right. But I also remember my first C. I wasn't used to C's.

My study habits did not change much at Berkeley. I continued to study primarily by myself, as I had done in high school. I would sometimes hear that students were getting together to study for a test. I'd never had the opportunity to study in a group, and now my work hours and lack of a car were not conducive to this kind of socializing.

I was also aware of the fact that some students used what were called Fybate notes to study. These were lecture notes that you could buy in lieu of attending lectures. I'd also heard that sororities and fraternities had banks of previously used exams for different classes that they used to prep their members.

I couldn't afford Fybates, and even if I'd had the money I probably would not have been inclined to use them as a substitute for attending class. I preferred to go to class and take my own notes. I knew Fybates were a help for some people, but I didn't think I needed them.

While I was conscious that my lack of money was a limitation, I was more conscious of a new freedom. Classes at Berkeley were more difficult than they had been in high school, but a lot of other things had changed as well. In Berkeley I was pretty much on my own. I didn't attend classes from eight to three. At most I went to two or three lectures a day. Only some of the small class sections met daily. I had more independent time between classes, and the challenge was to use this time wisely.

I had begun to learn how to gauge my progress in my classes. In high school it had been easy because, in most classes, we had weekly exams or quizzes that allowed us to measure progress and to know just where we stood. We also had daily homework. Every day we had to respond to such questions as "Did you do last night's translation? Did you complete last night's writing assignment, biology experiment, math problems?" If we did the exercises we got immediate feedback and always had some notion of the standard that was being applied. As college freshmen, we had to put all that behind us. Since the midterm was the only checkpoint between the beginning and end of the semester, we felt uneasy at not knowing where we were in terms of a grade.

For me, a major surprise was the fact that almost all my classes were lectures. In Wheeler Auditorium there might be three hundred students in one class. This was an environment of anonymity such as I had never before encountered. The lecture method also meant that I had to learn quickly how to take good lecture notes. I actually enjoyed teaching myself how to do this.

I listened intently from the very beginning of a lecture, attempting to identify clusters or chunks of information and sections of a lecture. I listened early on for what I thought might be main ideas and supporting details. I jotted down sentences as completely as possible, not trying to get all the words down but trying not to miss key words. I wrote rapidly. I would use space to indicate categories and subordination. These spaces would later also make it possible to insert additional information from my reading. This process of outlining was very visual for me.

I did all my note taking by longhand, since I didn't know shorthand. But I learned to write very quickly and to select key words so that the thought would make sense afterward. Sometimes when a concept seemed particularly complex or difficult to understand, I attempted to write down the professor's idea verbatim. After the lecture, I would study the thought and attempt to understand it.

I had a good memory, but my note-taking process helped me study the lecture material. I didn't like to cram for exams, so while I didn't study my lecture notes daily, I allotted myself sufficient time before an exam to study my notes. This process improved as I progressed in my education at Berkeley.

The library system at Berkeley represented still another major challenge for me. I had never seen libraries of the kind I saw at Berkeley. My reaction to Doe, the main library, probably best epitomized the sense of wonderment that the university evoked in me. Although it would not be entirely accurate to say that I gazed openmouthed at the architecture on campus, I can still conjure up the sense of awe that the buildings inspired—particularly Doe Library. My eyes were drawn upward by architectural elements such as windows and ceilings that I associated with cathedrals.

Walking into the library I felt very privileged. The number of titles and the range of topics in the card catalog represented a wealth of knowledge that had been inconceivable to me before my arrival on campus. The reference materials that lined the walls in the various rooms were forbidding in their sheer number.

The sense of privilege that I felt being in the library was not the privilege of personal or exclusive rights but rather of access to the ideal of excellence—an access that once gained carried with it the responsibility to work toward that ideal. I took this responsibility very seriously.

Initially I didn't make much use of the library. Perhaps I was a bit too intimidated by its size, its imposing physical presence. And I was put off by the lack of stack privileges for undergraduates. If you needed a book you had to request it at the main desk and then someone would go retrieve it for you. There was no opportunity to browse through the major collections.

Furthermore, I didn't care to study in a large library reading room with other students. I preferred the privacy of my own room. I felt that I could concentrate better. But little by little I became more familiar with the Berkeley library system. During my freshman year, I especially liked to use the smaller libraries on campus. There I could find books required for some of my classes and an environment more conducive to studying.

While at first I saw library work as a task, I ultimately got over that. I learned to appreciate the library as a resource and to love it. I began to understand why the Berkeley library was considered such a tremendous source of intellectual wealth. As a repository of knowledge, the library contained far more than I could ever access. Yet there was something energizing and reassuring about knowing that such resources were available even when I didn't expect to use them, or at least not most of them.

❧

My study habits, including my newfound library skills, aided me in surviving academically that first year. Yet it was a humbling experience.

While I was used to being an A student in high school, I had to adjust to the fact that this was not going to be the case at Berkeley. While I received some A's that first year, I also received some B's and even some C's. Overall, I recall that I achieved a B average, which I was proud of even if not fully satisfied. What was important was that I had made it through my freshman year.

That first year at Berkeley marked a major transition for me. It was a maturing experience that exceeded anything I could have imagined or anticipated. I had come to Berkeley from a small farming community where the concept of a city meant Fresno, which was still relatively small with the two-lane Highway 99 running through the center of town. Even though I had been to San Francisco once during my years of migrant work, I was a small-town girl, a country girl.

Given my background, I was surprised at how quickly I was able to adjust to Berkeley. I set my sights on the practical and the doable. I came to terms with what I saw as reality. I lost the sense of the future as some undefined time of unlimited opportunity. The sense that I was there totally on my own to make a life for myself was very real.

During my senior year in high school, college was less a reality and more a feeling that I was aspiring to this great something. I was just reaching out. But when I actually went to Berkeley I hit cold reality, and I had to make a quick adjustment. Part of this adjustment was the realization that I was on my own, that I was now making all my own decisions knowing that I would live with the consequences. I had to depend on myself entirely. And since my parents could give me no financial support, and there were no government student loans, I had to be resourceful about making do with the money I received from the scholarship.

There was something empowering about making a life for myself at age eighteen. Living and studying among twenty-five thousand students afforded me a glimpse of the many different ways in which people functioned. There was no right way or wrong way. There was only what you chose to do, what worked for you. You could potentially be anything except that there were no nurturing teachers to guide you. The choices were in all directions.

But there was an impersonality about the place. You found your own boundaries. I came to love and appreciate this freedom. You were even free to fail. And some did.

To me Berkeley was like living in a major city. The range of differences among the students was greater than anything I had experienced. But I could find a sense of community if I sought it out. The students I met represented an incredible diversity of interests. It was a learning experience. You couldn't help but learn.

Anywhere you might pause to observe the mass of the student body on a typical day, you were aware of the range of interests they represented. True, the faces of African American and Hispanic students were not visible. But that's the way things were. I understood that.

I was able to adapt to Berkeley, but I knew or know now that part of the reason I was able to do so had to do with my family background. My parents had in a sense unconsciously prepared me for Berkeley. They had always given me a lot of responsibility for making my own decisions, whether they were about school matters, clothes, or my work outside school.

I think, too, that the fact that I had started to work at an early age gave me a sense of being responsible and serious, and it provided me with a work ethic. Where the demands of work were concerned, I had been treated like an adult when I was young and I responded by learning to do things on my own without having to fall back on my parents as a crutch.

My parents' experiences also served as an example and an inspiration to me. My father had also, at an early age, left his home in Mexico and come to this country to work. At age sixteen or seventeen he was on his own. My mother, after she married my father, made the decision, also at an early age, to leave her home in New Mexico and come to California with my father.

My parents faced an uncertain future in the San Joaquin Valley during the Great Depression. While I did not fully understand or appreciate the hardships they had overcome, I recognized their tenacity. They had set an example for me.

Although I communicated infrequently with my parents that first year, I continued to see them as an anchor in my life. In other respects, I had made a break with Visalia. I returned home for Christmas, but that was the only time I returned that year. My time was fully taken up by my studies and my job.

The trip back to Visalia was a long one, and I didn't look forward to it. By Greyhound bus, it usually took an entire day. I couldn't take an express bus to Visalia but instead had to board a bus headed for Los Angeles and then transfer at some inland bus stop on Highway 99. From Berkeley, the bus stopped at every small town along the way.

By the end of that first year, I was becoming more and more used to living in Berkeley. As I made tentative plans for my sophomore year, I looked back at that little valley community, and I knew that I would never return, at least not to live. Too many of my twelve years of valley experience remained a source of both anger and frustration. With these experiences behind me, I felt free.

EIGHT

Settling into the Berkeley Ambiance

Early in my second semester at Berkeley, I decided that I would stay and try to find a summer job in the area. I also decided that I no longer wanted to live as a live-in servant in return for room and board. I felt that with what I would earn from a summer job and with the renewal of my scholarship, I could afford to find a different living arrangement.

I now had greater confidence in my job-seeking skills and decided to try office work. By midspring I started checking out possibilities, and by the end of the semester I had found a job at the Sears store in Oakland. I worked in the credit office for thirty-five dollars a week, more than I had ever earned. My work involved checking credit references. It was not exciting, but it was different. In fact, when I let myself think about it, I had to admit that it was downright boring.

That summer I came to learn about clock-watching. I would work and work, then look at the clock. It would only be three P.M. Two hours left to go. I'd work some more, then I'd look at the clock again and it would only be five after three. "God," I thought. "If it's bad for me, what must it be like for these other poor people who must do this year-round?"

The workers—all women—would appear for work in the morning listless. They would spend most of their first hour fussing with the papers on their desk. Then they would check their makeup—lipstick, eye shadow, whatever. By then it was time for a coffee break. When they returned, more makeup. By then it was lunchtime. After lunch the routine would start all over again. And everyone would stare at the clock every five minutes.

This routine was very painful to observe, so I tried to busy myself with my own work. Somehow I got through that summer.

More exciting that summer was finding a new living arrangement. Although boarding in the Berkeley hills was working out fine, I did feel somewhat ill at ease. I felt constrained by having to live in someone else's home. It was like being a perpetual guest while having to earn my keep. With my first year at Berkeley behind me, I felt secure enough to look for different housing.

That summer, before going to work at Sears, I checked over the listings in the campus housing office and found a rooming house that seemed agreeable. Besides your room, you also had access to a community kitchen and bathroom. It was an all-girls house, although it became mixed during the year that I lived there. It was on Parker Street a couple of blocks off Telegraph Avenue.

I had selected my room on the basis of its listed double-occupancy price. What I didn't understand was that I was supposed to provide my own roommate. Fortunately for me, the rooming house manager, Miss Brothers, a retired northern California school official, was very kind and understanding. "It's all right for now," she said. She let me have the room to myself at half-rent until another roomer showed up later that year.

Although the rooms had initially seemed spacious, as did the downstairs communal kitchen, the house began to feel crowded as soon as the other roomers started arriving. The noise level began to rise. By the start of the new school year, all the rooms had been taken, and the house never quieted down.

On the first floor, where I lived, there were individual rooms, while on the second floor there was a large apartment that housed several people. The second floor was the noisiest. This bothered me at first even though I had grown up in a large household. Perhaps because I had grown up with noise, I resented having to deal with more now that I was on my own. This resentment, however, didn't last long. I soon became adjusted to the living conditions in the rooming house and to the collection of fellow tenants there. Some of them were, in fact, very interesting, and I learned a lot from them.

When the house became mixed, men and women, I made friends with a couple from Iraq and with their young Iraqi friend, Saadia. Lateef and his wife occupied one room and Saadia another. They were graduate students, apparently from wealthy families and different from anyone I had ever known. The guttural sounds of their language intrigued me. Their dark good looks were dramatic. I was surprised by how quickly we formed an ethnic bond.

"What do you speak? What's your name?" they asked right away. When they learned that I spoke Spanish, they seemed delighted. "Oh, Spanish! We're brothers and sisters!" they exclaimed. They invited me to share meals with them as "brothers and sisters."

I knew nothing about Iraq and very little about that part of the world in general. The only connection I could quickly make was my general knowledge of the Arabic people who had occupied Spain for many years. Perhaps this is what they also connected with. For whatever reason, they saw me as one of them. It was comfortable being with them, like being with family. They were very open in talking about themselves and their background. I was surprised to find many similarities between their culture and what I had experienced growing up. I could connect emotionally with what they were saying when they talked about the status of women in Iraq and about the taboos around the subject of sex.

I marveled at this young couple, only in their late twenties, and traveling all the way to Berkeley to be students together. The wife seemed very Latina in many ways. When she talked, it was like listening to one of my aunts.

"The best part of marriage is the courtship," she would say. "That's a time for romance. After marriage, it's different."

Lateef didn't agree. He said that the whole point of courtship was marriage, the physical union of two people.

"That's what marriage is," he said. "And it's wonderful!"

I enjoyed watching them disagree without anger or rancor. Their relationship seemed very egalitarian, despite what they told me about Iraqi customs. Lateef was very matter-of-fact in describing life in his country, with men and women having distinct roles and obligations. All this had a familiar ring. I could identify entirely. What I liked about Lateef is that he recognized how unfair the system was for women.

I also remember a brother and sister living in separate rooms on the first floor. They were from out of state and not very friendly. He professed to be radical, belonged to the IPP, he said. "The Independent Progressive Party," he explained, when I asked him what IPP meant.

It was difficult for me to talk to him. He reacted to anything I asked him with a barrage of ideas that I couldn't understand. My main impression of him was that he liked to hear himself talk. On the other hand, I was intrigued by the fact that he spent hours alone in his room playing the cello.

From him I learned how immersed in political ideology some students could be. He and his sister were probably my earliest definition of campus "radicals." They were contemptuous of what they considered mainstream students, students who exhibited school spirit. That seemed to include me.

For example, I remember how disdainful both he and his sister were when they heard me talking about wanting to attend football games that fall. I had never had a chance to go to games while in high school because I worked after school as well as on Saturdays. Likewise, my first year at Berkeley I attended few games because of my job responsibilities. I was not overly enthused about athletics in general but loved the pageantry of a big college game. Our two house radicals were scornful. They thought that students who attended football games were mindless juveniles. The brother, especially, hated anything that sounded like the "rah-rah" spirit.

Some time later that fall semester or into the spring I finally got a roommate. Relying on Miss Brothers's generosity, I hadn't looked for a roommate but was eventually informed by Miss Brothers that she had rented my room to another girl and that I would now have to share it. I didn't mind, since all that time I'd enjoyed having that large room all to myself.

My roommate proved to be unique. Eve was a Jewish girl who had been adopted by a French couple after the war. From France she had been sent to the United States to live with a wealthy family. She resented her adoptive parents, she told me, because they had paraded her like a prized possession—like a monkey in its finery. Eve had come to Berkeley from Los Angeles. She was kind of an angry, confused girl and could be sullen at times. Yet I saw a wistfulness about her that was very appealing. She was slim and had short, dark hair with bangs that framed the fine features of her face. Her dark brown eyes would light up when she smiled, which wasn't often. She had a beautiful smile.

She had had a horrible past. At the time, I had little understanding of the Holocaust. I didn't know history well enough to get the full implication of what had happened to the Jewish people in Europe. But through Eve I began to get some understanding of what had happened to displaced little girls like her. She spoke of her home in Los Angeles with no sense of connectedness.

She seemed to like me, and I liked her. She would say things like, "You're better than I am." She thought that I was more privileged because I had been born in this country. This sentiment was new to me. She loved to talk and to express her feelings to me. Mostly I listened, guessing that she needed to get a lot out of her system.

She was very bright and generous. Her acts of generosity were a revelation. Once, for example, when I announced that I was going to Visalia for a visit, she said, "Here, wear this suit."

It was a very expensive, beautiful brown glen-plaid wool suit. When

I hesitated, she insisted that I take it because it no longer fit her. That was not true, of course, but she wanted to give it to me. "I don't need these clothes," she said. I didn't know what to say when I accepted her gift. I felt uneasy taking the suit, but she seemed happy to see me wearing it. It fit perfectly. I don't think that I understood this gesture entirely, but for the moment I empathized with her and felt very close to her. I wore her suit for a long time and treasured it.

Besides her suit, she wanted to give away all her expensive clothes. She never wore them, preferring to wear a modest outfit—a pleated skirt and white blouse—which she wore all the time. She was a special person, wondrous in some ways, and I've never forgotten her.

Since I had been hired at Sears only for the summer and since I needed additional income, I looked for work early that fall semester. I was able to find a job at a boarding house off campus, where I earned lunch and dinner in return for serving meals to the boarders. No wages were involved, but the free meals meant that the money I saved on food I could use for other expenses such as rent.

It was an all-boys boarding house run by a Mrs. Slevatz, an outspoken, warm-hearted divorced woman who had a small child about age six. She made a living by managing the house. She planned the meals and did some of the cooking herself, although she also employed a full-time cook.

I served dinner in exchange for the two meals a day. When I took the job I didn't anticipate just how much fun this experience was going to be. It was fun because of the rapport I enjoyed with the other three students who also worked there.

I was the only girl in our small group of servers, or "hashers," as we were called. There was one guy about my age who was from the South, perhaps Tennessee or Kentucky. "Gil" we called him, probably short for Gilbert. He could do a wonderful imitation of a stereotypical hillbilly. He enlivened his corny stories with a wonderful drawl, which he would add to his speech when least expected. He was a likable guy: cute, thoughtful, and loving. He spoke with great affection about his girlfriend back home.

Then there was Victor, who was an older student and perhaps divorced. It was hard for me to tell what the facts of his life might be. I never did learn the spelling of his last name, but it sounded Eastern European to me. He was vague about marital details but loved to regale us with stories of his lovemaking escapades. He was a graduate student in his thirties.

Victor possessed what we considered a ribald humor. But with Victor, such humor seemed forgivable, for he really seemed to care about women. The scenarios he created seemed more the products of his imagination than actual events in his life. He spoke lovingly of women and told us how he was happiest when cradled like a baby in the arms of a lovely lady. He knew all the dirty jokes and had a worldly wisdom, or so it seemed to me at the time, about sex, women, and life. He joked about these topics, but he was not hurtful. The jokes were usually on him. I never felt offended by what he said, because he seemed to care genuinely about people.

I remember Mike, another graduate student, very Irish in appearance. He was studying Asian languages. I can't recall whether his area of concentration was Japanese or Chinese. He had lived in a monastery in Asia and had studied there.

I was fascinated by the way he ate rice, which was frequently served at the boarding house. He brought the bowl of rice up close to his mouth and scooped the rice with his fork. I guessed that he had learned this way of eating rice in Asia.

He was a very scholarly type. He didn't talk much but was a good listener and seemed happy to answer our questions in his own enigmatic way.

"What's it like living in a monastery?" we wanted to know. "You get used to it," was his response. We got along well.

I had a good time working with this group of students, because they were relaxed and friendly. I looked forward to the meals we shared as a group before serving dinner to the boys who lived and boarded there. Lunch was served buffet style and was more informal. Overall, the atmosphere was very friendly both because of the boys who lived there and because Mrs. Slevatz seemed to enjoy her role as a mother figure to everyone.

As I became more familiar with Berkeley in my second year, I became even more aware that Berkeley represented a sanctuary for differences.

I thought of myself as coming from a fairly homogeneous community with racial and ethnic differences being primarily between Anglos and Mexican Americans, both geographically and economically. I had been aware of the Portuguese and Armenian communities in the valley, but they had seemed less ubiquitous.

In Berkeley, I was exposed to a much greater range of differences than I had ever known. One aspect of that difference was that, even in the midst of McCarthyism, Berkeley hosted students and even professors who were considered radicals. One example I knew well, of course, was the student in my rooming house who said he belonged to the IPP. He was clearly antiestablishment.

Such radicalism, however, was not at the same level of intensity as that which characterized the upheavals that would explode in the 1960s during the Vietnam War. But though more subtle, the disaffection could be felt on campus.

Radicals at that time didn't necessarily look different from most other students. Although they didn't look like your average fraternity or sorority type of student, they were indistinguishable from most other students in attire and appearance. Long hair was not part of the radical look, as it would be in the sixties. Nor was the hippie look, with the unkempt appearance and the ever-present aroma of patchouli oil, part of the radical persona.

There were some serious leftist students at Berkeley, some who might have been Communists. I became aware of the alleged Communist conspiracy, because this was the era of the loyalty-oath controversy, a time when professors were being asked to take an oath of allegiance to our government.

I never met anybody who claimed to be a member of the Communist Party. But I did become aware of people of various political persuasions. They were serious, but there was not the spirit of advocacy that would exist in the sixties. There were some agitators, but they generally confined their activities to the Sather Gate area on the south side of campus, which was as far as the campus extended at that time.

I don't recall particular political controversies in my class discussions, but I do remember that there was open discussion of topics, including political ones, that would have been considered too controversial outside the university.

I still remember, for example, the sense of discovery with which I read some of Friedrich Nietzsche's work. Readings in philosophy, in particular, were helpful in giving me both a sense of focus and a sense of the possibilities for examining concerns that had never been discussed in my formal or informal schooling.

The significance of Nietzsche's aphorisms—on truth, guilt and sin, good and evil—was not always obvious to me, but he never failed to provoke reflection. Many of my old assumptions were challenged, and I remember thinking about religious authority figures from my childhood. Had they read Nietzsche as I was doing? What had been their response?

Examining and questioning ideas was what the university seemed to be all about. It would be a long time before I would begin to understand how threatening the challenging of long-held beliefs can be for some people. While at Berkeley, I was relatively unaware of the generalized mistrust and even hostility with which some people outside the university viewed the supposed activities of professors and students on campus.

Although readings on socialism in general and Communism in particular were not specifically included in any of my course work, these kinds of materials were, of course, sold along with other political texts in the local bookstores. I had heard that there was a "little red bookstore" in Berkeley and I was intrigued enough to look for it. When I found the store I thought I was looking for, I stopped to look in the windows but never got enough courage to go inside.

I was generally aware of the national fear of Communism, but nothing in my campus experience indicated to me that some professors could constitute a threat to national interests. On the contrary, my sympathy tended to be in support of those professors who had apparently had to choose between acting on principle by not signing a loyalty oath, thereby facing dismissal, and violating their conscience to retain their livelihood.

The closest I came to being with someone I thought was a Communist was the time I chatted with a graduate teaching assistant whom I met during my second year in one of my class sections. He was from Spain. At some point, perhaps out of a sense of shared cultural interests, he became friendly with me. One time he invited me out for coffee after class, and I agreed to join him.

There was an ease about our conversation initially and I felt very comfortable. Then I became conscious of him gazing at me with what seemed aggressive intensity. Our conversation very quickly turned to politics. My lack of knowledge about Spanish politics was obvious. I simply had a general awareness about the struggle between Fascism and Communism. I listened intently and thought to myself, "This person must be a Communist—that must be what he's talking about." But that didn't put me off. It intrigued me.

What did surprise me was that he also invited me up to his apartment. He did so with an "I'll show you what I mean" attitude. He worked fast. I was disappointed. I had trusted him up to that point. "I'd better get out of this right now," I thought. "I'm not in his league."

Radicalism existed at Berkeley, but it was not in vogue. You were aware of it, and it was part of what gave Berkeley some of its particular ambiance, but it was not as pervasive as it would become after the Free Speech Movement in 1964.

I was neither antagonistic toward nor supportive of radical politics as I observed the action. I listened to some of the proselytizers at Sather Gate, and for the most part their ideas didn't impress me. I tried to deal with ideologues with a healthy amount of skepticism. My upbringing, including my religious training, had been characterized by a great deal of absolutism. There had been little room for compromise or alternatives. I knew enough by then to be wary of anyone who professed to have found "the truth." I was willing to listen, but I wasn't swayed by any one argument. I was cautious. I was not seeking conversion to a new set of precepts.

Radicals in the late forties and early fifties at Berkeley had to contend with the anti-Communist sentiments that were increasing as a result of the cold war. The times, rather than giving rise to a generation of radical students, produced instead what was called the "silent generation."

I didn't think of myself as being part of a particular generation and didn't like being defined that way. What was clear to me was that I was becoming increasingly aware of national and international political views and that this was an important part of my Berkeley education.

In my second and third years at Berkeley I took a variety of courses. I became convinced that technical fields were not for me. I had to choose a major, and I ruled out mathematics and science. I had never been oriented in that direction despite that fact that I especially liked science in high school. I loved languages and I loved literature. It was not a coincidence, then, that I found myself particularly favoring language courses and ultimately majoring in languages.

In my major I focused primarily on English, Spanish, and French literature. Some classes I enjoyed more than others, but I always approached my classes with a sense of discovery. Education became an opportunity for me to go beyond the small, provincial world I had known as a young girl.

Perhaps the best way to describe what literature meant to me is to reiterate that my personal world, the world I had shared with my parents in New Mexico, in the migrant camps of the southern San Joaquin Valley, and in the barrio of Visalia was truly a private world. It was neither reflected nor affirmed in any book available to me or in any course work.

Though this world was private, it was not secret. It was vibrant and widely shared by the Spanish-speaking community. Nevertheless, it was a world in which the dominant society did not participate.

As a result, even American literature to me was not much different from European literature in that I experienced almost no sense of real life or actual identification with some of the material I read. I had almost no direct experience with much of what was being depicted in these novels, short stories, poems, and essays, irrespective of what country they represented. To me everything seemed foreign.

I obviously knew English. By now it was my primary language. I was familiar with place-names such as New York and Georgia. Yet I didn't really know places like New York or Georgia. They were abstractions. Hence, all American literature was undifferentiated in that sense. America, beyond my limited experiences, was a world that I was discovering in the same kinds of ways I was discovering everything else— through reading, observation, and personal contact.

In my American lit courses I was introduced to and read the standard authors: Herman Melville, Mark Twain, Theodore Dreiser, F. Scott Fitzgerald, Ernest Hemingway, William Faulkner, John Steinbeck, and Robert Penn Warren.

But even though I found American writers engaging, I found myself even more intrigued by writers from other lands such as Europe and Latin America. Perhaps because of my limited experiences I found it more rewarding to read literature of times and places far removed from me.

With non-American works, I discovered that I didn't have to cut through the filter of cultures with which I was supposed to identify to get to the essence of the text. I could more easily focus on universal aspects of the material and absorb and enjoy the rest on the basis of context as I was able or inclined to do.

While I enjoyed American literature I don't think that there were any particular American writers whom I really warmed up to. By contrast, I fell instantly in love with Russian writers, for example. Tolstoy's *War and Peace* gave me a real feel for Russian history. I never felt that American writers conveyed a sense of history or that they understood it.

Other European writers fascinated me for different reasons. The Spanish essayist and philosopher Miguel de Unamuno was among them. "Let them sleep" is a phrase that I recall from one of his essays. I could sense the frustration he felt toward individuals inclined to live the "unexamined life," victims of ideas that go unchallenged, individuals who are, in essence, "asleep."

I was young and impressionable, and Unamuno seemed like a wise elder. He had the detachment of a philosopher and the compassion of a father figure. The Spanish language had never seemed more rich or more beautiful.

I have never gone back to those early readings to check my impressions, preferring to retain my image of the philosopher. In his detachment, Unamuno saw with clarity what is obscure to us. He cared and had the courage to challenge our complacencies. This image was very comforting to me.

Religion had been such a pervasive part of my upbringing that I felt compelled to come to terms with my position on the subject before I could feel truly free to go on with my life. When Unamuno had written his essays, he had been addressing a world far removed from mine in time and place, yet his ideas made sense to me. He provided me with one way of getting at some of the religious issues that had been nettlesome to me for a long time.

Plato, especially his *Republic,* also made a major impression on me. It was illuminating for me to immerse myself in a closed philosophical system that ostensibly had nothing to do with my life yet seemed relevant to aspects of my growing years.

I could remember having felt frustrated by my inability to understand why things were so difficult at home. There had been times when, as a young girl, I had really despaired. Our economic struggles seemed without end. I don't think I had much of a notion of cause-and-effect relationships, and there were times when I had no practical way of dealing with my frustrations. It was probably to my parents' credit that they simply put their faith in God and were determined to survive by dint of their efforts.

But their determination didn't explain anything to me. If God was listening, he didn't seem to be responding. The *Republic* did more than years of schooling had done to give me a sense of how a closed system can work to define a person's life. I realized that, in some ways, I felt I had grown up in just such a system, which in some ways had been very hurtful. I just hadn't known what to call it.

Some of the more interesting as well as frustrating experiences I had in my literature classes involved my Latin American and Spanish professors. These were not Latinos from the United States but from Spain and Latin America. I particularly recall taking classes with the very distinguished literary critic Arturo Torres-Ríoseco, who was from Chile.

In later years, when I read his whimsical, picaresque little book, *El Frijolito Saltón,* I thought about Professor Torres-Ríoseco. The book relates the adventures and misadventures of a Mexican jumping bean trying to survive as a little being trapped in the home of a wealthy Mexican family. This delightful creature demonstrates amazing wit, courage, and skill as he fends off the attacks of the nasty, mean-spirited child in the family. The little bean is eventually overcome—but not really. He is smashed by the little boy, but he doesn't die. Instead, he becomes a beautiful white butterfly and can be seen, even today, so we're told, fluttering across the blue skies of Mexico.

In contrast, the professor I remember was not whimsical, and he lacked the lightness of spirit that characterized the clever little bean. Though he would chat about his country quite a bit, his interactions with students were brief, even perfunctory, and he seemed a bit standoffish. I remember feeling disappointment and even anger at the way he conducted his class and frustrated at the students' reaction to him. He would lumber into the classroom, sit at the teacher's desk, and, looking briefly over the assembled group of about twenty-five students, ask, "*Pues, ¿qué leyeron anoche?*"

From the deathly silence that ensued, it was clear to me that the other students lacked the language skills to respond to such an open-ended question. "What did you read last night?" could be an intimidating question for undergraduates who, like me, were products of an educational system that did not place very high value on learning foreign languages and that furthermore relied on a grammar-and-translation approach to the study of these languages—which were most likely taught by nonnative speakers.

I sensed in our professor a lack of sympathy toward the *americanos* whose lack of oral skill in Spanish was obvious. He would wait out the silence, a faint smile on his lips and a dismissive look on his face as he avoided making any eye contact with his students. Invariably, I would speak up and get the discussion started. But I resented him for making me feel that I had to initiate it.

I derived no satisfaction from sitting among students rendered mute by Professor Torres-Ríoseco's teaching methods. My resentment toward him extended to my not taking any opportunity to engage him in private conversation, despite the fact that I was intrigued by the question of how a Chilean ended up in a place like Berkeley. His book, which was the text for our class, was indicative of his impressive knowledge of Spanish and Latin American literature. I surmised that he could have had a job in any major university in Latin America.

Even after I had begun to appreciate the importance of his position as a literary figure, Arturo Torres-Ríoseco remained for me the stereotypical model of the Latin American who is scornful of the *americanos'* effort to cope with Spanish. I personalized the experience—another piece of the puzzle of my self-definition. I wasn't "foreign," but Spanish was my language as much as his. I had no idea what the basis might be for his apparent unfriendliness toward us students, but I didn't like it.

In retrospect, of course, I recognize that he probably felt as frustrated with the class as the class felt with him. His gray hair indicated to me that he was well past fifty, and our small group of underclassmen could hardly have been the high point of his day.

Another Latin American professor who made a poor impression on me was a Peruvian who I think was a guest lecturer in a cultures class. I recall how he introduced himself. He expressed delight that the classroom was packed with eager students, but noting that the room was stuffy, he attempted to open a window. It refused to give, and in the ensuing awkwardness, he went into an impromptu little speech about his difficulty in dealing with mechanical matters in this technologically advanced nation. His point was that in his native Peru matters of the spirit were valued above the merely technical, and opening a window was hardly anything he would be expected to do. It was a weak joke.

To me it came across as a left-handed compliment to his host country. He seemed to be asserting his country's moral superiority. I personalized the little scenario and surprised myself as I recognized a stir of nationalism within me. Again, I was experiencing my private world as a dilemma of split allegiances. I was unable to appreciate the humor in our shared circumstances.

Although I enjoyed most of my Latin American and Spanish literature classes, I did not associate the content, the professors, or the books we were reading with my own background. For example, I couldn't relate to a professor from Chile as a "fellow Hispanic." He was to me no different from a professor from Poland who came via France to Berkeley.

They were from another land, another country. Nothing those Hispanic professors said or seemed to represent was directly related to my experience.

But I did have two favorites among the various language scholars I met. One was an erudite Galician, an older figure who enjoyed poking fun at his own *ceceo,* a pronunciation unique to his native Spain, which he took none too seriously. For me, Professor Buceta was a fountain of knowledge, with a sense of humor. I was flattered when he politely invited me to look at some of his books, and I promptly accepted. He was friendly but formal. He lived about three blocks from campus. I had no misgivings about what seemed like a harmless invitation. The experience proved to be rewarding.

The walls of his apartment were lined with bookcases, and he had so many books that they seemed to spill onto the floor. In the entryway was an impressive stack of periodicals and newspapers. I was too dazzled by the wealth of materials to make an assessment of what I beheld, but when he offered to give me a book I managed to make a selection. I still have my copy of the slim volume, *Antología Poética de Francisco de Quevedo.*

I also remember with fondness a professor of Italian and Spanish who was probably one of the most caring teachers I had in my four undergraduate years at Berkeley. Regretfully, I can no longer remember her name, although it may have been Professor Schotti.

She was a large woman, formal in appearance and manner. She dressed somberly and didn't seem to smile a great deal, but there was a gentleness in her manner that made her very approachable. She had a good rapport with students and a way of asking questions to make sure we understood her. I think that it was from her that I began to acquire a sense of what life in academia must be like.

I remember one particular occasion that was significant for me. She had invited another student and me to her lovely home in the El Cerrito hills, a short distance north of Berkeley. I was impressed with her large formal dining room, the long table suggesting that she entertained large groups.

In talking to us about the work she was doing, she conveyed a sense that as a woman she felt isolated in her department, in the minority due to the mere fact of being a woman. When I remarked on the impressive amount of writing she was doing, she said, "I don't get credit for this. I do it because I love my work."

She did not speak with affection about her colleagues. Although I heard her words, I missed their full significance at that point. For me, the fact that I saw mostly male professors at Berkeley was simply a reflection of the world as I had experienced it. I focused more on what she said about the "publish-or-perish" phenomenon, and because of her I began to feel greater appreciation for the time professors were investing in our education.

Probably the reason I remember with affection those professors whose homes I visited is that they gave me something I never could have obtained from books—a sense of the human side of the academic world and, by extension, a sense of how a person's life work can be personally rewarding as well.

I think, for example, of Professor Raleigh, the English professor who invited our entire class to his beautiful home in the Berkeley hills. I felt special sitting in his living room with all the other students. The seating arrangement was informal. The furnishings, the art work, and the books all seemed to suggest that here people lived personally enriched lives. There was some polite talk and an informal discussion of our class and of literature in general.

But equally important to me was meeting the professor's wife. She was an attractive, gracious young woman—seemingly the perfect partner for him. I have forgotten what she did professionally, but I remember being impressed by her intelligence. And I couldn't help reflecting, momentarily, that this was probably what a good marriage partnership could be all about.

At the conclusion of that evening, I even made up my mind that I was going to work harder at appreciating the English poet John Donne, whose assigned works in that class up until then had been a chore.

By my second and third years at Berkeley, I rarely thought of returning to Visalia even for a visit. I was busy with my studies and my work, and I had little time for the long bus ride home and back.

Because my family was poor, because raising the rest of the children remained an economic struggle for my parents, I knew that I had to fend for myself. I had to focus on taking care of myself. Even if I had wanted to go back to Visalia, I couldn't. There was nothing there for me economically. Seasonal field labor remained the work available to Mexican Americans. In Berkeley I valued my independence, my freedom to make choices. I knew that my parents trusted me to be all right on my own.

Although classes and working occupied much of my time, I did continue to manage a little bit of a social life. I dated, but infrequently and never seriously, at least during my first couple of years at Berkeley.

Dating at that time was friendly and casual. It involved going out for coffee, a movie, a football game, or just a bus ride to some event. Very few students I knew had cars, so most socializing occurred either on campus or in close proximity to campus. My dates were mostly with young men I met in my classes or at Newman Hall.

Dating to me was getting to know other people. I never saw it as engaging in anything else. I was worried about getting "serious," meaning that I never put myself in a compromising position. I had grown up with an unstated but understood prohibition of premarital sex. I didn't intend to "go all the way," as it was called, and I feared pregnancy outside marriage. My guess is that I was no different from most other girls in that respect.

For me dating was not falling in love and it was certainly not sexual.

I recall one date with Don, a fraternity boy who lived in the interracial fraternity on campus. The possible sexual implications in this instance were clear. He took me to a party at his fraternity house and, when we arrived, he showed me around. I remember being surprised by the low lights and the hay strewn about the upstairs rooms. I assumed that those rooms would be used for making out—or more.

I walked briskly through, and fortunately for me he didn't say anything or make any moves on me. We walked back downstairs, where we socialized. However, I remained in a state of shock the rest of that evening, alarmed by what I had seen upstairs. To his credit, Don avoided any reference to the subject, and I was grateful. I don't recall any guy ever attempting to actually force himself on me.

I don't know if my experiences were typical of those of other female students at Berkeley, but I suspect the concern about sexual matters was more common than not. There was one girl, for example, with whom I was friends for a while. She had been forced out of her sorority because she had gotten pregnant. It was clearly a big loss for her. She was teary eyed when she told me that she wanted to marry the boy but now wasn't sure what would happen.

I had met her in one of my classes, and she told me her story one day while we were at coffee. She had grown up a lot as a result of her pregnancy and felt pretty bad about it. I don't remember if she'd had an abortion or had put her baby up for adoption, but she didn't keep the baby.

I felt sorry for her, but her unfortunate experience didn't surprise me. I was aware of the dangers of becoming sexually involved—and I intended to avoid the danger. I believe most girls then had been taught to fear pregnancy outside marriage. However, the fact remained that contraception was not discussed publicly.

In my case, the Church promoted abstinence before marriage and the "rhythm method" in marriage. I knew of no office or clinic where you could get advice on birth control. If Catholic people used birth control, they did so quietly and didn't admit to it. It was a subject that you avoided. I suspected that many Catholics opposed the Church's positions on contraception and abortion, but few voiced these kinds of opinions publicly.

For my part, I wouldn't have known where to go ask about contraceptives. Since doctors weren't readily available when I was growing up, I wasn't used to going to them. I wasn't really ready to deal with these subjects. I knew that birth control was prohibited by my Church, and even though I had some intellectual reasons to question these prohibitions, I didn't go beyond this. I had no substitute for the code of behavior, the moral framework, that had been instilled in me.

For me at that time, life came in absolutes, in this case, either abstention or promiscuity. I possessed no countermorality that could justify sex outside marriage.

NINE

New Vistas and New Connections

By the time I became a junior at Berkeley, I had decided that I wanted to pursue teaching as a career. I was also aware that, at least at Berkeley, a teaching profession was not held in high esteem. Since Berkeley was a research institution, it appeared to favor research-related professions over teaching. There was a school of education at Berkeley, but it did not possess anywhere near the prestige that other schools and programs on the campus did. I considered all these factors but remained firm in my decision. I was attracted to the idea of becoming a teacher. Teachers had been role models for me even in Visalia.

But teaching was also part of practical reality for me. I wanted to go to graduate school but I needed to start working once I had completed my undergraduate degree. I thought that perhaps I could work and also take summer classes toward an M.A., possibly in literature. However, I discovered that this was not practical or permissible. To get a master's degree you needed to be in residence during the regular academic year, not just during the summer.

When I considered all options, I had no difficulty making my decision. I would apply for admission to the school of education, where I could receive my teaching credential in one postgraduate year.

✧✦✧

I thought I had my life fairly well planned for the next few years. But what I did not anticipate was falling in love.

Sometime either at the end of my sophomore year or the beginning of my junior year I received a letter from an Ed Tywoniak:

"Dear Fran, I know it's been a while since we met but I'd very much like to see you again, if that's possible. I hope you remember me."

I certainly did remember him.

During the summer when I worked in the mountains, I had met Ed. He was working for Pacific Gas and Electric Company and was living in Pacific Grove. At the time I met him he was on vacation and staying at the resort.

At the end of my summer job, I had decided to try to get a ride back to Visalia rather than take the bus. Ed offered to give me a ride, saying it was not out of the way for him. On our way to Visalia, I learned that he was originally from the East Coast, that he had served in the Pacific during the war, and that upon his return he had decided to get a job in California. His home office was in Monterey.

As we talked, we discovered that we shared some interests. We both liked music. I also shared with him my enthusiasm about going to Berkeley.

Before I knew it we had arrived in Visalia. I had enjoyed the ride with Ed and I sensed that he had also enjoyed my company. I was grateful to him and thanked him. He now knew my address in Visalia and promised to drop me a note. I never expected to hear from him again.

It was through my Visalia address that he contacted me in Berkeley. I was pleased that he still remembered me. I was pleased but not surprised. I think that because my time at Berkeley had gone so fast it didn't really dawn on me that it had been almost a couple of years since I had seen Ed.

He had been one of numerous people I'd met while working at

Shaver Lake in the summer of 1949. Those who came to the large main resort-complex area included vacationing families staying in the nearby cabins, young singles, including a few college students, and local residents. There was an overall pleasant and relaxed feeling about the place. People were friendly, and Ed, too, had seemed like a very sociable person. At the time, the little I saw of him simply indicated to me that he was a nice guy.

In fact, "meeting guys" was the last thing on my mind that summer. I remember one college student staying at the lake for a few days who told me that he was a student at a private college somewhere in the Bay Area. Before leaving the resort, he had given me a picture of himself and an address. He was interested in my plans to attend Berkeley and had said, "I'd like you to write to me when you get there."

At the end of the summer, I remember feeling very guilty when I threw away his photo and note. I didn't know what else to do with them. I wasn't interested in him. I was focused on beginning my studies at the university, and I had no plans to work on developing this type of social relationship. Besides, he had seemed aggressive, and I didn't feel comfortable around him.

Ed, on the other hand, simply impressed me as being friendly. It's only now, many years later, that I've begun to understand what was really happening.

By the time I was eighteen I had unconsciously come to the conclusion that boys my age or close to my age were of interest to me only if I could relate to them academically in the natural process of socializing with them.

Peter had been and would remain the great love of my life. Our relationship would retain its magic because it was unconsummated. It remained alive in the realm of the ideal, the much-desired but ill-defined world of unfulfilled possibilities. And it marked the beginning of the end of my adolescence.

My relationship with Ed was entirely different. Older than I, he had a self-assurance that put me at ease. I admired what I saw as his maturity and judgment gained from years of experience. He could discuss knowledgeably and with sensitivity subjects that were of importance to me. Since we shared a love of music, I could empathize with his sense of loss at not having been able to pursue his musical interests when he was young. Music remained his love all his life. I didn't understand the significance of it at the time, but Ed could make me feel that it was OK for me to be a woman and also a full person. I could be a woman and also be intelligent.

And so it was with a sense of renewed interest that I received word from him. In his letter, he informed me that he was now living in Oakland, which is why he had written. I wrote him back and told him I would welcome seeing him again.

We arranged to meet in Berkeley. I don't remember where we went. I know it wasn't a movie because we spent most of our time talking. I think we just stayed home and talked in the living room.

Although I was pleased to see Ed again, I was also a bit apprehensive. I wasn't sure he would be the way I remembered him. It wasn't like I hadn't dated before, for I certainly had met other boys, some of whom were also from the East Coast. The difference was that Ed was unlike these other boys.

In fact, he wasn't a boy at all. Ed was seventeen years older than I and was already well into his thirties. He was a World War II veteran who had gone into the navy in the 1930s and had been in China before the war. When he served in the Pacific he had attained the rank of lieutenant commander. He was different from any other man I had ever been with.

But despite my apprehension, Ed very quickly put me at ease. He told me more about his war experiences and about his plans to go into business for himself. He hoped to open a bar/restaurant. But he was also very interested in my experiences. "I just work and go to school," I told him. But he really seemed to want to know more about me.

So I talked about Berkeley and about my first two years there. I told him about my having to work to supplement the scholarship I had been able to maintain. I was now not only working in that boys' boarding house but had also secured a job as a theater cashier at the Campus Theater in Berkeley.

As I talked I got the sense that Ed was interested in me as a student. He wanted to learn more about what I was studying. I couldn't help thinking, as Ed and I talked, that he reminded me a lot of Peter, who had also respected my desire to acquire an education. They even looked alike in some ways.

We both had a pleasant time. The fact that he was much older than I didn't bother me after this initial date. I appreciated his maturity. In fact, it was very attractive to me.

We eventually began seeing each other fairly frequently, about once a week, usually on weekends. "Hi, brown eyes," would be his usual cheerful greeting. Our dates were simple. We would take walks, sometimes around Lake Merritt in Oakland, go to a park, or have something to eat at a small, inexpensive restaurant.

Sometimes the only occasion I could see Ed, what with studying and working, was when I went to Mass on Sundays. Although I learned that Ed was not religious in any formal way and not a practicing Catholic, he agreed to accompany me to Newman Hall for Mass some Sundays.

I also remember visiting Ed at his place in Oakland, a small apartment in a complex with all the units facing a common lawn where we sat and talked. He once prepared dinner for me there. These visits were all perfectly innocent, although a little bit rushed because I had my job responsibilities.

Yet after some weeks of seeing each other, it was becoming clear to me—and to Ed also—that our relationship was becoming serious. This was beginning to complicate my life a bit, but I didn't know just quite what to do.

By that time—I was well into my junior year—I had moved into a new rooming house where there were more single girls like me. I became good friends with two girls in particular. Helen was a Japanese American student from Richmond, California, and Betty was a Chinese

American student from Arizona. Among the things we talked about were marriage and sexuality.

"I intend to graduate, but I'm also very involved with my boyfriend. I love him, and he's coming to visit," Betty told me. Her boyfriend was out of school, lived in Arizona, and was driving up to see her.

"But how do your parents feel about your boyfriend?" I asked her.

"They don't know about him. They're not here, and so it doesn't matter."

I learned one day just how involved Betty was with her boyfriend. I had to take an exam at nine o'clock one morning, and I knew that she also had an exam at that time. Sometimes we would walk to campus together. But on this particular morning I didn't see her, so I knocked on her door. There was no answer. I knocked again. Still no answer. After a couple more minutes of knocking, I gave up and left, not wanting to be late for my own exam.

Later that day when I ran into her, she gave me what I thought was a lame excuse for not answering when I knocked. "I overslept," she told me. Then I realized what had happened. I felt foolish about my own naïveté. Her boyfriend had come into town and had obviously spent the night. I had never had a guy stay overnight with me. It didn't occur to me that she would have the courage to do it with our rooms so close together. I was shocked, but more at my own ignorance than at her behavior.

When I discovered what was happening in my own rooming house, it made me acutely aware of my own confused attitude toward sex. It was OK for Betty to have her boyfriend stay overnight, but this wasn't something I could do. If I had started having sex outside marriage I would have felt very guilty. My feelings were totally tied up with the way my parents had brought me up and their silences concerning sexual matters as well as the religious prohibitions I had been taught.

Although I was exposed to new and more liberal views at Berkeley, I was still very much bound up in my early socialization. I could accept intellectually what other people did—Betty's sexual activity, for example—but I was still compelled to be guided by what I had been taught about "right" and "wrong" where my own behavior was concerned.

Besides the moral issues involved in having sex with a boyfriend, there were the practical considerations. I grew up—as did most of my contemporaries—with a fear of pregnancy out of wedlock. A baby born out of wedlock would have been a shame, a disgrace, and a disaster.

It was during my time in Berkeley or shortly thereafter that a huge scandal developed around the actress Ingrid Bergman, who had mothered a child out of wedlock. Although she had been much loved in this country until then, she became the focus of tremendous opposition, so much so that she stayed out of the United States for several years.

There had been occasions when I had been physically very close to a boy, in a car, for example. I might have been able to have sex, but I drew the line. This was automatic behavior. You never crossed that boundary, or at least I didn't. This was because of fear—the fear of becoming pregnant and of violating the religious principles that had been ingrained in me.

One could, of course, take precautions and use some form of birth control, which was probably limited then to a boy using condoms. But this wouldn't work for me either, because taking precautions would have simply been premeditated sex. This was unacceptable.

What was an option for me was marriage. This was the natural way of dealing with sex. For the first time, I openly talked about marriage. I didn't discuss it with Ed, but with my two girlfriends.

"You're very much in love, aren't you?" Helen asked me.

I didn't know quite what to say. But the more I thought about it the more I admitted to myself that I liked Ed very much.

"I guess so," I replied, with great hesitation.

I was both strongly attracted to Ed and amazed at myself. How could I, who had so completely rejected the notion, be even remotely contemplating marriage? And yet that's precisely what I was doing. It would take me a little time to admit it, but I liked this new self. In my grow-ing years, I had unconsciously internalized the notion of marriage as a lifetime commitment, and now that's exactly what I wanted.

I wanted to be with Ed, and I knew this was a life choice. I was ex-cited and probably as giddy as any girl can be when she's in love.

⁓⁂⁓

As our relationship evolved, both Ed and I sensed more and more how close we were getting and, I guess, how much closer we both desired to be. At a certain stage in our relationship, without any fanfare, we just decided to get married. My best recollection is that, at some point, we looked at each other and said, "What are we going to do?"

And we agreed, "I guess we're going to get married."

We jointly came to this conclusion. There was no formal proposal, nothing like what I had seen in the movies. This wasn't a fantasy. Ed was real. I loved and admired him, and, yes, the feeling was mutual.

It was with Ed that I ultimately defined my life. Even now, more than twenty years after his death, he remains an integral part of who I am.

Our engagement was brief. We shopped for a ring together. We could have gotten married almost immediately, but we decided to be somewhat practical and to wait until I had taken my fall semester exams midway through my junior year. We decided to get married in January.

My parents and Toni didn't know that I was seeing Ed. I hadn't told them. Nor did I seek my parents' advice or permission, notifying them of my plans only after Ed and I had made our decision. My parents accepted my decision, even though they hadn't met Ed and would not meet him until several months after we got married.

I was in a bit of a fog, because everything was moving so fast. But I never regretted my decision. Nor was I frightened by it. I didn't think about the possibility of dropping out of school or of what would happen if I got pregnant after we married. After marriage, pregnancy didn't seem to be an issue. I was totally fearless. Ignorance is bliss!

We decided that we would drive to Reno and get married there. I asked Toni if she could come with us and be my maid of honor. She happily agreed to do so. She was not surprised at my actions. Both of us had been raised to be fairly self-supporting and to make our own decisions. Toni's agreement to come to my wedding was one more way that, as my older sister, she continued to support me. I appreciated that very much.

We drove to Reno with Toni and with Stan, a good friend of Ed's who was going to be his best man. When we got there, we had no idea just where we would actually get married. We had agreed that it should be a Catholic service. Although Ed was not particularly religious, he had agreed to get married in a Catholic church, partly because his mother was Catholic.

We drove to the University of Nevada in Reno and asked directions to the Catholic chaplain. We told the chaplain that we had just driven up from Berkeley and wanted to get married. The chaplain seemed stunned at first.

"What parish do you belong to?" he asked.

"Well, I don't actually belong to a parish," I said. "I go to Mass at Newman Hall on the Berkeley campus."

"But that's not a parish," he replied. "You have to have permission from your parish to marry outside of it."

"So now what do we do?" we asked the chaplain. More than a question, it was a plea that he do something.

He agreed to make a telephone call to find out what parish I belonged to in Berkeley. He was told that St. Joseph's was my designated parish, but the chaplain could get no help for us at St. Joseph's, because I wasn't registered there. He sat quietly for a while, absorbed in thought. Then, looking at us knowingly, he said, "This is what I need to do."

He then set about making calls to church officials in the archdiocese of San Francisco. Within about an hour, he had everything arranged. I was both impressed and ecstatic.

The chaplain directed us to go to the Church of St. Albert the Great, which was about a mile from the campus. We would be married there that afternoon. We were grateful to that chaplain and thanked him. I was amazed and delighted by what we had been able to accomplish.

In those days, under normal circumstances, a Catholic wedding did not take place until after the banns of marriage had been announced or published for a month before the ceremony. Banns were the official announcement of a proposed marriage. At that point in my life, I felt that rules of this type were rules that I would question. I knew that as a Mexican American at Berkeley I was already an exception. I was prepared to question social conventions. So I believed that a priest could marry us without the "mandatory" banns.

In fact, it was doable. We were married by a priest that afternoon. The church was completely empty except for me, Ed, Toni, Stan, and the priest. There were no flowers. There was no music. For me there was magnificence and dignity just in the sanctuary of that church. We stood before the main altar, two people exchanging vows.

I didn't wear a wedding dress. I wore the wool suit that Eve had given me in my sophomore year. I gave no thought to the fact that I wasn't dressed in traditional white. I was very calm and completely happy.

We spent very little time in Reno, because we all needed to get back to Berkeley, and Toni had to return to her job. It wasn't until that summer that Ed and I had what amounted to a honeymoon when we went to Catalina Island for a few days.

The fact that I had married someone other than a Mexican American got attention. This, too, was not the expectation, but it seemed right for me.

In the normal course of various social or business interactions, if I had to give my new last name, I would invariably be asked to spell it, which I would do. Then I'd be asked to repeat it. My face would be scrutinized, and I would then be asked, "Is that a Korean name?" Other guesses included Hawaiian, Japanese, and even Aleutian one time.

These were the days when, even in the Bay Area, people stopped to stare at mixed couples, particularly Anglo/African American couples. It's likely that Ed and I drew curious stares as well. He was tall, fair-haired, and blue-eyed whereas I was just a couple of inches taller than five feet and dark-haired. However, I don't recall that our differences were a problem to me in any sense.

My life, at that point, didn't fit the expected pattern, and I felt that I was continuing to take the initiative in setting the direction for it. My marrying Ed and assuming the name Tywoniak was the right thing for me to do, because he was the person with whom I wanted to be. The fact that I was crossing ethnic barriers was not a consideration. It was a decision he and I made with confidence that it was the right decision for us.

Ed and I never dwelt on the ethnic aspects of our backgrounds. That our backgrounds were vastly different was obvious. His parents had immigrated to this country from Poland. He had joined the navy at a young age and had trained at a naval training facility in Alameda, California, expecting to make the navy his career. As a seaman, he had been to cities that I'd never heard of. He spoke fondly of Asian people with whom he had made friends while he was in the navy. His worldview was inclusive.

I do recall that, years later, when our daughter had grown up, she asked, "How did you and Dad happen to get together?"

"I think it was just a classic case of 'opposites attract,'" I told her. My response was spontaneous and probably quite accurate.

As a World War II veteran, Ed had experienced combat in the Pacific, and as a result had left the navy not by choice but for medical reasons. It was not easy for Ed to talk about the war, but he told me enough to give me a new perspective on it. With reluctance and only at my request, he would share some of his war experiences, images of war I had never imagined.

"What was it like on a battlefield?" I wanted to know. His answer shocked me. As I recall, among Ed's worst nightmares were the memories of young men enclosed in a big gun emplacement and obliterated as the gun misfired, trapping them in a tight compartment. Death in an unintended burst of explosives.

The war had not always progressed as smoothly as I had envisioned it from the distance of my adolescent years. In fact, in the glimpses of war that I gleaned from Ed, the unexpected seemed to be the norm.

Ed also shared his memories of spending time on a special assignment in a submarine somewhere in the depths of the Pacific Ocean. This involved hours of waiting, in silence, watching the vessel "breathe," the hull of the submarine visibly contracting and expanding under the pressure of the ocean's depth.

Why was it that Ed retired from the army as a lieutenant colonel if he had been in the navy? I was curious. I learned that the war sometimes called for unique responses to special needs. Ed's skills as a naval commander had been needed by the army transportation services in the Pacific.

The war that Ed and I discussed was not the war of historical facts that I had grown up with. It was a war of injuries and powerful and highly personal psychological implications. It was a war in which men believed in and responded to the call of duty.

Those of us who had experienced the war through posters, patriotic songs, and newsreels had had a very different experience. It helped me, talking with Ed about this, to put my own stressful adolescence in perspective.

When I've been asked if, in marrying Ed, I was rejecting my father, I've had difficulty responding. The question seems to have as much to do with the person raising the issue as it does with me. At the simplest level, such a question seems to assume that, when you marry, your choices are between someone who embodies the attributes you associate with your parents or someone who, presumably, is the antithesis of these attributes. For me, the matter has been a bit more complex than that, yet I hesitate to engage in psychological analysis except in the most tentative way. I recognize the pitfalls.

That I was rejecting something is clear enough. That's the easy part. To the extent that I knew my father as an autocratic head of a household, I rejected his example. But my mother was the complementary side of the equation.

When a decision called for action, my mother was likely to say that the matter called for *mano de hombre*. A "man's hand" was needed. The man's actions were always authoritative. The woman served a cohesive function. She could keep situations from disintegrating.

That I resembled my father had been made abundantly clear to me. I'd grown up hearing from my mother how much like my father I was—quick temper, stubbornness, you name it. What wasn't mentioned was the fact that my stubbornness also reflected some of my mother's own tenacity. Not surprisingly, though in some ways I was very much like my father, in other ways I was more like my mother.

In fact, tenaciousness is probably the one characteristic that defines all us siblings equally. Toni, for example, has reminded me that she gets chided by one of her daughters for her "head-in-the-sand" attitude when she refuses to consider alternatives. But she can chuckle over it. "That's probably why I was a happy military wife," she says. "As long as the family unit was intact, I was intact."

The late thirties and early forties, years that were a time of deprivation and increasing alienation for me, were not a problem for her. "The fact that our family was together was important to me," she says. I remind her of how her placid demeanor used to enrage me. Her response is, "I knew that all I had to do was to pretend I was going to tickle you, and you'd back off." She recalls that invariably her response to adversity has been: "If I can't do anything about it, why worry? I do the best with what I have, and then I let the Lord take care of the rest."

In contrast, I rebelled against my father's domineering role, and I also rejected the role to which my mother appeared to be consigned—subordinate in the marriage partnership and limited to a sphere defined by family demands. I could not imagine myself in the role of submissive wife.

But rejecting something is different from identifying what will take its place. That, to me, was the important question. What kind of life could I rightfully expect? I must have asked myself that question in numerous ways, innumerable times. I was open to searching. I was open to questioning.

Toni and I did share this motivation to get away from our immediate environment. Although temperamentally we were markedly different, we had shared life experiences in our early formative years. There were unspoken assumptions between us. For example, we had similar perspectives on the subject of marriage. Toni says, "Mexican boys were too restrictive. I did not want to be considered just the woman in the house. For me, being a wife and mother was a matter of choice. It was not something I did because I was forced."

Shortly after I married Ed, a retired naval officer, Toni married a serviceman on active duty in the air force. "Oh yes," she remembers, "we admired our servicemen. They represented all that was good in our country. They were courageous, self-sacrificing, caring, and responsible. They were a symbol of who we were as a nation."

◦◦◦

Getting married and expecting to remain a student at Berkeley never seemed inconsistent to me. I never thought of dropping out of school just to be a wife and have children. My image of myself was that of a Berkeley student, and that implied earning my degree, completing a year of graduate work, and going on to a teaching career. My plans were consistent with the fact that I had always worked and I expected to continue working after getting married.

I never saw myself as content to remain limited to the traditional woman's role. Ed shared my feelings. Not only did he not ask me to drop out of school, he actually encouraged my studies. His support meant a lot to me, and, as I've mentioned, in this regard Ed reminded me of Peter. But more important, the connection between the two was that I felt as comfortable talking to Ed about my aspirations as I had once felt talking to Peter. Neither of them was threatened or put off by my hopes for making a life for myself. The marriage partnership did not preclude it.

Over the years, I continued to look to Ed and to trust him where matters of my academic and professional welfare were concerned.

"Ed," I would say, "I've been asked to take on a new responsibility, a new assignment."

Without fail, his response would be an approving, "Sure, if that's what you want to do."

The tacit understanding between us was that my new responsibilities would likely mean, again, a rearrangement of our home responsibilities. And we continued to share all chores at home as our time permitted. He never begrudged me his time in this regard.

The idea of dropping out of school would also have been inconsistent with the way my parents had raised me. My parents weren't quitters. The notion of my being a quitter never entered my mind. My father was, in his own way, goal oriented. He always saw a job through to its conclusion. My father had a "can-do" attitude about work. I learned a lot from him, a sense of coherence, of wholeness, of work being part of living. My mother was also a role model in this regard. She could be very single-minded in her support of her children's education. What both of them gave me was a sense of what it is to have a goal and to work to achieve that goal. It was that simple.

I also saw myself as setting an example in my family. I was the first to go to college, and I was in a position to demonstrate that it could be done. My marriage changed none of that.

Being married, of course, did mean some changes in my life. I was no longer living alone, and finding suitable housing was a little more difficult. I left my boarding house, and we found an apartment on College Avenue near Ashby Avenue, quite a distance from campus. We lived there for about eight months before we could find an apartment on Durant Avenue, which was closer to campus.

Although living with Ed did mean an adjustment, it was not a radical change. I resumed my classes as soon as the spring semester started. I also maintained my job at the movie theater. In between classes and working, I managed to find time to read and study. My irregular schedule did not cause Ed any problems.

I was fortunate. Ed and I agreed that our marriage would not be traditional. We never expected that he would be the main breadwinner and that I would have to be the homemaker. From the very beginning, we both had jobs and we also shared household duties, including cooking and housecleaning.

Ed's work facilitated this shared responsibility. He was operating a bar in Oakland, and his hours, too, were irregular. While this meant that he came home at a late hour some nights, at the same time his schedule gave him flexibility during the day. This meant that when I needed to be in class, he could be home.

I don't think a traditional marriage would have worked for me. While I respected my parents, I rejected the type of traditional/patriarchal relationship that they had. My father was quick to anger, and his moods dominated our household. This type of marriage was not acceptable to me. I could not accept the self-abnegation that seemed to define my mother's life.

"*¿Por qué se deja tratar así?*" I would ask my mother. "Why don't you assert yourself? Talk back to him!" I remember saying to my mother, but only after my father was safely out of earshot. My frustration would turn to a seething anger. My mother's resigned silence, a shrug of the shoulders, conveyed only defeat to me. As I saw what was happening,

I continued to conclude that my mother's inability to express or assert herself was inextricably tied to her role at home. My father had authority at home as well as on matters that extended beyond our home.

It would not be until many years later that I would recognize the strength that my mother had demonstrated during those incredibly stressful times. Years later, when economic pressures had eased, their life became more tranquil. I could then look back with greater understanding of what it had meant for them to live through the Great Depression and the harsh living conditions in the San Joaquin Valley.

Even though I was determined to have a very different marital relationship from that of my parents, I had no intention of separating myself from them. Shortly after we got married, Ed and I visited my parents in Visalia. Although I was a bit apprehensive about this initial meeting, everything turned out fine.

My parents liked Ed and made him feel at home. Ed reciprocated this feeling. Because he was older, he behaved with them as if he were dealing with peers rather than with parents-in-law. The language difference didn't prove to be a major barrier. My mother, of course, knew English and my father, by now, had also picked up sufficient English to converse with Ed. The fact that he was no longer so insistent that only Spanish be spoken at home helped.

Needless to say I was relieved at how comfortable our initial visit turned out to be. Although we didn't go back to Visalia any more frequently than I had before I got married, our later visits were always festive occasions. Ed and I would go out shopping and bring back food, and we would help my mother prepare a nice dinner. Our visits became like small family parties.

That my parents readily accepted Ed was not a surprise to me. In asserting their cultural values they had never demeaned others. In fact, they remained close to the Mexican American barrio church while also nurturing ties to the mostly non–Mexican American members in their nearby parish church.

Because Ed's family lived in the East, it was not possible to have the same relationship with them. I didn't meet Ed's mother or other members of his family until a few years after we were married. We didn't have the money to fly there for a visit. What relationship we had was at first conducted through the telephone and written correspondence.

While I didn't get to meet Ed's family until after our wedding, I did get to meet some of his friends. These were people older than I and closer to Ed's age. But I felt comfortable with them and they with me. I had always seen myself as older and more mature than my peers anyway, so relating to Ed's friends was not a problem.

∾※∾

I entered marriage without any trepidation. As far as I was concerned my life would go on pretty much as it had before. It never dawned on me that something might happen to change all this—like getting pregnant. Getting pregnant was something with which I didn't concern myself. I didn't give it any thought. Ed and I never talked about having children. We weren't opposed to it, but we didn't plan on it either. We were focused on each other.

For me, contraception was unthinkable. Ed understood this. Catholic friends would sometimes tease me and ask, "Are you still being a good Catholic girl?" We understood that our lives were dominated by the Church's moral strictures on this matter. I might challenge other things, but to me, birth control violated the principles of natural law. I had been taught that it went against our nature as human beings.

Abstinence and withdrawal were our only choices. This was the rhythm method as I understood it. We had to accept that whatever was going to happen would happen.

Well, it did happen! We were married in January, and in September I discovered, much to my surprise, that I was pregnant. It must have happened during our delayed honeymoon in Catalina that August.

I had always had difficult menstrual periods and had gotten used to my painful monthly cycle. It came with regularity—except that September, just before the start of the fall semester. At first I didn't really notice. I chose not to think about it. What I didn't know I wouldn't have to deal with. I think that I assumed that I was just having some problem with my period.

I was concerned enough, however, to discuss this problem with Ed. He tried to reassure me but understood my concern. Fall classes were about to begin. He was equally concerned but tried not to let on.

That weekend, we had a dinner engagement in San Francisco with a friend of Ed's. Ernie Tsang owned the Cathay House, a restaurant in Chinatown at Grant and California. Ed and Ernie had been friends for several years. He wanted to know how we were doing, and Ed mentioned my "problem."

To my amazement, Ernie started to laugh uproariously. I was puzzled that he would find such humor in my dilemma.

"Why are you laughing?" I asked.

"Because there's nothing really wrong with you. You're pregnant!"

"Pregnant?" Ed and I shouted almost in unison.

"Yes. You're perfectly normal," he said. "I'm not a doctor, but I know what's happening to you."

"Well, of course. He's being logical," I thought. "Why wouldn't I be pregnant?" I hadn't wanted to consider that possibility. Common sense should have dictated that I consider it. Ed was delighted. I was apprehensive.

Ernie insisted that I should see his wife's gynecologist in San Francisco, so we called Esther, who reassured me and said she would make an appointment with her doctor. Within a few days I visited the doctor, whose office was on Post Street in downtown San Francisco. Parking was difficult, and we were on a tight schedule. Ed left me off at the curb and waited in the car.

The doctor was a white-haired older man who practiced medicine with his wife, also a white-haired physician. Ernie had guessed correctly. The tests were very simple and routine. I was pregnant, and the doctor estimated I would give birth the following April. I was awed by my situation. I had lost control of my life. Something else had taken control of my body. I wasn't prepared for this. I would need all the support I could get.

The doctor was very kind. He treated me as if I were the first pregnant lady he had ever dealt with. He was interested in every symptom. He listened sympathetically to everything I needed to say. "Will I be able to stay in school?" I needed to know.

"Of course," he said. "There is no reason why you can't go on with your normal life."

This was the first extended doctor-patient relationship I had ever experienced. He proved to be a counselor as well as a doctor. I felt reassured and could begin to relax.

I was beginning to allow myself to get excited. My mother had given birth to eight children, and I was aware that she treated birth as a natural process. I had taken it for granted. But now all of a sudden it was happening to me. I had to deal with the specifics of being pregnant. Suddenly I was fascinated by all the details the doctor could offer me. He made me feel special.

I rushed out and gave Ed the good news. He shared in my joy. He, too, made me feel special. I called my parents that night. They were very happy for us.

During the next few months, as we anticipated the baby, I didn't think about whether it would be a boy or a girl. Ed and I didn't discuss a preference. I was certainly aware that boys were preferred among most American ethnic groups, including Mexican Americans. But as far as I was concerned I would value either a boy or a girl. What I thought about most was not the sex of the baby but having a healthy baby.

To put it more accurately, I was still in the process of maturing into my role as a parent. Most of the time I was focused on my studies. Parenthood was an abstraction more than anything else. Ed was solicitous. Ernie wanted to be kept informed about my well-being. And I felt that I was the center of their attention. It was as simple as that.

I thought a lot about what name we would give our baby. This consideration carried heavy religious portent for me. It had been the custom in my family to give a child the name of a saint who was commemorated on the child's date of birth. Another dilemma. Would I be the first in my family to break this time-honored custom or would I go with the religious calendar no matter how esoteric the name?

I liked the idea of a biblical name. I didn't want some cute fashionable name. I purchased a book of names and recall pestering Ed about possibilities. Finally, having heard enough, he said in a firm but kind way, "If it's a boy, we'll name him Edward."

I said, "Oh, OK," relieved of the name burden. That he didn't offer a name for a girl was of no significance to me. He was now willing to help me with my name dilemma, and that was what mattered to me. Ed had a wonderful way of taking my most nagging perplexities and reducing them to the simple and practical.

My pregnancy did not hamper my school routine. I went to class up to the day before I gave birth. Toward the end of my pregnancy going to class did pose some difficulties and elicited some interesting reactions. Since the campus is so hilly, I would get very tired going from class to class. There was also no elevator in our apartment building, and we lived on the third floor. I had to climb three flights of stairs when I got home. After climbing hills and stairs I would walk into our apartment and just collapse into a chair or on the bed.

I was also the object of gentle jokes about delivering in class from some of my professors who weren't used to having a pregnant woman in school. I don't recall seeing any other pregnant women on campus. Nevertheless, the students in my classes were very accepting and considerate of my condition. Since Berkeley was such a huge and diverse campus, the unusual was not particularly surprising. Helen, with whom I'd remained friends after leaving the rooming house, even sewed a couple of maternity smocks for me.

I expected the baby in mid-April of my senior year, which would be just fine since, if the baby was on schedule, the birth would coincide with our spring break. Other than taking care of myself, there wasn't much else to do to prepare for giving birth. There was no such thing as Lamaze classes then. My doctor gave me a couple of anatomy books, which were intended to enlighten me about what was going on inside my body but taught me very little about the actual childbirth experience.

We did begin to accumulate a few basic things that we would need such as a crib. A few days before the estimated delivery date, Toni came to stay with us to help.

As the doctor had predicted, within a couple of days after my sister's arrival, my water broke at around five or six in the morning. I couldn't have picked a more convenient time—I would have caused a problem if it had happened in class! Ed got up, made coffee for the three of us, and called Ernie, who had asked to be notified. Since I was not yet in labor, we sat around the kitchen table in a happy mood drinking coffee.

After we dressed, Ed drove us across the bay to Children's Hospital in San Francisco, where my doctor had arranged for me to give birth. It was in the parking lot of the hospital that the first serious labor pains hit me. They were quite sharp, and I had difficulty walking. I'd take a few steps and stop and allow the pain to sweep over me.

Eventually we made it to the hospital entrance, where Ernie was waiting for us. I was placed in a wheelchair and wheeled into the preparation room, where I remained until the last few minutes before delivering. Toni, Ed, and Ernie stayed with me throughout, Ed and Ernie on either side of my bed holding my hand.

I was in labor for about six hours, not a particularly long time. Still, it was a far more painful experience than I had imagined it would be. A nurse would come in periodically to check on me.

She would ask me, "Is it very painful?"

I would say, "Yes, it is," getting increasingly frustrated at not knowing what to do, what to expect. The not knowing is what made the pain seem unbearable. Not having been prepared to take an active part in the process, I felt helpless.

Every time she came into the room the nurse would make some comment about the "progress" I was making. I had no way of judging. The periodic contractions were undifferentiated pain. In between contractions, I lay tensed up waiting for the next one.

At some point, when she judged that I had made enough "progress," the nurse again asked me about the pain.

"It's very bad," I said, or pleaded, really.

"We can give you an injection," she said. I could see that the doctor was now in the room.

Of course I agreed, giving no thought to what the injection was or what its negative implications for the baby might be. It was at this point, when the pain was becoming a horror, that the nurse came up to my bedside with a large chart depicting the normal progress of the birthing process. As she drew my attention to the normal progression illustrated on the chart, I began to feel the effects of the injection that the doctor had just given me. I drifted off.

I regained consciousness and felt as if I were being thrown onto what seemed to be a precariously narrow delivery table. I had been transferred to the delivery room. Everywhere I looked I saw shimmering white walls, overhead a blindingly bright light. The lower part of my body felt like a dead weight, with no sensation.

The nurse began shouting commands at me, and I did my best to comply. I had lost track of time. Not long thereafter, or so it seemed, I heard a flurry of excitement around me. I felt a rushing, emptying sensation. I relaxed, woozy and drowsy. I looked in the direction of the doctor, and he smiled.

"It's a boy," he said.

I watched as they placed my baby on a little table at a distance from me. My gaze rested on this little person. He lay there quietly, seemingly looking around the room. I smiled. Tired. Very happy.

It was a moment of wonder—to feel the baby's sudden emergence and then to see the new life to which I had just given birth. The pain suddenly seemed immaterial. I was overcome by the beauty of childbirth. I can still conjure up that memory and feeling. It remains one of the most positive experiences of my life.

Edward Tywoniak, Jr., was born on April 17, 1953. I was twenty-two years old.

I stayed only two or three days in the hospital before going home.

Ed, Jr. was the first grandchild in my family and the second grandson in Ed's family. In my family this made him the center of attention. In later years, this also made him a little extra special among various cousins. He was the oldest. As the older brother, he has also played a special role in the lives of my two younger children.

Although Toni had to leave right after the baby was born, I was fortunate in that my mother was able to come up to stay with us for a few days. My father didn't see the baby until a few months later when we visited Visalia. It was helpful having my mother there. She was a calming and experienced presence. She was very skillful in lending assistance without making me feel inadequate and without dominating. She would answer all of my "what do I do now?" questions with helpful suggestions.

It was my mother who pointed out to me how best to wash the baby's cloth diapers. When you consider that these were the days before disposable diapers, you can appreciate why I valued my mother's help. These were also the years before popular how-to books, and I had a lot to learn. But it was more than practical help that she gave me. She also gave me the moral support that came from her just being there.

After spending three or four days, my mother had to return to Visalia. I had to prepare to resume my classes. It was then that Ed and I began to feel the impact of having a baby. Our lives became quite hectic.

The routines to which we had become accustomed were now thoroughly altered. The baby's feeding schedule kept us both occupied with little time for anything else. Ed had suggested that I not nurse the baby, because he wanted to feed the baby also. I agreed. Bottle-feeding seemed to be the "modern" thing to do. But this meant that we had the additional task of sterilizing the bottles and preparing the formula.

The apartment had to be kept warm and the drapes drawn during the day when the baby slept, which was also an occasion for me or Ed to take a nap. In fact, napping became the only way we caught up on sleep since continuous sleep at night became a thing of the past. We shared all responsibilities. Whoever had time was on duty.

Night and day pretty much blended into undifferentiated time. The baby seemed to need attention twenty-four hours a day, so we lived twenty-four-hour days. Both Ed and I would stagger around in a daze. But somehow we adjusted. Unlike me, who needed a certain amount of sleep, Ed proved to be able to go without sleep for extended periods of time. And it seemed that he could sleep standing or sitting.

Everywhere you looked there were diapers. It helped that most of the diaper washing didn't need to be done by hand. The apartment house had a washing machine in the basement that the tenants could use. But there was no electric dryer, and we had to walk up two flights of stairs from our apartment to the roof to hang the diapers out to dry.

Consumed with all these activities throughout a twenty-four-hour period meant that we were living segmented lives. There were segments when the baby slept, when Ed and I took turns sleeping, when we made the baby's formula, when we washed diapers, when we bathed the baby, and when I went to class or when Ed went to work. And so it went.

The other tenants were sympathetic. The landlady was not. She raised the rent. "Extra person," she said when she rang the doorbell to deliver the news.

It helped that the baby had an even temperament. His crying was minimal, and we were spared colic attacks.

Since the baby was born in mid-April, I had only three or four weeks of classes left in the spring semester. Hence we only needed to adjust to my class schedule for a brief period of time. When I had to go to class, Ed stayed with the baby and fed him his bottle. When I prepared for my exams, I remember sitting with little Ed in one arm and my book in the other.

Our transition to parenthood was a joint venture. There was never any doubt about Ed's willingness and eagerness to help take care of the baby. We shared all the work. He fed the baby. He changed diapers. He bathed the baby. And he took care of little Ed when I had to go to class. Ed did at least 50 percent if not more of these duties. He was that kind of father.

After a few weeks of adjusting to our new situation, I had to focus on what proved to be something of a dilemma for me, something that troubled me. I had to make a decision about baptizing the baby. I had been baptized in the Catholic Church. The Church was an important part of my life.

I had been raised a Catholic and had been significantly affected in many ways by my Catholicism—my Mexican Catholic upbringing. I recognized this even though over the years I developed certain reservations about the Church and its inflexibility regarding a variety of issues.

As a young girl, I had been distressed by the seeming contradictions between what I had been taught by the Church and some of the uncharitable behaviors I observed among parishioners who attended church regularly. It was inevitable that, as a university student, I would reflect on these dilemmas. Furthermore, I could not easily separate my allegiance to my parents from my allegiance to a Church that they so devoutly believed in and that I now questioned.

I continued to feel very much a Catholic, but I sought my religion out in my own way. For me, the chaplain who had arranged for Ed and me to marry within the Church personified what the Church is really about. I liked a priest who, I felt, understood that God is not a bureaucrat.

I had been taught to believe in absolutes, and now I saw other possibilities. Looking ahead even to the near future I tried to envision the religious education that I would give my child. I had to make a decision about his baptism. Church practice required that a child be baptized as soon as possible after birth. Ed didn't have an opinion one way or another on this subject. In matters of religion, he respected my opinions. He trusted my judgment and left the decision up to me.

I deliberated for several days, at one point even secluding myself in my room to express my feelings in writing. I wrote and wrote—not in a journal or a diary, just stray random thoughts about what I was feeling at the moment. I tried to separate out those emotions more associated with my childhood and adolescence from those associated with my new responsibilities.

This sorting-out process helped. I felt comfortable with my decision that we should arrange to have our baby baptized within a month. What I had needed to do and had done was to begin to define for myself the kind of parent I was going to try to be.

I achieved a kind of peace within myself when I made this decision. Ed, Jr., was raised a Catholic and went to Catholic schools as would my other two children, Richard and Rebecca, who are both also very special in their unique ways.

My senior year at Berkeley was not what I had envisioned two years earlier. Rather than it being a clear and direct path leading to my graduation, it became paths diverging and converging as I juggled responsibilities to my marriage, to my baby, and to my studies.

As such, graduation seemed anticlimactic. In fact, I didn't even attend the public ceremony. It wasn't for lack of interest. I was simply too busy and too exhausted, despite the fact that I had dropped two classes from my spring schedule, which I had to take in the summer before I could officially receive my degree.

A public graduation ceremony—commencement—had been important to me in high school. I had needed that ceremony to validate everything that I had worked for. By contrast, I didn't really need that type of ceremony in 1953 when I graduated from the University of California at Berkeley. What was important and meaningful to me after four years at Berkeley was what those four years represented.

I had been in an intellectual environment associated with the highest standards of excellence and had come to identify closely with the university. Berkeley had been a liberating experience for me. My four years there had been a time for me to mature intellectually, socially, and emotionally.

Those of us who arrived at Berkeley as freshmen in 1949 had been reminded by upperclassmen that we were not to be seen wearing high school paraphernalia, particularly honor pins, on campus. Indeed, the pace of university life had not allowed for dwelling on past glories. My own small-town background had also receded in importance as I adjusted to campus life.

I had achieved a high degree of comfort in Berkeley and had enjoyed my experience there. More important, the ideals of knowledge and service that I believed Berkeley represented were becoming a reality for me. I looked forward to a teaching career.

Berkeley had opened up many vistas for me. There was a wealth of academic resources there. You couldn't be a student at Berkeley and not be conscious of the major research being pursued there, of the richness of the curriculum and the distinction of the faculty, and of the strengths of the libraries. There was so much intellectual wealth at Berkeley, and I felt that I had shared a small part of it.

In a sense Berkeley had become a new home for me both literally and symbolically.

In completing my education at Berkeley, I had a sense of accomplishment. I was proud of the fact that I had made it largely on my own. Being young, I felt that I was in control of my life and my future. This sense of confidence about what I was doing was due, in part, to the fact that ever since I had been a junior in high school I had been making adult decisions for myself. At Berkeley this was even more the case. I had been responsible for myself. I had been self-supporting and self-directing. I was literally free to do what I wanted. I didn't have to answer to anyone.

And yet, it wasn't just self-confidence I felt. I also recognized how important my parents and family had been to me. My family had been a major influence in the first eighteen years of my life. My sense of independence had been nurtured at home in ways that I was just learning to appreciate.

I recognized at the end of those four years that I had not totally divested myself of my background. The fact was that I could not have survived and succeeded at Berkeley without my family's moral support. Earning my degree was a way of validating my parents' trust and faith in me.

My parents shared in my accomplishment. This was especially true of my mother, who had always stressed the importance of education and who had empathized, perhaps more so than my father, with what I had gone through at Berkeley. My mother came from a large family, and she enjoyed keeping our relatives informed of her children's progress in school. Certainly a highlight was my becoming the first member of our family to graduate from college.

I knew that what I had achieved at Berkeley was not just an achievement for me but for my family in Visalia and for my new family in Berkeley as well. And although I didn't particularly dwell on it, I was also aware that I was one of the very few Mexican Americans to have graduated from Berkeley in 1953. In fact, as I look back at my senior yearbook, besides myself, I am able to identify only five or six others who might have been Hispanic or Mexican American.

I had known before I left home that to make a life for myself I would have to make a break with Visalia. But I also came to recognize that making a break with Visalia didn't mean breaking with my family.

It would be years before I would come to fully appreciate what my parents represented in their own ways. It is true that by leaving Visalia I had rejected a way of life that I believed constrained my parents, particularly my mother. I had asserted my right to live my own life free from rigid role expectations. I did not feel, however, that I was rejecting my parents or the love that they had for me. It was my good fortune that they lived a long life. There were many occasions when I was able to tell them how important they had been to me.

I think that by graduating from Berkeley as a married student and as a parent I gained a greater appreciation of my parents, an appreciation that has steadily increased over the years and even more after the death of first my father and then, more recently, my mother.

I did not always recognize, for example, how much I had unconsciously absorbed my mother's influence. There was a dignity about my mother as well as a strength. She was reliable. I associate these characteristics with a person who is solid. My mother was such a person, and I value those characteristics in myself. As I had children and raised them I came to recognize how much I was repeating my mother's experiences.

Although I had been critical of my mother's subordinate relationship to my father, I didn't appreciate until much later in life that I had not considered my mother's life in its full context. Her life reflected the time and the circumstances in which she lived. My mother's options were extremely limited.

In 1953 Fran Tywoniak, nee Frances Esquibel, was different from the person she was in 1949 and even more different from the person she was in 1943, when my family moved permanently to Visalia. In 1953 I had come of age, and my own professional career of some forty years as a teacher and school administrator would shortly commence. I think that by becoming a teacher I was giving something in return to the very profession that had inspired me to achieve both in high school and in college.

Even though I was only twenty-two in 1953, I felt that I had a keen sense of the direction my life was taking. The alienation I had felt in Visalia had attenuated over time. I was channeling my energy toward integrating my life. I didn't feel the need to seek escapes anymore.

I had not yet bridged fully the disparate parts of my life, but I had begun to make the connections. And, in a way, as I look back on my life, I sense that perhaps this process had begun even as early as those wondrous years in my beloved New Mexico.

POSTSCRIPT

After receiving her teaching credential in 1954, Fran Esquibel Tywoniak commenced her career as a successful teacher and administrator.
Her first permanent teaching assignment was at Lowell Junior High
School in Oakland. From 1955 to 1975, she was a teacher, counselor, and
administrator at Mission High School in San Francisco. From 1975 to
1981 she was the principal at McAteer High School in San Francisco.
And from 1981 to 1991 Fran served the San Francisco school district in
a variety of administrative capacities, including as area superintendent,
program manager for certificated personnel, and supervisor of curriculum and instruction. She retired in 1991. Her husband, Ed, died on September 18, 1976.

Mario T. García and Frances Esquibel Tywoniak.
Photo: Jane Scherr.

Text:	11/15 Granjon
Display:	Granjon
Composition:	G & S Typesetters, Inc.
Printing and binding:	Maple-Vail Book Manufacturing Group